GOLD BUCKLE

GOLD BUCKLE

The Grand Obsession of
Rodeo Bull Riders

JEFF COPLON

HarperCollins*West*
An Imprint of HarperCollins*Publishers*

A portion of Gold Buckle *was originally published in the* New York Times Magazine, *April 12, 1992.*

The preface was adapted from an article in Men's Journal, *November 1993.*

The lyrics of "Rodeo," by Larry Bastian, are quoted with the permission of Rio Bravo Music, Inc., BMI.

HarperCollins West and the author, in association with The Basic Foundation, a not-for-profit organization whose primary mission is reforestation, will facilitate the planting of two trees for every one tree used in the manufacture of this book.

 A TREE CLAUSE BOOK

HarperCollins Web Site: http://www.harpercollins.com

HarperCollins®, 👜®, HarperCollins*West*™, and A Tree Clause Book® are trademarks of HarperCollins Publishers Inc.

Library of Congress Cataloging-in-Publication Data

Coplon, Jeff.
Gold buckle : the grand obsession of rodeo bull riders / Jeff Coplon.
ISBN 0–06–258545–2 (cloth)
1. Bull riding—United States. I. Title.
GV1834.45.B84C66   1995
794.8'4—dc20   95–12563

95 96 97 98 99 ❖ RRD(H) 10 9 8 7 6 5 4 3 2

For David,
who's always helped me cowboy up

and for Suzanne,
who is missed

When you're on one of those ninety-point bulls and you're tapped and in the right position, the higher they jump is a little too low for you. The faster they spin is a little too slow. . . . You jump off, and the crowd is roarin', your heart is poundin', the adrenaline's flowin'— there's not a high in the world that can take its place.
Gary Leffew,
former world champion bull rider

You don't want to get on those damn animals unless you feel you'll bounce. And once you've landed and broken you're not as sure about the bounce any more.
Giles Tippette, The Brave Men

CONTENTS

Photographs

Preface

"*Sack Man!*"

I know who's calling before I look up from my eggs. The throaty shout, the rakish grin, that rolling stride through Jocko's (the café of choice in Nipomo, California): it can only be Gary Leffew, a.k.a. "the Guru," TV rodeo analyst and tenured professor at the bull-riding school that bears his name.

Leffew is forty-eight years old, but his body is stuck in middle-age denial; he is craggy in all the right places. He wears epidermal Wranglers, a four-hundred-dollar black Resistol hat, and seven-hundred-dollar pointy ostrich boots. A promotional T-shirt ("Feel the *Rush*") hugs his biceps and trucker's tan. At his trim middle juts an ornate belt buckle slightly smaller than a stop sign. It's the gold buckle, the trophy of trophies circa 1970, when Leffew "won the world" as the best bull rider in the land.

He takes a seat and sizes me up in my own gray Resistol, his eyes crinkled behind burnt-orange aviator sunglasses. Leffew's been calling me Sack Man for a year now, ever since I began to waffle about joining his five-day school. "Got to show some sack," he'd coax—*sack,* of course, being western slang for a tender part of the male anatomy.

Fact is, I'm still unsure. Bulls are nothing to trifle with. Twice as heavy as horses, they are the middle linebackers of the animal kingdom, an in-your-face mix of mass, quickness, and mean spirits. They kick you when you're down, and those cloven hooves can crack a man's rib cage like a one-pound lobster; those horns can cleave an artery.

"Tell me again," I put it to Leffew, "how I am going to do this without getting killed."

As earnest as a Jehovah's Witness, my instructor reminds me that his arena is rototilled before each school: "It's just like the beach. When you fall, the sand absorbs the shock." Besides which, beginners like me are matched with "bunny-hill bulls that just lope around out there. They're not mean, they don't hook. We've got an old bull named Tiny who just barely gets around—in fact, you have to keep hollerin' at him or he'll stop."

I nod and smile . . . and recall the release I have signed should I go home with fewer body parts than I came with: "I AM AWARE THAT BULL RIDING IS VERY DANGEROUS."

For the sake of argument, I venture, what *if* gentle, old, fifteen-hundred-pound Tiny were to step on me accidentally in just the wrong spot?

"This ain't tiddlywinks," Leffew says nonchalantly. "You could die. Definitely." He wolfs his biscuit and grins anew. "Let's go see the flock," he says.

Five miles of snaking gravel road later, past foothill glades of western oak and a grazing cow or two, we find the flock gathered outside Leffew's rough-hewn arena. They are baking in the dry June heat, joking down their jitters, swiping at tribes of flies.

There are forty-six of us. A handful are fantasy campers on leave from real life—a public-works official, an investment banker. The rest are in their teens and twenties, country jocks and ex-marines, feed-lot hands with fancy chaps and one-track minds. They've driven thirty hours and more, forked out $325 apiece to feed their dream of a six-figure income and cult-figure status on the Nashville Network—or, at the least, to beat the boys back home for fifty bucks and bragging rights.

After two years on the beat, I've come to know scores of bull riders, from San Francisco to South Flyspeck, Texas, to Albany, New York. I've met champs and green amateurs, black cowboys and Navajos, women and adolescent boys, even inmates at the state pen in Oklahoma. They all sing different songs, but the chorus rings familiar. They share a passion that makes no sense till you're inside it.

Some people get hooked on fast cars, or the racetrack, or the ocean's mad surf. But in whatever remains of the wild, wild West, there is no thrill like riding a bull. Obsessions are costly, and even the young ones pack baggage. "This is my first bull in two years," confesses a cleft-chinned ex–high school star, now all of twenty-three, who ponied up a month's wages for tuition. "My guts was a-rottin'. I was layin' on the couch and not doin' nothin'. My wife said that I'm a half a man now, and maybe when I come back I'll be a full man again."

One hell of a way to play double or nothing, I'm thinking.

It's time for Leffew's daily lecture, which meanders from bawdy anecdote to paeans to positive thinking. Back in 1967, during the worst slump of his rodeo career, worried sick he might have to find a *job,* Leffew came upon a copy of *Psychocybernetics,* by Maxwell Maltz. He devoured it whole. Soon he was spouting Maltzian jargon about mental programming, visualization, and "the law of attraction," the notion that subconscious mental energy—positive or negative—brings luck in the same direction.

After a two-month layoff, Leffew returned to ride his first bull in high-spurring style. The next year he placed second in the world. He claimed he had "hot power," that he could get a winning, spinning ride out of the most worn-out bull by scraping an "X" in the dirt in front of the bucking chute. "What people think about you may be right or wrong," he lectures my class, "but if they think it, it becomes true. Because life is an illusion anyway."

Laying "moon talk" aside, Leffew turns to technique. The secret to bull riding, he tells us, is constant forward momentum. A well-positioned cowboy will seem to be climbing the bull's shoulders, never sliding back to "the house of pain" to feel every whipping ounce of the beast's force.

"I can tell a great rider by how much daylight he has under his ass," Leffew claims. "When you're up above, the bull *floats* under you. You don't muscle bulls, you balance them. It's like a Zen deal: you become one with the animal."

That afternoon we enter the gray-planked arena, an oval about fifty yards at its longest point. I roost on the fence and watch my fellow students bounce off the boards and land headfirst in the hoof-pocked dirt, only to jump up and scramble to Leffew's shaded perch for a critique.

My bull debuts with another novice. Tiny is hornless and humpless, low-slung and stunt-legged; if he's 90 percent Black Angus, as Leffew suggests, the rest must be dachshund. "He's been used so many times he's gotten complacent," Leffew observes. Tiny looks to be hopping along quite fast enough, thank you, especially after Brett Leffew, Gary's first-born son, buzzes him with a low-voltage hot shot.

"Did you *have* to do that?" I complain. "Now he's going to be pissed off."

"He won't buck that good with you," Leffew soothes me. The next hour passes quickly, till my teacher warns that Tiny's sixth in line again—"a little time to get your adrenaline up." Quelling a stab of panic, I dash to the chutes. I don a left-handed deerskin riding glove (Leffew counsels righties to ride lefty, saving their dominant hand for balance), dust my loaner rope with a rosin sock, then scrape my glove over the rosin to make it sticky. I fix one spur upside down, till a classmate corrects me.

But it's when I swing myself up and over the coffin-shaped chute, lowering my knees onto Tiny's back ("Watch those spurs, now!"), dazed without my glasses, that I feel truly helpless. For all my regalia, I might as well be naked. I have no bridle, no saddle, no stirrups. It's just me and Tiny and the yellowed rope that joins us for this moment, the rope that a hired hand named Stinkweed is pulling tight—alarmingly tight—over my gloved palm.

"Cowboy up, Jeff!"

"Bear down, Jeff!"

And then the gate swings open, and the hands' shouts and the clanging bell and my bull's laboring snorts dissolve into a buzzing cloud. All I can see is Tiny's thick, bobbing neck. All I can feel is this dense pulling surge beneath me. It is like driving a Lincoln without steering wheel or brakes, forget about seat belt or air bag. It is like plunging to the center of the earth.

After two jumps I've slipped to the right, and now my car is a car wreck, careering past the point of no return, each second stretched into time warp. At the third jump I flail at Tiny's neck with my free hand: automatic disqualification. By the fourth I am falling sideways, but cling a tad longer—out of pride, perhaps, but mostly because *I'm having such a great time.* . . .

At its most violent moments, life turns simple: you hang on or you fall off. You live or you die. Maybe that's why we love Westerns so; maybe that's why the ranks of top bull riders are littered with brawlers and borderline drunkards, but nary a neurotic.

My ride seems to last forever. In fact, I hit the dirt—as soft as advertised—within four seconds. "It was just your first one," consoles Stinkweed, rescuing my flown hat from among clots of greenish bull dung.

"You had good form going out of there," says Leffew, ever positive. "You've just got to get that little rocking motion."

My classmates greet me like a brother. "Welcome to the club!" shouts a chunky fellow with a bent owl feather in his hat. "You're a *bull* rider now. There are those who talk about getting on and those that get on—and you got on."

This was just a magazine assignment, but now it's become something more.

★

My next two tries I fall off even faster, and Brett Leffew takes me under his wing. To compensate for my height (I'm six-four), he tells me to "shoot" my left shoulder toward the center of the bull's head with each jump. Since Tiny always circles counterclockwise, the shoulder move will put more weight on my inside (left) leg, averting my slide to the right: "You'll ride him all night, I guarantee you."

Brett's father focuses above my neck. "Writers tend to be real cerebral," he says. "You need to get on and just nod your head, and let your subconscious feed you the right moves. Quit thinking and just *do* it."

Our classwork is taking a toll. Ace bandages are in fashion; guys are gulping Bufferin like malted milk balls. And I've discovered why cowboys walk so funny: their groins are always strained.

This time I pull my spurs on with time to spare. I stalk up to Tiny as the dumb creature waits in line, glare at him through a gap in the planks. "You're already *rode*," I hiss, just like Leffew taught me. "Your fat ass is *mine*."

"Get that lion heart!" Brett calls out. I board Tiny's back with new comfort, even ask for an extra pull of the rope. And then, to signal I'm ready, a jaunty "Let's go, boys!"

The gate swings wide . . . and everything clicks. My mind blanks clean; my body shifts to automatic pilot. I follow Tiny's lead without strain or calculation. We're no longer sparring, we're *dancing,* two hearts beating to one herky-jerky tune.

I've flown to some higher state of perception. I feel my hat fly from my head—I even feel my hair decompress. I smell the dust we're raising and the musky undertone of a large animal exerting itself. It's the hyperawareness that visits young lovers and true athletes, and for eight seconds it's visiting me.

Twelve jumps from the start I sink triumphantly to the ground. The whole deal seems effortless, except that I'm sweating and huffing like I'd run half a mile.

"I'm proud of you, pardner!" says Brett, high-fiving me from behind the chute, as the gallery whoops and hollers. Legs a-tingle, I raise my hands to acknowledge the cheers, then sheepishly flip my hat to the sky.

"We done it!" the Guru exults. "You kept your chest out, you stayed square with him—that's a major accomplishment. And it was an inspiration to the class, that a New York City boy looked fear in the eye and took care of business."

There would be more surprises before school was out. I could tell you how I advanced to a loping sixteen-hundred-pounder named 88 with the mother of all goiters for a hump . . . how I rode him to first place in a beginner's jackpot on getaway day, netting nineteen dollars and a ten-year-old's admiring gaze. But what lingers in memory is that first full ride on Tiny, when the bull and I were one and nothing else mattered, nothing mattered at all.

Acknowledgments

This book began nearly four years ago with an article on Tuff Hedeman for the *New York Times Magazine*. Tuff proved to be the ideal subject, one who threw himself into my work as a partner. From the start he was my willing guide and mentor in all matters cowboy, including my western wardrobe. I came to rely upon his generosity, his candor, and his patience; I was never disappointed.

The top bull riders were, without exception, remarkably open in allowing a tenderfoot into their world. Especially helpful were Cody Lambert, Ty Murray, Clint Branger, Charles Sampson, Cody Custer, and Buddy Gulden.

Don Gay and Bryan McDonald were free with their time and insight—a break for me, as there's no one smarter about this game or the men who play it.

Gary Leffew actually taught me to ride a bull, no small trick, and told enough terrific stories to stock a second book. George Michael and Bob Tallman shed fresh light on their friend Charles Sampson, each in his own inimitable style.

Jim Shoulders, Harry Tompkins, and Larry Mahan were major influences—not just for their interviews, but for the bull-riding heritage they've sustained. The historical portions of this book were also enriched by the extensive files and library at the National Cowboy Hall of Fame in Oklahoma City, which showed me every courtesy.

Dr. J. Pat Evans never wearied of discussing the cowboys' injuries—a full-time job—and allowed me liberal access to the Justin Healer room in Las Vegas.

Among the stock contractors, John Growney put me up at his ranch and taught me more about bulls than anyone else. And Sammy Andrews proved that nice guys can finish first.

Among others lending a bed to this wanderer were Lynn Birleffi and Phil Noble in Cheyenne, Pat and Dorothy Ryle in San Francisco, Michael and Paula Gaughan, Steve Fechser, and Steve Carpenter at the Gold Coast in Las Vegas. Their western hospitality kept my spirits up even when my boots pinched.

Steve Fleming, director of communications for the Professional Rodeo Cowboys Association, got me into the locker room at the National Finals, an invaluable window onto the bull riders' world. Sherry Compton and her good-humored crew provided all the data I asked for, even when my research bordered on the compulsive.

I never met Lane Frost, but by the time I finished writing I felt I knew him as a friend. Six years after his death, he remains a vivid presence in rodeo; he'll be remembered as long as bulls buck and cowboys try. I'm especially grateful to Clyde and Elsie Frost for their friendship, and for sharing memories of their extraordinary son. And to Kellie Macy, who never ducked an old question even as she made her new life.

My editor, Joann Moschella, showed a rare gift to shape, without ever squelching, the work of a writer known to go over the top; her talents shine from every page.

Acknowledgments
=================

I am grateful as well for the extra-mile efforts of assistant editor Beth Weber, editorial associate Julia Barfield, production editor Lisa Zuniga Carlsen, copy editor Carl Walesa, proofreader Karin Mullen, and art director Shelly Meadows.

Kelly Riley, a gracious ex–bull rider and Tad Lucas's grandson, checked a draft of this book for accuracy; any remaining errors are the author's responsibility, and his alone.

I must also mention Peter Richmond, whose story on Lane Frost in the *National* helped put me on this trail; Robert Vare, then my editor at the *Times Magazine;* and Michael Carlisle, my agent, whose hard work and confidence kept this long-shot project afloat. Much-needed moral support came from Frank Mobus, Barry Tubb, Paul and Denise Castro, and Pat and Tony Garcia.

Of the many good books that touch upon this sport, the most valuable to me was written by a veterinarian-turned-anthropologist from Massachusetts. In *Rodeo* (University of Chicago Press), Elizabeth Atwood Lawrence shows how modern bull riders are direct spiritual descendants of the nineteenth-century cowboys.

Finally, I'm thankful I married a native Texan; Gracie was one person in our Brooklyn circle who found my new interest perfectly natural. She didn't merely put up with my travel and odd hours; she came to care about "my" cowboys with her typical curiosity and warmth of spirit. Along with the enthusiasm of our sons, Steffen and Jake, her support kept me going down the road.

CHAPTER 1

Riding Ugly

*F*OR TUFF THE BULL RIDE
began as any other: with whiplash. With that first jolt from the
yellow chute like a freeway collision. With two more jumps,
wild to bursting, when a cowboy must think from his spinal
cord and trust sheer reaction, till the blur subsides and the
blunt force beneath him heaves into a pattern. Then the fun
begins, the boxing match, *mano a toro,* and may the better
mammal win.

They fought this particular bout in Las Vegas in 1990, on
the sixth day of December. It was the seventh of ten go-
rounds at the National Finals Rodeo, or NFR, the make-or-
break World Series of the sport. In one corner, from
Avondale, Colorado . . . Copenhagen Stinger, weighing seventeen hundred pounds and sporting a pair of foot-long
horns, four sharp hooves, the spring to rise five feet in the air,
and an inbred resentment toward any object on its back. In
the other, from Bowie, Texas . . . Richard "Tuff" Hedeman,
weighing a thick-legged 175 (give or take a pre-ride chili

dog), and armed with a belled rope, two spurs, and the muscle memory of a thousand rides in a hundred burgs in an eight-year pro career.

Bull riding is plain as a gunfight, quick as a sprint. The rider wins—or at least scores—if he sticks on the bull for eight seconds. (To "ride," as cowboys speak it, is to last and "make eight," not just get on and pray.) The bull wins if he bucks the cowboy off before then, and gets a freebie to skewer any man on the ground. The game is rigged for the bull. A rank, rough-bucking star like Stinger, with G-force to daunt an astronaut, will sling 80 percent down before the eight-second whistle.

Tuff had carved a career out of beating such odds. Vegas was his town. Each year he won big and stayed sound. While others limped into the neon night or exited on stretchers, Tuff never got hurt bad enough to mention. Clint Branger, his less bionic traveling buddy, would marvel that Tuff was "a bull," the highest praise. But even iron men are at risk in this business. The casualty rate mushrooms at the Finals, where each bull is an all-star: cat-quick, ox-strong, not noted for mercy.

A cowboy from central casting—crooked grin, squared chin, sandy bangs, and a brisk, bowlegged, tippy-toed gait—Tuff had topped enough bulls to win the world in 1986 and again in 1989. He'd laid aim at a third championship in 1990, taking two of the first six go-rounds, when a funny thing happened six seconds into his joyride on Stinger. Tuff got tipped away from his gloved riding hand, his left, which gripped the flat, braided rope, and "into the well" of the bull's clockwise whirl: a script for disaster. Your typical pro cowboy might have cut his losses, pulled the tail of his rope, freed his hand, and braced for landing—to eat some dirt and ride another day.

But Tuff was the stubborn sort. For most of his twenty-seven years he'd denied fear and pain and the limits of his gifts, and he wasn't to be fazed by some piddling law of physics like centripetal force. He would hold on. "He just tries so hard, goes so far over the line when he's riding," a friend reflected. "He don't quit till it's too late."

The stress was telling—in the bulged tendons of Tuff's neck, in his grinding bicuspids. And then, suddenly, Tuff was thrown—all of him save his left hand, which had rolled over and jammed in the rope's handle. Tuff found himself jogging along on foot, an offense to any self-respecting cowboy, and worse yet when you were fused to a ton of sirloin at pains to sever the relationship or your limb, whichever came first.

A bull rider rarely gets "hung up" more than three jumps before he works free. In extreme cases the predicament might last ten seconds. But this time Tuff was stuck. The son of a Mexican fighting bull, Stinger bared his raw power. Suddenly Tuff was skimming flush to the ground, still stemmed to the beast by his left arm, orbiting like a carny plane ride. The rodeo clown Rob Smets—the toughest man in rodeo, a Mafia hit man in a former life—took Stinger on horns-first and ricocheted like a duckpin. A dozen off-duty bullfighters streamed out of their seats, led by Tuff's older brother, Roach, who flung himself over the bull's back to grasp the snagged handhold. The crowd was in bedlam, horrified and half delighted, as when a circus cat swats the whip away and steels to pounce.

"I was settin' with my folks in the stands," recalled Tuff's wife, Tracy, "and I've never had that feeling before. Everybody was going wild, and I was just watchin' it, in a zone."

After thirty seconds of chaos, Tuff managed to find his footing without getting tromped on. "It was like running through a war," he'd say later, in his reedy twang. "It just goes on and on, takes every ounce of energy you have. You can't even breathe. You keep workin' to get your hand out, and then when it doesn't come, doesn't come, doesn't come, it starts feelin' hopeless."

It took another half minute for Tuff to cut loose. By then Stinger had worn out and petered to a stop. Though physically unharmed, the animal would never be the same. Rodeo

bulls are fragile inside their savagery, and Stinger had lost all heart for bucking.

Tuff made off unaided, to check with the on-site doctor and hear what he already knew: a few bruises, nothing more. He was still the iron man. "Ain't nothin' but a hangnail!" he blustered to the press, as friends and family milled about in tears. It struck some as hard-hearted, this drumming of chest, but Tuff would have to ride again in twenty-four hours, and Stinger had cracked the bedrock certainty he'd need to survive.

It is no small leap of faith that brings a man to board a bull's back and feel that he belongs there. Tuff knew that any ride could be his last, that the minefield was loaded—that what had happened just the year before in Cheyenne, to the best friend he'd ever have, could happen to him. But he believed his state of grace would last one more night, one more jump. Tuff had to believe it or he'd never see a ride through. To shout out his defiance was to keep that faith.

The next night he rode without moment and tied for first, cashing more than seven thousand dollars. Sometimes the bull got you, but sometimes you got the bull.

They'll tell you that rodeo is for Everyman, in the frontier tradition, and that all cowboys are created equal. But they won't be telling the truth, for pro rodeo has its own caste system. At the pyramid's base are the workaday ropers and wrestlers, good ol' boys built like Hoss Cartwright. In the middle sit the saddle bronc and bareback riders, heirs to the classic image of a man on a bucking steed, average-sized men who take moderate chances.

And at the top strut the bull riders, the sport's marquee outlaws. Other rodeo folk might see them as little men with big egos, less than dependable and not quite sane. But to their fans they are knights without armor. By reputation, bull riders are the slickest dressers, the biggest spenders, the heaviest gamblers, the hardest drinkers—the macho princes of their realm. No one travels lighter. No one roams freer. And no one pushes the envelope so recklessly, whether in an all-night, hell-for-leather drive to the next town, or atop a raging bull ten times their weight and toting a grudge for good measure.

Where ropers and bronc busters get respect, bull riders share something more: the mystique that shrouds a man who puts death on his dance card a hundred times a year and lives to dance again. Which is why bull riding comes last on your rodeo program—to trap the crowd to the end, to sell that last Coors and corn dog and leave everyone buzzing.

Bull riding is easy to get. There is one basic rule: you can't touch the bull with your free arm. Unlike saddle bronc, bull riding docks no one for Arthur Murray infractions; no one cares how you time your spurring or turn your toes. While the judges may shade a point or two for balance and control, you are scored, first and last, for your bull. The higher he bucks, the harder he kicks, the crisper he spins—the more you win. You need technique, to be sure, but the drill is to hang on.

And bull riding is most spectacular. To the casual viewer, bronc rides are so many variations upon a manic hobbyhorse, with little to set them apart. But a rodeo bull awes even at rest, with its porterhouse bulk and ominous hump. In action he overwhelms. Within a single trip the bull may nimbly spin right and then left, charge out at some oblique angle, drop its front end like a sledgehammer, and throw in a belly roll or two for good measure—all in tommy-gun, multitrack sequence.

The top cowboys have seen these tricks a thousand times. They know how to counter like they know their own ropes. But to move in the blur of the moment, to sustain this pas de deux with a partner from hell, is something else again. Riding a rank bull, said Walt Garrison, the old Dallas Cowboys fullback and collegiate rodeo hand, is "like reachin' out with a hay hook and grabbin' a freight train goin' sixty." A great bull ride is eight long seconds of loosed anarchy, jammed with unforeseen crises and unlikely comebacks. No two trips look the same.

At bottom, though, bull riding is most popular because it's most dangerous. The peril comes from the nature of the beast. Bulls are bigger and stronger than horses, and the good ones just as fast; when carting two thousand pounds at forty miles per hour, they parlay more mass and velocity than any creature in the hemisphere. Even with no harm intended, a rodeo bull can sling a fellow into the next county, or plant him like a pile driver. And where broncs shy from fallen cowboys, bulls are most lethal *after* riders leave their backs; they'll charge for the joy of assault. That threat of gore keeps the turnstiles whirring. Bull-riding fans, proposed Lewis A. Cryer, commissioner of the Professional Rodeo Cowboys Association (PRCA), "have a stock-car mentality. They go to see a great race, but they also go to see the crashes."

It's older than history, this match of man and animal, and the boys who dare revive it make the rest of us breathe more deeply. Peaking quick and quitting young (eight years make a handsome pro career), they play out a daily drama of luck, pluck, and human failings. Bull riders have mortgage payments and marriage woes like the rest of us, or more so. But they also have something, *know* something extra: that we all hang by threads twixt sky and ground.

"In the storm that is the psyche of a bull rider," said Stephen Baldwin, the actor who played Hedeman in *Eight Seconds*, "there is a calm . . . a control . . . the purest, humblest sense of fearlessness I have ever encountered."

Not every macho prince is a horseman. There are bull riders who dread the Grand Entry, the Finals' nightly prelude, who yank and slap their nags and still screw up the parade. But for Tuff it's like coming home. He grew up in a town, El Paso, where horses were everywhere. It felt good to roost high in a saddle, especially when you were the last of seven children and short for your age, an awkward, stocky-legged kid in hand-me-down shirts. On horseback Tuff had freedom to roam, and a rough equality. On foot he was a nearsighted runt with no clear talent, least of all for rodeo.

Not that it stopped him. He tried his first calf at the age of four, and soon he was telling any adult who cared to ask that, yes, he knew just what he'd do when he grew up: win a gold belt buckle, the world championship trophy for each rodeo event. The boy might better have wished to quarterback the Cowboys, or knock out George Foreman. He might as well have wished for the harvest moon, except for one odd omen. . . .

Young Richard was six years old when he hopped into a pickup with a family friend, a horse trainer named Tater Decker, on his way to pick up some feed. Tater reached over to shut the door and caught a funny look on his passenger's face. His eyes trailed to the boy's limp right arm, to the small trapped hand. Tater hustled to open the door, swearing his apologies. But the child never made a sound, never dropped a tear, though his hand would soon swell and be tender for a week.

"Well, you're a tough nut, ain't you?" the trainer exclaimed. And as Tater knew something about good nicknames, he decided that "Tough Nut" was just right for the boy. It inevitably shrank to "Tuff," and though Hedeman hated it and hid it for years, the name stuck.

The boy had to be tough, if only to handle his weekly frustration at amateur rodeos in the neighborhood. He'd barely come to terms with five-hundred-pound steers when he turned thirteen and moved up to twelve-hundred-pound "junior" bulls. It was a vicious transition—a shift from Disney to Stephen King. Tuff stood less than five feet and still weighed in double digits. He was simply overmatched. "He couldn't ride a stick horse," said Barry Tubb, a boyhood friend and junior bull-riding champion. Tuff set an unofficial

El Paso record for the most consecutive one-jump buck-offs. Each time, he'd snatch up his rope in a spit storm of curses and self-loathing. Wouldn't he ever learn? Wouldn't he ever grow?

"We just never noticed him much, to be honest," said Cody Lambert, who was a year and a half older and hung with Tuff's more athletic brother, Roach. "I remember coming back from a high school rodeo in New Mexico when Tuff was fourteen or fifteen, and we stopped at a jackpot bull-riding contest. And Tuff rode one bull three jumps, close to two seconds, and was proud that he rode him that far. Nobody gave him any chance to go anywhere."

That low estimate nagged the boy forward: Tuff became the Little Brother Who Could. His failings ate at him, made him testy and mean-mouthed, but never discouraged him. He couldn't afford discouragement; that was a luxury for people with money or looks or talent. Tuff wouldn't quit, he *couldn't* quit, for there was nothing to fall back on if he did. He would rise on blind persistence. He never lacked fuel for his furnace; he needed only to watch someone who rode better. For many years he hadn't far to look—to his big brother, to Lambert, and then to a flashy dynamo named Lane Frost, who was tearing up the junior rodeo circuit.

In Lambert—a future top-fifteen cowboy in both the bull riding and saddle bronc—Tuff had the ideal mentor, one who liked to teach almost better than he liked to win. And in Tuff, Lambert found the model student, with a malnourished ego that kept him hungry for guidance. "Everything I learned about riding bulls was from Cody Lambert," Tuff said much later. "I seen the success that Cody had, and it gave me the drive and desire—I wanted to do that. It just took me a long, long time to get competitive, and I think that made me a better cowboy. I realized how hard it was to do good."

It finally began to happen for Tuff at sixteen, after he made his high school varsity. Slowly he passed boys who'd once smirked his way. Now they were casualties of burnout and beer, of Little League fathers and small-pond smugness, and Tuff kept turtling by. But even after winning the state bull-riding championship in New Mexico, he kept his sights low, to one rung at a time. He bought his PRCA permit and went about earning the thousand dollars he'd need to become a full-fledged pro: "I thought if I got my card and got to go to the PRCA rodeos, that would probably be as good as I'd ever do. I would have been happy with that—I would have been content. The National Finals wasn't even in the vicinity."

In the fall of 1981, Tuff wangled a rodeo scholarship, his only avenue to college, to Sul Ross State University, in Alpine, Texas. He wouldn't accept much money from home—"The first year I liked to have starved to death"—and made a few bucks breaking horses at nearby ranches. Nor would he take much coaching, even as he floundered in competition that first semester and worried that he'd lose his free ride.

"He'd had to scrape and fight for everything he had, and he really had a chip on his shoulder, trying to prove to everybody how good he was," said John Mahoney, his college coach. "He was real standoffish, real defensive about everything. I just more or less left him alone.

"But I liked him. I'd never known anybody, *ever*, to have as much determination as he did. I really liked him, but I didn't try to get close to him."

As seventh man on a six-man squad, Tuff outpracticed all comers, rode five bulls in a day just for fun and instruction. Every so often one of the team regulars would bash a knee or strain an elbow, and Tuff would plug the gap. In the spring he began to get better. "He's a good college cowboy because he can ride the pretty-good bulls," recalled Lambert, a year ahead of Tuff at Sul Ross and then the top collegiate cowboy in the nation. "Nobody knows—not even our team, not even myself—that we've got a guy here that's going to ride *everything* because he tries so hard."

When Sul Ross made the 1982 National Collegiate Finals in Bozeman, Montana, Mahoney chose Tuff to fill the team's last slot—over vocal protest from several teammates, who'd lobbied the coach to pick a senior pal of theirs instead. After getting past his first two bulls, Tuff drew a seldom-bested National Finals veteran known as 222 in the final "short" round. A national team championship teetered on the line. It was Tuff's first chance to rise to a great occasion, to hush the skeptics without and the doubter within. Then the chute opened, and the bright lights kicked in for him. Tuff rode the hair off 222, won the short round, and clinched the title for dear old Sul Ross.

When it was all over but the whooping, Mahoney found his favorite in back of the chutes, alone. Tuff looked at his coach, and for the first time anyone remembered, he cried. He told Mahoney, "You're the first guy that ever believed in me."

If a man's life could have one simple turning point, that was it for Tuff. He rode brilliantly through his sophomore year and won the '83 college finals. He could be ignored no longer, though he surely didn't look like a star, with his bad teeth and black-rimmed, Coke-bottle eyeglasses and a haircut out of Mayberry. More to the point, he didn't feel like a star. Tuff was only as good as his last ride, and if that conviction made him hard to live with, it was also a mighty wedge against complacency. He would never take a bull for granted. He would never forget that success was twinned to struggle, and that struggle was the one thing he did better than anyone else.

When Tuff turned pro full-time in 1983, he was tempted to follow Lambert, now his traveling partner, in competing for the prestigious all-around title. He'd excelled at saddle bronc at Sul Ross and had a talent for team roping as well. But Tuff knew at his core that bull riding fit him best—that the bulls alone blessed all-out desire over style or technical correctness. "Fuck the form and get the horn" went the bull rider's motto, and it might have been tattooed on Tuff's forehead.

He entered the PRCA mature in his craft and a cut above the crowd. Most any professional rider could handle "cupcakes" or "sweetie pies," the nice rhythmic bulls that turned back to spin right in front of the chute. But even the top-tier cowboys had holes in their game. There were strength riders lacking the touch and subtlety to last on bulls that whirled away from their riding hand. There were finesse men who thrived on those but faltered on mighty, "stout" bulls that bucked *into* their hands. Some cowboys gave in to "droppy" bulls that jackhammered each landing, or "welly" bulls that sucked men into the black hole of their spin, or "sun fishers" that mamboed their middles like cement mixers. What made Tuff special was that none of the above could count on evicting him. From the start of his pro career, he made the whistle more often than most anyone else. As the cowboys like to say, he kept his dirty side down.

The year he turned twenty-one, Tuff reached the Finals for the first time and finished tenth in the world. The next season he led from the wire and dominated "for three hundred and sixty-four days and twenty-three hours." After five go-rounds at Las Vegas, he was up twenty thousand dollars and ahead for the best average bonus. Had the rodeo ended that night, he would have won the world in a walk. "It didn't look like there was any way I could be beat," Tuff said. "But I was beat." He bucked off three of his last five bulls, while Ted Nuce, the life-is-lovely Californian whose strobe-lit style juiced the crowd (and could sometimes con the judges into "gifting" him a point or three), closed with a rush. In the acid-test tenth go, when the bulls are rankest, Nuce notched a ninety to win the round. Everyone else but Lane Frost fell off. Nuce snatched away Tuff's gold buckle by five thousand dollars.

If Tuff ever needed reminding that nothing he'd toiled for was secure, here it was, in spades. That Finals was his master's degree, his hardest knock. "That hurt. That's like ripping your heart out," he'd say. "That's like dropping a touchdown pass with no time left on the clock in the Super Bowl." He'd finished second, the agony spot, and had blown a big lead to boot. Rodeo people, the wily ones with hawk's eyes and chaw-stained incisors, knew that one of two futures would unfold. Either Tuff would be punctured, even wasted, or the near miss would goad him higher, make him great.

Tuff rode better than ever in 1986 and again swept into Vegas on top, leading Nuce by ten thousand. Then the unthinkable happened: he bucked off his first two bulls. The instant experts played taps. The kid was choking, again, and every drugstore cowboy and his uncle flocked by with free advice. Tuff dutifully ignored them, but it got a tad annoying. Finally Donnie Gay, who'd won the world eight times in the '70s and early '80s, took the younger man aside before the third go-round. "Just remember," Gay said, "you're the same guy that got here."

Pressure? Pressure was having four kids and no job. Pressure was going down the road with just enough money for gas or food, but not both. Tuff felt no heat in the arena because his gauges were internal. At every step he'd demanded more of himself than anyone else had. Big crowds, fat payoffs, world titles—these were but wind for his wings. They made him pay attention and soar. "With Tuff," Lambert noted, "the more there is on the line, the more comes out of him." When you had nothing, Tuff knew better than most, you had nothing to lose.

Tuff went on to ride his last eight bulls. He placed second to Lane Frost at the Finals, but won the gold buckle—based on total season earnings—by twenty-two thousand dollars. Tuff had never feared failure, and soon it grew clear he could handle success. For the next seven seasons he'd finish no lower than fourth in the world.

He had come a long way, inside and out. Tuff might not be Gary Cooper, but he wasn't Hoot Gibson, either. He'd kept growing well into his twenties, topping off at just under six feet. He was broad shouldered and thick chested, and those muscular legs finally seemed to fit his body. He capped his teeth, fired his barber, and traded in his Coke bottles for contact lenses. He grew a taste for combed cotton and Mont Blanc pens and cowboy hats with enough beaver fur in them to swathe a fair-sized woman.

But even as he entered the 1990s as a rugged fashion-ad model, the old Tuff, the least likely champ in the neighborhood, kept peeking through. You could hear it in his sarcasm—wry and hilarious on his good days, mean and self-scorning on the bad, the way of a man who wouldn't let you hurt him if he could do it first. You could see it in that strange stiff way he moved. "Tuff is the most uncoordinated person I know," said Ty Murray, the stylish wunderkind who rode in all three roughstock events, and was en route to his second straight all-around title in 1990. "I don't care what it is, from shootin' pool to golf, he looks funny. He's not a natural in anything."

You could glimpse the old El Paso Tuff most of all in his form on a bull: hardscrabble, unprettified, crudely aggressive. Tuff made all the right moves, but they were rough and hamfisted. He had his rope pulled tighter than a prison guard's smile, to take each jerk undiluted. Donnie Gay put it simply: "He rides ugly."

There was a death grip to Tuff's riding that leapt to the mezzanine and left you spent for the viewing of it. What beamed out at those moments was *try,* a cowboy noun, a compound of effort, courage, and unsinkability. All cowboys required some measure of try, but bull riders wanted the most. It was their antidote to fear and its first cousin, paralysis, their spur to push on when others stopped. It kept them going when homesick and slumping, in chill rain or desert sun, when they had the flu and their legs screamed for lounge chairs and a bull with Flintstone clubs for horns was playing crush-your-knee in the chute.

Try could be learned, but it couldn't be faked. All the top pros knew who had it, and how much. They saw who played safe and who gutted rides through, or who ducked a mean bull by "turning out" of a rodeo. A few had snared gold buckles with ordinary try, getting by with smarts and skill or a hot run in Vegas. But the legends of the game, the cowboys' cowboys, were the ones who sweated the stuff through their shirts, who gave out before they gave in. Donnie Gay had ultra-try, and Freckles Brown before him. Lane Frost had it, and it was already clear that twenty-one-year-old Ty Murray had it, too. At the National Finals the try quotient was high all around. But no one tried harder than Tuff Hedeman.

"He hates to lose so bad," Murray considered, over a teen-dream Vegas lunch of chicken fingers and french fries. "He's got it here and here"—the prodigy tapped a finger to his forehead, then his chest—"and those are the places you better have it."

If you asked Tuff to name his favorite ride, he wouldn't cite his highest score or the biggest-name bull he'd beaten. He'd tell you about the third go-round at the '85 Finals, when he mounted a strapping black Brangus known as 313. The bull blew out away from his hand, centrifuging him from the first jump. His good seat gone, Tuff flailed out with his free arm. The bull felt the slip, knew the man was in limbo, moved to finish him off. Tuff flailed again, fighting the drag of his torso. Hadley Barrett, the mellow-toned announcer, egged him on: "C'mon Tuffy, c'mon Tuffy, c'mon Tuffy, stay *with* him!" Now the bull was peeved and bucked still harder, kicking near over his head, and Tuff desperately responded, and so the two lurched to the horn and might be lurching still if the rules had allowed it. The judges gave eighty-two points, no showstopper, but Tuff cherished his effort that night. Other cowboys might have tried as hard, but you could count them on your thumbs.

"I see guys who have a lot of talent and ride real correct," Tuff said, "but they don't bear down all the time. You just have to really want to do it, deep down in your heart, and you have to want to do it all the time, not every now and then.

"Nine times out of ten, when a guy gets bucked off," he said flatly, "it's because of a weak heart."

Like most professional sports, rodeo contains two worlds: a regular season and the play-offs. For eleven months of every twelve, the cowboys drive a thousand miles at a clip or hop planes the size of kitchenettes—sometimes to major-league productions in Tucson or San Francisco, more often to wind-blown corrals in Deadwood, South Dakota, or Elk City, Oklahoma. Here is what romantics call "goin' down the road": a blizzard of one-day stands, fast food, and speeding tickets. By chancing your ligaments and future generations, you stand to win up to a few thousand dollars—but only if your bull or horse, picked by random draw, feels like bucking on some bleached afternoon out of *Death Valley Days*. Nine of ten contestants finish out of the money, out their motel bills and plane fares, out of luck, and, finally, out of time.

Sixty or so bull riders survive this winnowing to ride full-time all year long. Of these, only the top fifteen money winners get to the second season, the Finals, their lone hope for a real living. In 1990, Tuff made fifty-eight thousand dollars down the road—just about right to pay his travel costs and entry fees. In ten days in Vegas, not counting the bets he pressed at blackjack (Tuff gambled like he rode, never flinching), he earned fifty thousand more, his net rodeo income for the year.

"You go maybe two hundred twenty-five days away from your family," Tuff said, "and lots of times you'd rather be home. But every day reminds you that you're headin' to the National Finals. It keeps you goin' all year. It's the eighth year I've been here, and I'm just as excited as my first time."

Every cowboy worth his chaps craves to join him, and any who get there dwell on getting back. The Finals is a field of dreams. In rodeo country, the lore of great rides at the NFR—

such as Freckles Brown's conquest of the unridden Tornado—
is passed from father to son, like tales of Babe Ruth's called
home run.

The Finals can spoil you for any other rodeo. The fans love
it because they get to see high-octane action every night. All
ten shows sell out a year in advance.

The stock contractors love the NFR because they get
about two thousand bucks for each bull or horse that makes
the cut, plus trucking costs, plus a free hotel room and all the
free beer they can chug, which by most accounts is enough to
float a silo.

The cowboys love it most of all because the Finals, as Donnie Gay said, is "the only truly professional rodeo we have all
year." The purse is unparalleled. In 1991, each round paid
more than ten thousand dollars for first, down to about
twenty-seven hundred dollars for fourth. The six bull riders
accruing the most points overall would also share a liberal pay-
out for the "average," up to twenty-three thousand dollars—a
royal sum in this business.

But it isn't just the cash. The Finals spells a chance to rest a
man's vagabond legs. For ten days a bull rider need drive no
farther than the two miles from the Gold Coast Hotel &
Casino to the Thomas and Mack Center, normally home to
the Runnin' Rebels of UNLV. He competes with the best
cowboys, on the best bulls, with the best bull fighters at the
ready, in front of seventeen thousand true-believing fans. And
after his short day's work is done, it's into the night for a
hero's welcome wherever he saunters. In Vegas each December rodeo cowboys are a tourist curiosity on a par with the
genuine simulated volcano at the Mirage (eruptions every fifteen minutes) or the nightly jousts at Excalibur.

It wasn't always this way. The NFR was born in Dallas in
1959, then swung to Los Angeles for a three-year run that
nearly closed the show. (One night the sponsors' flag girls—
the ones who canter in the service of Justin Boots and Bull's-

Eye Barbecue Sauce—came out in strapless evening gowns, and flopped off their mounts like skateboarders in an earthquake.) In 1965 the event settled in staid Oklahoma City, home to the National Cowboy Hall of Fame, and many presumed it was there for keeps.

But two decades later, from the other end of the earth, came an offer hard to refuse. The civic fathers of Las Vegas promised to double the Finals' purse, hike attendance by half, get the big media in tow. The NFR would no longer be some quaint ritual, but a state-of-the-art *happening*—a Super Bowl with spurs.

The lobbyists went to war. The chairman of Oklahoma City's chamber of commerce harrumphed that rodeo was "red-white-and-blue, a family affair"—all that Las Vegas presumably was not. PRCA directors were quizzed by the FBI as to whether a Nevada high roller had bribed them to sweeten the pot. But in the end it was no contest, for how could you keep 'em down on the farm after they'd split aces at Binion's? In 1985, the year Tuff appeared headed for his first gold buckle, the up-at-dawn, put-out-the-hay, low-falutin', straight-shootin', God-and-country world of rodeo embraced the capital of glitz, vice, suicide, and lung cancer. The Baptist deacon of sports had eloped with a showgirl.

"We've growed up," explained Bobby DelVecchio, the Bronx-bred bull rider who blew kisses to the crowd. "It's time to move on."

Or as Tuff liked to croon, "If you've got the money, I've got the time."

For Vegas the marriage was a godsend. A hundred thousand people dropped in for the Finals and left $75 million behind each year, turning a slow month into a hot one, swelling hotel occupancy by 10 percent. Ranch society, meanwhile, came round to see that Sodom wasn't such a bad place once a year, not when it threw in valet parking and three-dollar buffets.

For their part, the bull riders fit right in. There was no false romance in Vegas, no frontier nostalgia. There was just a clockless series of gambles, which was how the riders lived their lives year-round, and they figured they might as well get paid for it.

☆

As Las Vegas continued to boost the Finals purse by up to 8 percent each year, it also altered the flow of rodeo's season. In the Oklahoma City era, a hard driver like Donnie Gay could wear out the competition by August, get on so many bulls and build such a big dollar lead that he couldn't be caught. But by 1991, the Finals would dole out two and a half million dollars; the next richest rodeos, in Denver and Cheyenne, paid less than four hundred thousand apiece. There was so much money to be won or lost in Las Vegas that every championship was up for grabs. A twenty-thousand-dollar lead, once as good as checkmate, could now be wiped out on two bulls. Rarely would a gold buckle be settled before the last go-round.

And so the pressure on each man grew. Lord knows it's terrible hard just to make the Finals, to stay sound and sharp and ahead of the pack. But that's just the ante. A cowboy has to win big here to run for a title, and maybe to cover his heating bill in lean months sure to come. He has to prove himself before maiden aunts and high school classmates, and the wife who comes to vacation after fifty weeks of rodeo widowhood.

At the Thomas and Mack each bull rider stands exposed. Before it's over he'll have to mount every conceivable type of bull, from tea-party spinners to no-rhythm "eliminators." The smallest technical flaw will surface. The slimmest sliver of a qualm will unseat him. For every Cinderella story there are a dozen stepsisters who can't get their big toes into the damned slipper. The Finals, warned Gay, "can either make you or ruin you."

In answer, the bull riders reveal themselves. Tuff and muscle man Jim Sharp switch on in Vegas like latter-day Frank Sinatras. Clint Branger seems to cramp and shrink, as if he can't afford the table stakes. Ty Murray, the purist, rides just as he does in Pecos or Ponoka: with unbridled, tunnel-visioned effort.

And each year there are sad cases who fail to finish, who get danced on and packed out, whose bodies buckle under the stress of ten tough bulls over ten straight days. By the last go-round, it's odds on that at least one bull rider will fail to answer the bell—which likely means he can't walk.

That was bull riding, buddy. Plenty pain and adversity, and then it got harder.

On December 5, 1991, one year after Tuff's tussle with Stinger, he joined fourteen other joking finalists for a photo on the eve of the first go-round. Seven stood on the custom-mixed clay and sand trucked into the Thomas and Mack. The rest perched behind them on the top rail of the empty bull chutes, soon to hold their portions of crossbred rage. Nine of the bull riders hailed from Texas, two from California, one each from Oklahoma, Arizona, Montana, and Australia. All wore the cowboy uniform: hats of fine, brushed felt (twelve black, two cream, one white); brashly patterned, open-necked western shirts (in Tuff's case, a lush paisley number from Panhandle Slim, his main sponsor); ironed Wrangler jeans, so tight they accordioned at the knees; and a zooful of designer boots: ostrich, lizard, elephant, kangaroo.

Bull riding is a young man's game. Only three of the fifteen posers had passed their thirtieth birthdays, and Tuff was a veteran at twenty-eight. It's also a small man's game; the average finalist stood five-nine and weighed 150 pounds. A low center of gravity came in handy against the force of a gyrating bull. Tuff was trim enough, with a twenty-nine-inch waist, but he stood out like a third baseman among gymnasts. His jokes drew the loudest laughs, partly 'cause they were the cleverest, partly 'cause his frat brothers listened harder when he spoke. As a PRCA official noted, "Right now he's just the stud."

From the 1930s on, every ten-year era found one or two superstar bull riders, but this generation had deep depth, out of the boom in bull-riding schools and the lure of bigger money. In 1991, only one big name, the star-crossed Charles Sampson, had lost his season to injury. The result, by general agreement, was the strongest Finals field of bull riders ever— "fifteen guys who don't want to get off." On a given day any one of them could ride the rankest bull there.

In a typical year Tuff would target two or three cowboys he needed to beat for the buckle. This time there were at least five. First and foremost was Jim Sharp, one of Tuff's traveling mates, who rode stock-still and flawless as a Remington bronze: "When they turn on the lights in Vegas, he's tough to beat." Clint Branger, another partner, was overdue for his breakthrough Finals. Cody Custer, the born-again Christian cowboy, was "very underrated . . . a notch away from being a world champion." Ty Murray was "the greatest cowboy I've ever seen." And Ted Nuce still had to be reckoned with, even at the ripe old age of thirty.

(Nuce was a strange case. Gossip had it that he'd get psyched by staring down his own chubby image in the bathroom mirror, and shouting: "Ted Nuce, can you rise to the challenge? Ted Nuce, who are you? *You're a champion bull rider!*")

Modesty barred Tuff from naming the gold buckle favorite: himself. Despite ripping a knee in May, he'd entered the '91 Finals as the high money winner, the top seed. As the bullfighter Miles Hare would note, "The bulls are better than they've ever been, and the cowboys are better, and Tuff is still dominating. It's amazing that he can pull it off."

The old-timers will tell you facilities went upscale when the Finals left Oklahoma City. But the bull riders' dressing room was still pretty primitive: plain wooden benches, with open pine compartments overhead for their gear; a single padded folding chair; two toilet stalls and a sink; one mirror; and a small keg of Coors Lite. The linoleum floor was already splotched with Copenhagen/Skoal. ("I only chew three or four times a year," Tuff confided, "and it about makes me sick.")

On this first Friday night a mimeoed sheet of the night's draws papered one cinder-block wall. A green chalkboard bore a crude scrawl, the complete primer on cowboy philosophy: "Ride!"

At other rodeos bull riders pulled in whenever they pleased, often with minutes to spare; Branger once groused to Tuff that he hadn't heard a national anthem all year. But in Las Vegas they had to be primed at seven sharp to join the Grand Entry (no-shows were fined $250), leaving eons to stew before they went on.

An hour before the bulls' debut, the riders funneled tension into ritual. They scraped rosin chips down their bull ropes, spraying fine showers of amber dust. They hammered the locked rowels of their spurs to roughness, to grip a bull's hide without cutting.

"Sounds like a bunch of little elves in here," quipped John Growney, one of the few stock contractors the riders could stand to look at. Then a short, stocky, impish man, resplendent in gray tweed and diamond horseshoe neckerchief pin, blew into the room with an unmistakable Lone Star blast. "Is it a wake, or what?" bellowed Donnie Gay.

Two years after his no-fooling retirement from riding, now a thirty-eight-year-old contractor with three bulls in the Finals, Gay would spend every minute he could here. He'd held court as a contestant at thirteen Finals, till he seemed a part of the furniture—if furniture moved at 140 miles per hour. Gay would not go gently into the contractors' hospitality room down the hall. Over the next ten days he would function as wise mentor, obnoxious big brother, and master kibitzer; as a conscience of the game and the living emblem of try.

Gay also worked wonders as an icebreaker, and the riders eased into their routines. Ted Nuce stretched his hamstrings. Branger drilled a pet move, his free arm flowing like a martial artist's. Tuff slapped his left forearm, the one that would hold him in place, and that was that. He was high on his chances. He'd placed twice before on his draw, the feisty Tiny Tim—a stripling at thirteen hundred pounds, three-quarters the norm.

At 8:30 Tuff set a strip of tape on the palm of his riding hand, to protect it inside his soft deerskin glove. At 8:35 he donned his gaudy pink and silver chaps. Tuff didn't take to being rushed; he did everything in his own time, and tonight he trailed the line tramping out to the arena. As the cowboys receded down the corridor, to wait their turn behind the chutes, the bull-flattened bells that anchored their ropes set off a melancholy clanging. "You guys do good!" Gay called out. He looked out at their backs, his envy transparent.

CHAPTER 2

Chasing the Grail

"*I* SURE *HATE* TO GET BUCKED off," Clint Branger said, glowering as best he could through drooping lids. His voice was low, each syllable forced through a rigor-mortised smile. Twelve hours after he'd walked the plank on his second-round bull, a dirty dealer named Hammer Time, Branger steamed like water on a griddle. "There's nothing I hate worse—I can't accept it. I'd rather see my mother disown me than buck off."

It was past ten o'clock. Branger was late for Sunday breakfast at the Monterey Room, the Gold Coast coffee shop, where canned Christmas carols backed the slot machines' winter bells and the murmured urgings of high-heeled Keno runners. Without his cowboy hat, in a gray T-shirt and new Nikes, Branger looked even shorter and scrawnier than he had behind the chutes. He rubbed his eyes, but the fatigue stayed put: "I'm just lazy. I can't ride and I can't get up. I can't do nothin'." He'd slept badly on both ends of the night. Three times his phone had rung that morning, and three times he'd started awake with visions of Hammer Time. "I can't get it settled in my system," he said. "It'll just eat on me until I can get on another bull."

A waitress delivered the day's first caffeine—a tall Coca-Cola, heavy ice—and Branger looked up to ask for steak and eggs: "Rare, over medium, a glass of milk with that." Rodeo cowboys, like the old Egyptian kings, would gobble beef thrice a day if they could get it. Call it real food for real men, or a bull rider's revenge. As one man remarked over a sausage burrito, "I don't feel like I've eaten unless I eat meat."

Order taken, Branger went back to brooding. "There are some bulls that I just can't ride," he said. "They just don't fit, you know. That bull last night, he's just one I try to avoid. I wouldn't of won anything on him—I wouldn't have been enough points, not with those other sons of bitches turnin' back and *stayin'*. He was *leavin'*.

"I want a bull that bucks hard, and the only way he's gonna buck you off is if he *bucks* you off—not one that just sneaks around and waits for you to get tipped one way and then lunges the other way. It wasn't no fair, you know. I needed to ride him, of course, but what do you do?" The cowboy scowled. "I want to talk about something else now."

At twenty-seven, a year younger than Tuff, Branger still got carded at the big country bars. His face, pale and narrow, hardly had room for his features: heavy brows over hangdog brown eyes, a long, winding nose (broken three times, par for this course), a stubborn lower lip and defiant chin. Branger's ears stuck out and his hair sprouted in several directions; there seemed too many teeth for his mouth. Yet somehow it all fit together, in a lost-boyish sort of way.

Of all the top bull riders, Branger is the least guarded. He says what he means and he looks like he feels, and his frankness wins you over even as it worries you. How could a man so close to the skin survive such a rawhide world? His friends call him "Roscoe," which suits Branger perfectly, even before you

learn that he lives in Roscoe, Montana. Out between the pur-
pled Crazy Mountains and Custer's Little Bighorn, amid hilly
stands of evergreens, Roscoe is a ranch community with a bar,
a post office, a café, and fifty western souls. Billings, the big
town, is ninety minutes away by pickup. Roscoe grows wheat
and cattle, and time to scan the vaulting sky.

They did things the old-fashioned way in Branger's hometown. At roundup all the neighbors came to help load cows
and calves into the corral. Then the calves were roped and
dragged out, wrestled down and doctored and branded. Some
kids liked the wrestling most, but Branger had dicier sport in
mind. "Hold him!" he'd shrill, and then he'd hop on the calf
and ride without a rope. While the little boy hung on as long
as he could, and begged to go again, the episodes swamped
him. Each time he would "black out," never see a thing till he
hit the ground.

Branger was six years old when he started riding—the
same age he chewed his first tobacco. He began to notice
rodeo on television, and heard tales of Montana's rich past in
the sport, going back to the Linderman brothers and Greenough sisters from nearby Red Lodge, Branger's birthplace.
His father rode broncs, "so he kinda raised me to be a cowboy," Branger said. "And it fit me, too."

He was still six when he entered his first local rodeo. The
calves were no bigger than at home, but the setting—all those
people in the stands, all those eyes on *him*—was a shock.
Branger bawled in terror. He clambered on, cheeks wet, and fell
off nearly before the gate opened, once more fading to black.

It took two years for the child to try it again. This time
something clicked. Branger was like the Little Leaguer who
could suddenly follow the flight of a pitched ball. "They
brought this calf in and I got on with two hands, and I rode
this one—I saw everything. I could see the calf's head, and his
up-and-down motion, and the ground. I felt it all, and that
was really what hooked me."

All the events came easy to Branger, from goat tying to breakaway roping. But from the time he was nine and rode his first big steer to win a rodeo, none could compete with the call of the bulls. "I got such a thrill after I got off of him," Branger said simply. "It still is, today, when I get off an animal. I wish I could find the words. There's nothing like it. There's *nothing* like it."

By the time Branger won the national intercollegiate bull-riding crown in 1985, two points were clear: he had a huge talent for the sport, and he was wildly unsuited for the life to which it led him. "He didn't age as quickly as some people—he's always been a little more immature," related Sybil Branger, Clint's mother, a handsome woman with such a soft voice that it helped to follow her lips. She sat at a table in her smallish room in downtown Vegas, at Binion's Horseshoe ("It's not fancy, but you won't find any place where they treat you better"), a few hours before the next go-round. With a glance at the balding man next to her, the plain ex–bronc rider who'd hoisted Branger upon his first calf, she went on, "Chris was like that—young at heart." She laughed like a wind chime in a spring breeze.

To meet Branger's parents was to meet Montana. You found their like in films from Ingmar Bergman, characters molded by expanse and long freezes. They were people whose pauses told as much as their words. When your nearest neighbors are a mile or more away, all that space can color life gray—and lend excitement to the chance encounter. Clint and his older brother had six cousins as playmates, "and that was it," Sybil said. "When we went to town, they hid behind our skirts. They weren't worldly at all."

Growing up, Branger was happiest on his horse in the quiet hills, or fishing the East Rosebud River. In Roscoe he was whole in his world and deeply rooted. For many, ranch life breeds a user's mentality about animals raised for slaughter. But Branger lived in gentler communion. As a young child he called the lambs his "honey babies." When he was nine years old he trekked outside one morning to find forty of his pets on the ground with their throats ripped—some dead, others writhing their last. A coyote bitch had come in the night to train its pups to kill. The family raised no more sheep after that.

In Roscoe, where society was so sparse, Branger kept tuned for the weakest signals. He read faces for worry and voices for pain. He never acquired the modern age's tunnel vision, the trick of looking past the old man sleeping out on the grate. His unbuffered heart worked fine back home, but pro rodeo was lived in closer quarters. Each week brought a crush of airports and big-city traffic and packed arenas, with fans constantly bumping up against him, demanding some response. The nonstop interaction sapped Branger; the perpetual motion, where you were always running late, frayed and dismayed him. He pined for open space and solitude, for land he could read without maps.

But Branger still craved the riding, those eight seconds when the world stopped. In his thumbnail profile in the PRCA's media guide, he chose this quote: "If I can go to a rodeo every day, then I'm happy." Like many eager rookies, he figured there was one way to win a gold buckle, the way Donnie Gay did it: go to every show you can and pile up the points. Falling in for a time with a frugal vet named Joe Wimberly, Branger chased sleep balled up in a two-door Mustang grungemobile, with Motel 6 as a treat. Yes, he truly loved to ride, but the getting there was murder.

Branger's life changed in 1987, the first year he made the National Finals. The official programs misspelled his name as "Bronger," but he didn't much mind because it made the announcers pronounce it right. He won two go-rounds and got invited to go the next season with the best in his business: Tuff, the self-made man with a skewer for a tongue; Lane Frost, every mother's son and the newly crowned world champ; and Jim Sharp, the pink-cheeked machine who rode with more authority than they'd seen in donkey's years.

In rodeo they tell you that winners go with winners. A travel team works only when each cowboy rides at about the same level. If three men cash like clockwork and a fourth stays broke, the green-eyed dragon soon intrudes.

Branger knew the score. He'd never tried so hard in his life; he tried so hard he'd fall off, then cuss himself out as the others critiqued him. As Tuff would say, "It's easy to take the compliments, but it can be hard to take the truth." It took Branger a good part of 1988 to relax—to see that these great men screwed up, too. And if his grit needed proving, he passed the test that July in Calgary, when he won the fifty-thousand-dollar jackpot with a bum leg.

Along the way, the new man also had to unlock his wallet. Tuff and Lane liked Lincoln Town Cars and Sheratons. When they chartered a plane to pepper four towns in three days, the rodeo grind wasn't such a grind anymore. Branger found himself in a Kerouac novel and loving the loose-jointed flow of it. "It was a never-ending adventure," he said. "You do it long enough, you get to where you don't even think about going back home. . . . It's just that feeling of being free, I guess. You're stopping long enough to ride a bull and make a little money, just to keep that thing *movin'* all the time."

That foursome laid waste to many a rodeo. On pulling up to an arena, they'd draw stares like the James Gang muscling the doors of a saloon. *There they are,* the journeymen and locals would whisper. *There he is,* they'd say, nodding at Lane, who outshone everyone around him. Where Tuff coveted Lane's appeal, Branger just about worshiped the lanky Oklahoman. Lane was the man he wanted to be: forthright, sensitive, attentive to each needy fan.

As a stylist, however, Branger was very much his own cowboy. The last word in finesse, he rode with fluid control, a perfect seat, and minimal upper-body movement. When Clint Branger rode a bull, it was like DiMaggio gliding to a fly ball: the most elegant solution to the challenge at hand. Branger was often compared with Sharp, but he went only five-six and

135 pounds to Sharp's five-eight and 145 (about half of it in the Texan's forearms and biceps), and that made all the difference. Where Sharp could lock down on a bull, get a hold with his legs that he never relinquished, Branger would make a smooth series of micro-adjustments. His style suited most any bull—small or stout, rank or nice, into his hand or away.

But it wasn't a style to suit the scorers. When Branger was on his game, he'd "get eight" on the baddest cats in the business without an anxious moment. If a judge keyed on the rider instead of the bull (a common error, even among the full-time pro officials), he might mistake Branger's ease with an easy animal. The Montanan would score two to four points less than the flop-and-pop set on the same bull, same trip. He'd be punished for understatement, for his superior skill. Branger owned not an ounce of flamboyance. He wore mono-toned shirts in a cowboy sea of faux Indian prints, like a fox-trotter at a disco, and asked no pardon for his drabness: "I let my ridin' do my talkin' for me, and if people don't like the way I look, they can kiss my ass."

However well he rode, Branger was never quite content. By 1988 he was the lone member of his gang without a gold buckle. The next year Frost was dead, gored in the heart at Cheyenne at the age of twenty-five. Everyone felt bleak—"It just let the air out of the whole rodeo business," sighed Bryan McDonald, the PRCA's bull-riding director—but Branger bore a special loss. Lane "would listen to you," Branger said, "and he was always positive. When we were driving somewhere together, just me and him, he'd always make me feel better. I really miss him, thinking about it."

With Lane gone there'd be no one to listen. Sharp was the strong and silent type, barely there. Tuff treated Branger like a brother, took him home for months at a time, but he wasn't much for heart-to-hearts. Bare a weakness, and Tuff would stomp it like a snake that threatened the trail crew. "He's got a very rough way about him, where there ain't no excuses for anything," Branger said. "Most of the time he's right."

In high school Branger had lost his closest friend in rodeo, Zane Yanzick, in a car wreck. Zane was Branger's first confidant, the kind ear he needed when the nights were too dark or the days too long. Ten years later, Branger still missed him so much that he'd talk out his troubles at Zane's flowered grave back home. And now Lane was gone, too, and Branger took it as a lesson: don't get too close. From that point on, he would "have a hard time telling anybody I like them, because they'll just probably turn around and tell me they don't like me. I ain't gonna let myself be that vulnerable."

"He's got," said Sybil Branger, "a soft center."

But while Branger might hold friends and lovers at arm's length, he couldn't stop reaching for a gold buckle, every bull rider's grail. As metalwork alone it impressed: a dense oval in three colors of ten-karat gold, girded in sterling silver. At its center, flanked by two small diamonds, sat a hand-sculpted cowboy on a high-kicking bull.

There were forty-one hours of engraving in that buckle, and seventy-five hundred dollars of retail value. But like the heavyweight belt or the Stanley Cup, a gold buckle had no price, for you couldn't buy the stamp of history. You might get crippled after you won it, or killed, or foreclosed on by a cool-eyed banker, but they could never take away your title. When a Donnie Gay or Tuff Hedeman stood tall with that buckle cinched on (and they wore it everywhere but to bed, and on wilder nights there as well), he was marked as a being apart. In an event that ground most men down, these few had been raised up.

The gold buckle loomed so large—"bigger than an Oscar, bigger than an Emmy, bigger than anything in the world," as announcer Bob Tallman would declare at the '91 Finals awards dinner—because winners and losers both knew what it took to come by. In any era, according to Bryan McDonald, there were only "three or four guys who could win it, because there were only three or four guys who are that breed of cat." The catch was that they made just one champion a year, and so a cowboy might be *great* and never win. One might be, as Branger once was introduced in Calgary, "a champion without a buckle."

Of all the famous bridesmaids, the most famous was surely Denny Flynn, Donnie Gay's great nemesis. A leggy fellow from Arkansas, Flynn had it all: dark leading-man looks, judge-pleasing flair, and a talent for big, sweeping moves—amazing moves—to regain his seat. Had you stood them side by side, the chunky Gay would have looked like the anchorman on a Kiwanis bowling team.

Flynn could ride the rank ones; he won the Finals average, and the world's second most coveted buckle, a record three times. He was also tough enough to come back from a terrible hooking in 1975 in Salt Lake City, where he pole-vaulted over his riding arm and onto a high, sharp horn that ripped through his abdomen and within half an inch of his heart. (As Flynn would report, "I knew I was hurt real bad when I reached down and touched my intestines.")

He returned, stylish as ever, to rank sixth in the world that year, but he no longer rode his best on the bad bulls, the ones with big horns and the spite to use them. Flynn had never liked hard travel anyway. Over time he took to turning out those bad bulls, a practice that infuriated Gay, especially when the animal in question—a bull *he* could have drawn—had enough gas to win the rodeo. Gay couldn't abide a wasted opportunity; Flynn looked to a shady porch on his Arkansas farm. And when it came time to tally their careers, Gay had eight gold buckles and Flynn not a one. It turned out that Flynn had lacked something, after all: the drive to be best. At the end he didn't quite care enough, and caring counted for something in this game.

While Flynn knew his limits, other riders were ruined by gold buckle dreams. Some years ago, one of them finished second by a small margin. Rather than savor the best season he'd ever had, he let the near miss gall him. He groused to his friends that the buckle should have been his: the judges had cheated him, the winner slapped a bull unseen. Whining was strep throat to cowboys, a germ to be avoided, and when the runner-up's friends stopped listening, he turned on them as well. He went to the Finals one more time, struck out, and was never heard from again. He'd lost his buddies, his confidence, and finally—most fatally—his joy in riding.

Tuff understood the obsession: "Before I ever won a championship, I thought I *had* to win one. I thought the end of the world was going to come before I won." Only after owning one did Tuff discover that he still had "the same worries and fears as everybody else. I'm no different than I was—and I think that's the biggest thing that people don't understand."

Branger, for one. He was absolutely accepted by Tuff and Sharp, who knew how good he was and how hard he tried. But each time he looked at them, with their Hall of Fame passports at their waists, he saw again what he lacked—that shining, taunting oval. There were times, many times, when Branger felt out of place. There were times when he felt like a homely little guy from Roscoe.

Once he bagged the buckle, Branger said, "I'd fit more. Sometimes I'm with Tuff and Jim and people are doing interviews, and they don't want to talk to somebody who hasn't won a world title—that's just natural. I just go over there in the corner for a while." He put down his fork, and his eyes turned molten. "I shouldn't let that bother me, but I do."

It bothered him most at the NFR, where gold buckles are won and lost. There were years Branger did well enough in Vegas—those two winning rounds in '87, or the time he rode nine of ten in '89—and still fell short of the brass ring. But there were others when his riding curdled, when he pressured up and the air turned toxic. Once a bull stepped on Branger's foot, splitting it open; the doc, short on supplies, sewed the flesh without painkillers. "That damn sure hurt," Branger admitted, "but the worst kind of pain might have been in 1990, when I didn't ride my last bull at the NFR."

To that point it had been the best of years. Branger ended the regular season sitting second, just behind Sharp. He came into the Finals keen and healthy. But as he prepped to do battle, he sounded anxious, almost desperate. "I'm scared, but I'm going to be trying my ass off," he said at the time. "I have the best chance I ever will. I'm not going to let this opportunity slide."

After riding seven of his first nine bulls, he led the pack into the final go-round with three others still in the running. The whole year had come down, as it usually does, to one bull: sudden death. Norman Curry rode his tenth straight—only the second man, after Sharp, to do so at the NFR. Tuff, three days after his draining slam dance with Stinger, got welled into his hand and dunked. Sharp beat the dangerous Wipeout Skoal—one of the less friendly draws in a hostile pen, a white-faced fury—for an eighty-six, enough to overtake Curry for the championship lead.

Then came Branger, on the last bull of the year. He faced a neat proposition. If he rode and beat Sharp's score, he was the champ. Buck off, and the buckle was Sharp's.

Branger had the best bull, the one he needed: Outlaw Willie, the big-shouldered Black Angus with just a drop of Brahma blood for temper. At seven years old, the bull was in the heart of his prime: old enough to gain from experience, young enough to be fit and feisty. Never mind that Willie was a "muley," born without horns; his power and speed were ample to intimidate. That season he'd been ridden but four times in thirty-eight tries.

Still, the cowboys liked his no-tricks approach. Willie just bucked and kicked and spun, high and hard and very fast, with the even timing that made for high scores. Bull riders had a saying about this caliber of bull—that you couldn't "stub your toe," make the smallest mistake. Not if you hoped to score.

That night the deal began to go bad as it often did, in the chute. Eager to fly, Outlaw Willie hammered the yellow iron panels, disrupting Branger's groundwork. The rider had his rope pulled and wrapped once, twice, three times. He knew that his balance would hinge upon the perfect centering of his riding hand, on his left pinky tracing the bull's backbone. After the third pull Branger thought his handhold was right. Or maybe the pressure of the moment—with ESPN's camera crew pushing its time limit, with the chute boss all twitchy, with those thousands of eyes on *him*—nudged the rider to rushing. It was time to go. Branger nodded, the universal signal to open the chute.

Not until Outlaw Willie's second jump, as the bull slashed to the left and rolled his hide, as Branger's hand slipped off center, did the rider realize his error. It amounted to a fraction of a centimeter, and to Branger's whole world. It threw him just an eyelash behind the bull's action, but a miss was a mile on a bull quick as Willie. The man from Roscoe had stubbed his toe.

To his credit, Branger never quit. At the third jump a to-the-moon kick whipped him off center, till he leaned forty-five degrees away from his hand. Branger threw his free arm back over his head, fought and recovered, but never quite solved the bull's frantic spin. By the eighth jump he fell behind again, and this time there'd be no recouping. Branger's arm chopped back, faster and faster, all elegance lost. He knew he was through.

Six seconds into the ride, Outlaw Willie finished his fourth full circle, a phenomenal pace. Just two seconds from engraving his name in gold, Branger whipped off into space. Still he clung to his rope for a long half second, his body flipping like a tumbler's, as if to put off the end as long as he could. He knew what hell he'd be waking to as soon as he touched the ground.

"Nobody could have tried it any harder than that young man right there," weighed the ESPN play-by-play man, as the ride unraveled on slow-motion replay.

"He is gonna be down too soon," replied the man's partner, with the only fact that mattered.

Branger peeled back to the chutes for safety. Then he knelt to the dirt, crossed his arms on one knee, and buried his head. His season was over; Sharp had his second title. It was, said

Sammy Andrews, the bull's owner, "the most heartbreaking thing" Outlaw Willie had ever done. To make his anguish complete, Branger checked with the judges. Had he ridden, he would have topped ninety. Had he ridden, he would have won it all.

"Does that mean he choked?" mused Cody Lambert, long after the fact. "I would never say that. Clint had a bull that is liable to buck him off anywhere, anytime. I would say he got bucked off by a real rank bull."

Branger had finished his best season, but he wasn't fit for society after that ride. He skipped the awards banquet at Caesar's Palace once again. "You're still a champion in my book," said Tuff, who well recalled the lash of '85, but Branger brushed him off. He dodged his parents and slunk back to Montana, to where no one could find him.

He'd gone on whiskey binges after past Finals, but none to match this one. For two weeks Branger stayed drunk, spinning into depression, his sole companion the man with the cork hat. Christmas passed, and New Year's, and still his pain wouldn't soak away. The more he drank, the worse he felt, and the worse he felt. . . .

At some point in that dim Plains winter, Branger might have understood a suicide's compulsion, the need to kick out an exit when all life's doors seemed bolted. But then the second week of January rolled around, and the National Western Stock Show & Rodeo in Denver—where, as it happened, Outlaw Willie would buck off Jim Sharp. A new season. Another gold buckle with nobody's name on it. Branger packed his rigging bag and hit the road, which was all that he knew to do.

Months later, when someone suggested it was no shame to finish third in the world, Branger winced and replied, "But it's not good enough." He was reminded of that harsh American fact—that you were number one or nobody—wherever he went in 1991. Riders who couldn't carry his rigging bag, fans who couldn't tell a bull's flank from its brisket, all itched to set

Branger straight. For rodeo announcers, known to milk a story line, Outlaw Willie was *the bull that cost Clint Branger the title!*

"I had to listen to that all year long," Branger said. "You want to put it behind you and do good, and come back and win it the next year, and they're talking about something negative." That black bull was Branger's white whale. That ride he'd relive beyond counting. He'd see himself sliding behind, scuffling for dear life. Never quite catching up.

For all that, he was once again the best bull rider of the regular season, and led the money-won standings till a broken ankle shelved him in early October and allowed Tuff to edge ahead. The doctors cleared Branger for action nine days before the '91 Finals. The ankle felt fine, but some wondered if he was ready from the neck up.

"Clint dwells on the negative too much," Lambert said after the second go-round. "You've got to acknowledge your mistakes, but you've got to enjoy the good things, too. You can be so worried about doing things wrong that that's what you program into your mind." Or as McDonald put it: "Clint wants to win it so bad that he can't."

The puzzle of bull riding is that the tougher the bull, the more relaxed a cowboy must be. You can clamp down tight on an average draw, but the great bulls demand moves that can't be forced. That goes triple at the Finals, where extra pressure fathers mistakes. The champions make mistakes, too, but rarely two in a row. They can try without trying too hard. They are better at riding one bull at a time, at evening their keel against each day's tides—especially in Las Vegas, where, says Donnie Gay, a bull rider's fortunes go "up and down more often than a whore's drawers at a weenie roast."

Branger understood the loser's syndrome but couldn't shake it. Each time he bucked off a Hammer Time, his anger was a Ouija board for old grudges, for all the dark voices clamoring inside him. Like a nightmare that gathered power with each worming visit, the Finals plot line seemed less and less likely to turn in his favor.

You could see it in his eyes, which smoldered holes into the dressing-room television at the second round's replay. ("Why in the hell you talkin' to me?" he once snapped at a writer. "Go interview the bull.") You could hear it in his voice at the coffee shop, when he vowed not to "screw up" again, and to ride the eight bulls left to him. Branger had a vision for this Finals: a rematch with Outlaw Willie, winner take all. "I'll guarantee you I'll have him—and I'll guarantee that I'll ride him this time, too. I just know I will. He owes it to me. Next year he's gonna be Outlaw Willie, the bull that *won* Clint Branger his first world title."

Did Branger trust his destiny? Or was he just panicked by the empty alternative—and where it might lead him? It was hard to be sure as he eyed the bone on his plate, what was left of his steak and eggs. "Here's my chance—I got to do it now," said the bull rider, lean and ever-starving. "I had to do it last year, and I didn't. I *got* to do it now."

CHAPTER 3

Try, Again

O₂ Sunday Tuff struck back with Kowabunga, a twisting spinner. The bull was "juicy" that night, and Tuff won the third go-round with an eighty-four. He seemed unfazed that Kowabunga's hooves had landed inches from his skull after a brief hang-up fouled his dismount. The win was real, the disaster only theoretical, and Tuff was the most happy fella at the Thomas and Mack. You saw just how much he lived to finish first.

"I always have this fear of coming to the National Finals and not winning a dime all week long," he said, moving double-time through the thronged concourse minutes later, spurs jangling at each stride. Inside the main entrance Tuff took a seat at some folding tables with the other go-round winners, to sign programs and posters for his starstruck fans. Middle-aged women gushed like schoolgirls. Young boys could barely mouth their names.

"Tuff, Tuff!"

"Getcher autograph?"

"That's the man right here, y'all!"

Tuff sparked something in people. It was more than his two gold buckles, or a bull rider's generic appeal; Jim Sharp had the same credentials but lacked the same tug. Fans pulled for Tuff because they believed he was like them, an ordinary joe and honest workman. "He's the man," said Randy Weeks, a young enthusiast who'd flown to Vegas from Muskogee, Oklahoma. "It's before he even gets on the bull—when they announce his name, eyes light up. He just gets in there and gets the job done."

As he scribbled his bulky cursive Tuff wondered about Branger, who'd had another siege of buzzard's luck. He'd ridden Desert Storm for an eighty and a tie for second, but the bull lost its footing at the horn and fell tail first on the rider's leg. The pain began when Desert Storm slid to Branger's right ankle—his good one—and twisted its bulk to get up. Dr. J. Pat Evans, the orthopedics man with the medical team sponsored by Justin Boots, sent the limping cowboy to the hospital for X rays. "In the worst case, it's the end of his Finals," Tuff said.

Back at the Gold Coast, Tuff found Branger in his low-lit room, hunkered down with a room-service steak and a horror movie. Branger's ankle, dressed and ice-packed, lay propped on a pillow on the coffee table. The X rays would be read the next morning. "It feels loose, kind of wobbly inside," Branger said. "They think I tore some ligaments or tendons, maybe broke a small bone."

"Oh, a small bone's not that bad," Tuff consoled him.

"I don't think it's serious," Branger said. "I think I can still ride."

Among bull riders, riding hurt was a given. If a man couldn't master his body, how could he master a bull? And so the highest virtue was to be "tough": to sneer at pain and go on. "It comes back to the same old thing," Branger said. "If it was easy, everybody would do it."

Or as seven-time world champion bull rider Jim Shoulders once considered, after splintering his leg in five places: "You can't stop something like this from hurtin', but you can damn well not let it bother you."

Shoulders was the John Wayne of rodeo, the bullheaded hero who'd eat a dozen bullets and never say uncle. Back in the tight-lipped 1950s, when cowboys scored horse pills from the vet to help them creak through the morning, Shoulders was king of the stoics. More than play with pain, he could win with it. He'd win with the palm of his riding hand torn and raw, layered with gauze and liquid ether. He'd win, spitting blood, after a hoof found his mouth and sheared off five teeth.

Toward the end of Shoulders's career, a head-fighting bull at Houston hooked back and caved in his face. The champ got so mad he refused to buck off, seventeen fractures notwithstanding. With his nose shoved under his left eye, Shoulders looked like a bad Picasso. The doctor told him he needed prompt plastic surgery to rebuild the nose and repair his squashed sinuses.

"But doc, can't you put off operatin' till after I ride tomorrow?" Shoulders begged.

"Good god, man, you can't ride with a nose like that."

"Hell, doc," Shoulders said, "I don't hold on with my nose."

Toughness is more than good form. Without it you can't feed your family, for rodeo has no disabled list, no three-year guarantees. And besides, to give in to soreness is to yield to the bull's pull and power. Yield at the wrong time and you may not greet the next dawn.

So bull riders frown at too much sympathy. Dwelling on a pal's suffering won't help the wounded, but it might distract you enough to join him. On Sunday night Tuff was up on the second bull after Branger got hurt. When he saw the mishap, he said, "I knew it probably wasn't life threatening, and you know, I just ignored it."

"You got to ignore it," Branger agreed. "Otherwise you ain't gonna do your job."

"You got to attend to business," Tuff concluded.

When Tuff hung up on Stinger the year before, Branger had "wanted to do something, but I was next to ride, so I finally just turned and walked away from it. It looked like he was gonna come undone, but I didn't want to have it bother me and maybe do the same thing, you know? I got to save my life, too."

Up until the early '80s, most rodeo injuries went untreated. Strains and bruises weren't worthy of mention. Rips and sprains were managed with a six-pack. Of course, it got harder to grin and bear it after that first bad wreck broke the news: you weren't bullet proof, after all. The tough guys kept gritting their teeth and nodding their heads, but hens would flutter in their gas tanks. At some point self-preservation would cut off their try, and then they were useless in the ring.

By the time Tuff and Branger hit the scene, Justin Boots' Healer program had gained the cowboys' trust. The bull riders know that J. Pat Evans won't keep them sitting any longer than needed. Still, they keep straining their limits. They ride with broken jaws and cracked vertebrae, with torn biceps and walls of fractured ribs. Bull riders, Evans said, "don't expect to be pampered." Pain is the coin of the realm they love.

"It goes this way," said Monty "Hawkeye" Henson, the three-time saddle bronc champ. "I was born naked, broke, and just had a fresh-ass whuppin'. They can't send me out no worse, isn't that right?"

Which brings us back to Branger, on his couch, holding his foot in perfect stillness and contempt. "It ain't gonna kill you to ride if your leg gets stepped on," he said, splurting tobacco into a plastic cup for emphasis. "As long as the bull don't smash it in the chute. . . ." After the horn, he went on, "I can get away from him the same as always. You don't have to be Carl Lewis to get away—just pick a spot."

Maybe it was Branger's foot, or maybe it was the beer he and Tuff were guzzling, but late that evening the talk turned to an absent friend, the missing cowboy: Lane Frost.

From the moment Tuff met Lane in 1980, at a national high school tournament in Yakima, Washington, they were natural rivals. Born seven months apart, they longed for the same prize: to be the world's best bull rider. Tuff was stuck in his ugly-duckling phase. In Lane he saw what he lacked: hair that stayed combed, a smile that lit the world, and a loose-limbed riding style all the Oklahoman's own, down to the brown eagle feather in Lane's hat.

Tuff finished out of the money in Yakima and watched Lane take second. The following year Tuff placed second to Lane's first. And so it went through their junior rodeo championships, and into their PRCA rookie year in 1983. Lane got the jump on Tuff that winter, clocked a ninety at his first professional rodeo, and nearly won rookie of the year. Tuff was still in school, still broke and playing catch-up, and he didn't much like it. "I was extremely jealous—sure I was," Tuff conceded. "Lane was the guy I wanted to be, and wanted to *beat*. In my eyes he was a lot prettier, and rode better. He was probably a lot friendlier to me than I was to him."

"Jerk," Branger broke in, to clarify the point.

"Not really," Tuff said, slurring a bit now. "Well, probably a jerk, but I was intimidated more than anything. I didn't feel comfortable with him because I thought he was superior to me. I thought he was the golden child." It wasn't until 1985, after Tuff was established in the pros, that he warmed to the idea of their traveling together. Then Tuff got to see Lane's first-magnitude stardom up close.

"He'd walk in the room, and you'd just feel it," Tuff said. "It was 'Lane, Lane, Lane'—not only with the fans, but the cowboys. He was the all-American boy; we'd be like heathens compared to him." Another swig. "He was just like me and Clint, though, wantin' to win every time. Once in Arizona he got bucked off, and we got in this brand-new white Lincoln and we're driving off . . . and all of a sudden Lane starts cussin' and kickin' the dashboard. That's stuff that nobody's ever seen. If he'd been bucked off tonight, he'd be kickin' the wall and throwin' this." For illustration Tuff winged a remote-control pad off the television cabinet.

"But he really liked people," Tuff went on. "He'd try to make everybody feel special, and they'd just flock to him. We'd tell him, 'What are you doing, runnin' for office?' But Freckles Brown—that's who Lane idolized—taught him that it was always better to make somebody feel good than feel bad. And that's what he tried to do." Till Tuff and Branger took to calling Lane "the King," after Elvis Presley, for the way folks next to fainted when they spied him.

As they went down the road, Tuff came to see that his partner was more than a pretty face. Lane was *tough*. He had a trim frame—about five-eleven and 140 pounds—and a habit of getting stomped on. His body wasn't built for the pounding he took, but he took it just the same. Pale with pain or shivering with grippe, he'd keep on entering—and, like Jim Shoulders, he always entered to win. At Lane's first Finals in 1984, it seemed he got slammed in every go-round. But each time he'd rise and shrug off assistance, never showing his hurt, never giving an inch. At the end he'd ridden five bulls and placed on four of them, just enough to rank ninth in the world, or one spot ahead of a vexed young man from El Paso.

Over thousands of miles, through good times and hard, Tuff and Lane built a bond. If Tuff was Huck Finn, the shameless bad boy, then Lane was Tom Sawyer, embraced by all. But their differences meant less than what they shared: a no-holds-barred drive to be great. Of all the bull riders of their generation, only Lane matched Tuff for total try. Two originals, they moved from cold competition to mutual fascination to a selfless comrades' love.

Tuff freed Lane to be rougher, to swear and spit like one of the guys. But where Tuff and Cody Lambert bickered like brothers, until they'd shout to stop the car to slug it out, Lane was unflappable. He liked a good laugh even when he was the butt of it. Once he rode a rank bull and gave the crowd his trademark wave—two hands raised overhead, flapping from the wrist. As he neared the chutes he found Tuff and Lambert waving back the same way. Lane was the best kind of folk hero; he never took himself too seriously.

For Tuff, it was his first and last intimate friendship. Lane was that rare unfiltered man—"This kid will talk about *anything*," George Michael exclaimed after their first *Sports Machine* interview—who somehow got Tuff to respond in kind. A videotape addict, Lane was also one of the few who could knock Tuff's riding without getting blown off or chewed up. Tuff knew that Lane had earned the privilege, paid the same dues.

For four years the two were inseparable. When Freckles Brown, Lane's mentor, died in 1987, Tuff flew out to Oklahoma for the funeral. The gesture might have seemed out of character, but Tuff's character had changed.

"You know, I have a lot of shortcomings; I can be negative and hateful," Tuff said. It was two in the morning and the beer cans were empty; soon it would be time for sleep. "Lane was the best thing that ever happened to me. I'm a lot better person from the things I learned from him."

On July 30, 1989, Lane slept in after an overnight drive from Helena to Cheyenne. Tuff brought him breakfast in bed: "I did things for him that I had never done for anybody else."

About six hours later, in a grim drizzle at Cheyenne Frontier Days, the world's largest outdoor rodeo, Lane took on a long-horned brindle named Taking Care of Business. He made a masterly ride and a decent dismount, but was slow to gather himself in the mud. Getting clear from a bull is like a three-step race with a grizzly bear, and this time Lane finished second. He was on his knees when Taking Care of Business

hooked him the first time, on his face when the bull came again, to dig a horn in his back. Lane staggered toward the chutes and motioned for help, then crumpled. A broken rib, or the horn itself—there would be no autopsy—had notched an artery.

Tuff rushed to his friend's side, but there was nothing to be done save follow numbly to the hospital. After they'd stopped the heart massage and the ventilator, and the monitor went flat, and all the doctors were gone, Tuff walked into the deserted room and gave Lane a last hug.

Lane went out in typical style, the cowboys nodded in years to follow. He'd scored an eighty-five, won a check he'd never cash. By dying at twenty-five he became the King forever. As the surviving alter ego, Tuff was flooded with memorial poems and hackneyed media nostalgia. He drank a little more, sowed a deeper mean streak. Lane had been the one who could set him straight, call him on some flash of pigheadedness. Now Tuff would listen to nobody. Now he would barrel forward like he used to, straight and hard for what he wanted, and if you got in his way you were liable to get walked on. "It was," Tuff said, "the toughest thing I ever went through."

It wrenched at him most in Las Vegas. The routes he drove, the places he stopped—all brought back what he and Lane had shared. But while Tuff would always shoulder his loss—"Oh, I'll never get over it," he said—he deposited his grief at the 1989 Finals, five months after Cheyenne. Tuff had already called his shot, audaciously vowed to win the title in Lane's memory. Once again it came down to the tenth bull. Tuff knew he had to score to claim the buckle. "He's not riding alone," Bob Tallman intoned. Tuff made the whistle—and then rode an extra eight seconds to honor his fallen friend.

On Monday night, an hour before his fourth bull, Tuff laid out his gear on a dressing-room bench for inspection:

One pair of scuffed, tan riding boots, of extra-tough hide.

Two leather thongs, to be tied above the ankle, to keep the boots from slipping off in the fray.

A pair of dulled steel spurs, with five-point rowels locked for traction.

A yellow glove made of deerskin, "because it feels so good on your hand."

A pair of leather chaps, which saved Tuff's legs in the chutes or in a spill, and made a show when they billowed in combat.

A twelve-foot rope, flat and braided, to be pulled tight—but not tied—on the bull. It featured a stained, arched handle and a loop for two battered cowbells. The bells rang to excite the crowd, if not the bull, and also dragged the rope to the ground when Tuff pulled its tail.

"It's real basic," Tuff said. "That's all you have and all you need." For a bull rider, the most critical item was the bridge between man and bull: the rope. Once made of hemp, now synthetic, bull ropes were treated like frontier horses, with care and possessiveness. Each had peculiarities, in its number of plaits or the shape and give of its handle. A rope lost or stolen spelled trouble, as it took several rides to break in a new one.

Tuff shook into his palm the contents of a leather pouch, a half dozen chunks of translucent rosin, to be scraped along the rope's handle and tail for added friction. He would use the rosin twice that night, once in the dressing room and again when he took his "suicide wrap" at show time, with the tail snaked twice around his palm and then wedged between ring finger and pinky. Tuff kept his rope stickier than most, as he was prone to having it jerked out of his hand. Which was as dire as losing your steering on the Pacific Coast Highway: "It's hard to make the whistle if you don't get ahold of your rope."

His point became prophecy after four seconds on Happy Jack, a smooth little Brangus with lots of action. Tuff had lagged behind the spin but was still in fair shape when his hand popped halfway out of the handle. He went down like a duck in season. Rob Smets darted between bull and rider to "pick" Happy Jack away, but slipped in the middle of his move. The bull checked his run. Like a shark in its strike zone, he'd caught a glimpse of Tuff and swerved back for the kill—"a very smart bull," the bullfighter Miles Hare would say later. By the time Hare and Smets restored order, Tuff had been plowed under by a one-bull stampede. He tottered out a nearby gate to the photographers' moat and collapsed to his knees in the sawdust.

Minutes later he was back in the dressing room, flush-faced from exertion. Aside from an eight-inch stripe down his back, scraped raw by a hoof, he felt fine, except that he felt like screaming. "He was just a real good bull," Tuff muttered, as he siphoned beer from the keg into a Diet Coke can.

Winners and losers filed to their stalls. Tuff paid his respects: "Good ride, Ted; good ride, Martin." Clint Branger limped to the bench, peeled off his orthopedic lace-up boots, and set five pounds of ice on his tortured ankle, blown to the size and color of an eggplant. After Branger's X rays turned up negative (they'd actually missed a bone chip, which would heal uncast), he'd spent the day on crutches, then ridden with a skater's balance.

Tuff took his front-row seat by the VCR, to see Ted Nuce wiggle his way to pay dirt and twirl his bull rope like a lariat to the keening crowd. "Michael Jackson, Michael Jackson!" brayed Donnie Gay.

"I hammed it up. I'm thirty, I got to think of something," Nuce said cheerfully.

"You're going for another endorsement—suppositories," Gay observed.

Tuff chuckled stiffly at the byplay, but his heart wasn't in it. He reddened anew when he watched his own ride on replay: "That's a strong-bucking bull. If I stay on, I should win a bunch." Aside from a fat check, Tuff had lost acreage in his title run; with this honest bunch of spinners, only three men had failed to finish. Plus he'd blown another chance to ride all ten Finals bulls, the one goal that still eluded him. "It's ridiculous," he said.

As Cody Lambert saw it, Tuff hadn't lacked for effort on Happy Jack. He'd been done in, instead, by his butcher-knife style: "The bull was going to the right, and Tuff made such a rough, hard move, such a twist on his body, that it turned his butt to the outside. And that put such a strain on his hand that it popped out."

But Tuff wouldn't probe the fine points of failure. When searching for blame after a fall, he invariably pointed his finger at the center of his chest. He'd never fault the draw or the weather or the judges, or his own athletic soft spots, for these he could do nothing about, and they might as easily unseat him the next day. Instead Tuff would flay his try and his courage, his smarts and heart: the elements he controlled. Tonight he'd conclude that he'd let down after the prior round's triumph, taken Happy Jack for granted, made "a big, big mistake."

And that he "wasn't aggressive enough."

And that he had to "get stronger," and "get off my ass and do something."

Tuff's judgments were harsh, but they guaranteed he'd come out swinging the next time. Once he'd purged his rage, he could take a cooler view. "You go from champ to chump in a hurry here," he said, as bull riders scattered into the vast parking lot and beyond. "One night you think you've *got* 'em, you're fixin' to blow 'em out of the water, and the next night something happens and you don't know if you'll get over it. But I've gotten to the point where I can shake it off pretty well."

To help in the shaking, Tuff and Tracy made a pilgrimage to the Stardust. For two weeks in December the casino's yawning conference center became a bandbox for the Grateful Dead of rodeo: Ricky and the Redstreaks. Friends and relatives in tow, Tuff was ushered to a front-row-center table for a packed-to-the-rafters midnight set. "Hey, Tuff, how ya doin'?" welcomed lead singer John Jackman, alias Ricky Zucchini, a blocky, balding cult hero with a walrus mustache and an arthritic hip. He launched into a zippy Pat Boone number and the bacchanal was on.

The "Streaks" were not your typical country band. To be honest, they weren't a country band at all. Aside from a crisp cover of the Blues Brothers' "Theme from *Rawhide*," they stuck to old rock 'n' roll, party songs from the '50s and '60s, enlivened by Ricky's lewd patter and a cache of props surely banned in Salt Lake City. Ever since crashing Cheyenne Frontier Days in 1982, the Streaks ranked as the number-one draw for rodeo folk. During the National Finals, Merle Haggard might play to 950 fans a night. Willie Nelson might croon to 1,100. But John Jackman and his cronies—a few homely guys in leather or powder-blue blazers, plus a voluptuous blond vocalist in red sequins (a rumored female impersonator)—would wreak havoc before 2,500 camp followers each evening. The cowboys loved the Streaks because they had no rules and never asked people to stay in their seats. Pay your five-dollar cover, in fact, and you could do anything short of a felony. At one casino where the band no longer played, management installed a two-drink minimum. Jackman told them it wouldn't fly: "To a cowboy, a two-drink minimum is an insult."

Tuff adored the nightlife—"I do my best work after midnight"—and had a personal history with the Streaks. Once he brought along his father-in-law, a front-row Baptist whose grown daughters shrank from drinking in his presence. When Jackman spied Tuff, he took to reminiscing—over a live mike—about the time in San Antonio when Tuff had come to hear the band and found a Wagnerian-sized singer instead, "and you were throwing beer cans at that fat girl on stage, and the cops came and started to drag you out." Tracy wasn't easily embarrassed by her man, but she'd never let him forget that one.

Tonight Tuff would behave. Not so the hordes of amateur ropers and western-wear marketing reps, who were living it up like Shriners on holiday. They pitched back their Coors Lites to Ricky's transvestite homage to Connie Francis, complete with fishnet stockings and pasties on Jackman's furry chest. They howled at the sight of Ricky lobbing and dodging items from his fabulous dildo collection. They stood and cheered the Streaks' signature tune, "It's So Hard to Say I Love You

When You're Sitting on My Face," clambering atop their tables to hoof it among the trembling bottles. They went totally mad-ass bonkers when the band batted an inflatable plastic love slave about the stage like a beach ball. It was a great night to be young and drunk and a cowboy, or even one or two of the three.

On his way out of the Stardust, in one of those endless Vegas anterooms that recalled a plane change at O'Hare, Tuff encountered a slight black man in a cowboy hat. As the man swayed a bit in greeting, it appeared that Charles Sampson, too, had hoisted his share. "He's a bull-riding mother!" Sampson roared, his voice whiskey-hoarse, his grin plastered in a stubbled beard. "He's a bad mother! He's a *tough* mother—that's Tuff!"

Sampson seemed insubstantial, even smaller than his listed five-foot-four: the Ghost of Finals Past. In 1982 he'd become the first black world champion in rodeo history, a tiny guy from Watts skimming past mean-eyed judges, redneck precedent, and any number of maladjusted bulls. He'd reached the NFR eight times in all, and this one would have made nine, except for a scalpeled knee and four months on the shelf. Sampson had given his all to the sport, put rodeo on a bigger map. He was *somebody* in this world, wasn't he? But now he'd been shunted aside. No interviews on ESPN, no invites to the VIPs' booth, naught to do but watch and burn. If Tuff needed any reminding, here it was—that fame was a wisp in time, and you'd better enjoy it while you could.

With the sixth round on Wednesday, the riders got their first taste of the rank pen, "the A Team," brutes with all the charm of SCUD missiles. Through the season these bulls had thrown more than nine of ten cowboys, and crippled quite a few, and so the Finals became a war of attrition, with bull riders triaged in the corridor outside J. Pat Evans's door. Only three men made the horn that night; the rest were lucky to leave with their skins.

In the dressing room Donnie Gay took Branger aside to gently chide him for "babying" his sore foot: "You're movin' but you ain't really stickin'." Tuff sat watching the carnage on video amid a sea of Ace bandages and ice packs. He wore a boot on his left foot and a sock on his right. "I *love* bull ridin'," he said. His own adventure had ended in a blink. Just after the gate opened, Dr. J had "hipped" himself as he made his quarter turn out of the chute, smashing into an iron panel. Tuff's spur snagged in the rail with such force it sheared off. His right ankle twisted backward before Tuff fell clear, and quickly swelled big as a fist.

Tuff had been durable and more than a little lucky over his career, but he held no illusions. "Rodeo isn't a matter of if you get hurt, it's when and how bad," he said. "It's a game of wrecks." Some assumed Tuff to be fearless, but that wasn't it at all. Every bull rider knows fear. The trick is to let the danger work for you, to use it for fuel. Or for static, to short out any last current of common sense. The trick is to drain away your doubt, fear's sour residue, and if you can't you better quit. Because that's how people get hurt, and worse.

As Tuff hobbled his one-booted way out the concourse, there stood Red Hedeman, his ever-patient dad. "Where's your boot, son?" he asked.

"Outgrew it," Tuff said.

Then he spied his six-month-old baby, Robert Lane (called Lane for short), a pug-nosed, wispy-haired boy who wouldn't stop smiling, even at 10:30 at night. Tuff doted on Lane without stinting, knew his age to the day. As Tracy took the wheel of the rented Lincoln, he winced his way inside with the baby on his lap.

"Look at him," Tracy said. It was Lane's first brush with world-class neon, and he was mesmerized.

"There's a whole lot of lights out there, aren't there, pard-ner?" Tuff said softly. He kissed his son and shared the view, far from the nearest bull.

The National Finals began to turn Tuff's way the next day. First came the news that he had a grade-two sprain but no fracture. He'd ride with it, of course. He spent the day resting at the Gold Coast, taking turns with Branger with a nylon boot filled with ice water to compress their swollen feet.

In his new Justin lace-ups ("They're ugly, but they feel good"), his right leg mummied from ankle to knee, Tuff took on three bulls that evening, including two rerides. He got bucked off once and didn't win a dollar. To add insult, his fancy shirt got stained from some "recycled alfalfa" on the arena floor. But Tuff also made a statement that Thursday night.

"That's where he gained momentum," Donnie Gay reck-oned. "The other guys are thinkin', 'Tuff's hurt,' and now he ain't hurt bad enough."

You needed to finish strong in Vegas to win a gold buckle. Since Tuff's first Finals in 1984, he'd ridden better than 80 percent of his bulls over the last three rounds, when the draws were toughest and the heat most withering. With poise and skill in hand, Tuff needed only a break. He got one in the eighth go-round by drawing Skoal Playboy Bunny, a "blowy" high bucker who'd thrown him earlier that year: more grist for Tuff's thrill.

Playboy plunged out of the chute as advertised, spinning wildly away from Tuff's hand, where a rider's feel counts more than strength or leverage. The bull's black-marble eyes were bloodshot and dilated; muscles churned beneath his hairy hide. Tuff weathered the noisy cloud of the first two jumps, when a bull moves from stillness to fission. Then Playboy found his rhythm, giving all on each mighty buck, and Tuff's mind cleared. The cowboy's seat was dead center, his free hand bold and true. He'd gotten "tapped off," the zone all riders strive for, where you no longer fight the bull's force but share it instead, like a sailor with a stiff wind.

Neither Tuff nor the bull would weaken that night. After the horn sounded, Tuff leaped off and Playboy trotted away, trailing drool and bad intentions. All eyes shot to the overhead scoreboard. Within seconds the judges returned their verdict: ninety-one. It was the best score at that Finals so far, and among the five highest of Tuff's rodeo career.

After placing second the next night, Tuff entered the final go-round Sunday afternoon in the lead. But to clinch the title he'd need eight seconds on a jumbo black Brangus named Copenhagen Thumper, a "big eliminator" thrown into the rank pen because he'd yet to be ridden in a brief pro career. Just the bull to break a cowboy's heart, among other organs.

To a cowboy, "big E's" were as welcome as grazing fees and vegetarian restaurants. They were trashy, awkward, distempered; they were the essence of bull riding. Thumper had snookered Branger in the sixth go by slamming the brakes and doing the cowboy in with his own momentum. Still, Tuff was optimistic as he worked on his second cup of black coffee in the dressing room: "It's a good day for him to get ridden. I just got to hang on."

A half hour before Sunday's game time, deep-country Sammy Andrews ducked into the room to wish the bull riders the best. "You all ready?" he asked.

"Don't know yet," Tuff said.

They'd all know, soon enough.

Thumper began by whirling left, as expected, then squandered the spin and died, just as he had with Branger. Countering bluntly, Tuff overrode the flagging bull. When Thumper threw in a belly roll, Tuff tipped into his hand, listing far to the left, till his torso swung nearly level to the ground. "I was as close to being bucked off as you can be," he'd say afterward.

Thumper had the rider at his mercy; had he chosen to veer right at that moment, Tuff would have crashed and burned. But instead the bull leaped forward, handing Tuff a chance to hop back to the sweet spot. The whistle would come three jumps later, but Thumper was as good as beaten. *Fuck the form and get the horn.* . . . As Tuff walked off, barely limping, he looped his hat toward the roof in triumph.

While the judges rated it a modest seventy-six, the ride would stand as vintage Hedeman. In those eight seconds Tuff had recapped a career, a life of stubborn struggle on the edge. He'd ridden ugly once again—and like a champ. He wound up about fifteen thousand dollars better than Ted Nuce, who'd climbed to second. Branger had faded to seventh.

Thirty yards down the hall, Tuff was comparing his three gold buckles for eager reporters. "In '86 it was more of a relief than anything, because I felt I should have won the world in '85," he said. "In '89, that was bittersweet, because we lost Lane Frost, my best friend, and there's still to me a void that he isn't here." And today? Tuff thought about that and smiled, and then he couldn't stop smiling. He might be the sorest loser in the world, he'd never argue that, but he was also one terrific winner. "Today," Tuff said, "I was just pretty happy."

Interviews over, he took a stiff, tippy-toed walk back to the empty dressing room, to lodge his personals in a canvas rigging bag: rope, chaps, rosin bag, tough-skin remover.

"My hero!"

Tuff turned to face a beaming Ty Murray, who'd tamed enough bulls and broncs to win his third straight all-around title at the age of twenty-two. Murray had finished sixth in the bull riding, but it was number six with a bullet. Ty was the future, of that Tuff was sure. "You're *my* hero," Tuff said sincerely. And then, after pausing to thank the Justin Healer team, he shouted down the corridor, to no one in particular: "How do you spell relief? O-V-E-R!"

Outside the arena, on the way to his Lincoln, Tuff was waylaid by a director staging impromptu screen tests for a Diet Pepsi commercial, to star Ray Charles. "You'll have to speak up, I can't barely hear you," the tester said. "What's your name?"

"Tuff Hedeman."

"What do you do?"

"Professional bull rider."

"*How'd* you do?"

"Real good today," Tuff answered. "I did good today."

But the glow wouldn't last long. Six days later he would head to Wichita for a bull-riding invitational, then on to Denver, where the title hunt would start again, and, as Tuff knew well, "the bull won't care what I did last week."

CHAPTER 4

The Joy of Bucking

IF TUFF'S FROM-THE-HEART struggle crowned the '91 National Finals, the most electric moment came five minutes earlier, when Cody Custer took on Wolfman Skoal, a pocket-sized black bull with a lacy white mask. At barely twelve hundred pounds after breakfast, Wolfman was John Growney's pride and meal ticket. The fastest bucking bull in captivity, he'd been ridden but twice in a two-year career.

Custer had been ready to pass on the A Team altogether. He'd decided to ride on Sunday only if he drew one of three bulls; he reckoned the other twelve in the pen to be too strong and apt to jerk him down, weakened as he was after getting stomped again the night before. When he heard he'd drawn Wolfman, the ideal pluck, the Christian cowboy took it as a sign from on high.

With Custer, Wolfman took off at the only speed he knew: full throttle. He burst from the chute in a crazy-legged rear, slinging back his head and stubby devil's horns, twisting his frame almost inside out. He bucked as if pent up for weeks, as if his hide could no longer contain him. His body language was simple to read: *Get—off—my—back.*

Two jumps out Wolfman veered left. Where other bulls spun, Wolfman whirled, like a toy wound too tight. His front feet touched down briefly as a deep-kneed Russian dancer's; when his hind hooves dusted the ground he'd wheeled more than 180 degrees. Then he shot up to do it again.

The rotation was into the man's riding hand, where a very good cowboy stood maybe half a chance, yet Custer couldn't help slipping a hair behind the bull's first corner. That was usually fatal with Wolfman: if you were late, you were done. Custer took a stab, a deft slash with his free arm up over his head. He caught up, then skidded ahead, but the bull came so fast it purged the error. Custer found himself "packed" by Wolfman's warp speed, lashed to the bull's axis. The cowboy's custom-tooled chaps—one heralding "Jesus Is Lord," the other "Glory to God"—flapped like kites in a gale.

And Wolfman went faster, impossibly faster, till he'd flown through five full revolutions, two of them wholly in the air. The bull was still zooming as the horn vaguely sounded beneath the crowd's roar, still pushing his tarantella up-tempo, till his feet were a blur and Custer slid off, dizzy and transported.

"That wasn't speed, that was hyperspeed," exclaimed Jade Robinson, among the judges who gave ninety-four points, second highest in Finals history.

For Custer, a main-event talent with an undercard past, the eight-second cyclone salvaged a trying week. It was pivotal as well for Wolfman and his handlers, Growney and Don Kish. It propelled the bull to top honors in his class at the NFR (worth a three-thousand-dollar bonus from Copenhagen/Skoal) and cemented his status. Wolfman might have been shy on power, but no bull was showier. That meant a lot in a star-hungry sport, where few cowboys—and fewer animals—could boost the box office.

Fame had first come to Wolfman six weeks earlier, in Central Point, Oregon, when he whooshed a pint-sized journeyman named Wade Leslie to what many thought would never, or should never, happen: a perfect, hundred-point score. "The only thing the bull didn't do was cartwheels," Growney crowed at the time.

But the Custer ride, before everyone in rodeo that mattered, proved the theory that Growney had bet his California ranch on: that a bull's bucking traits, like a Thoroughbred's speed, could be passed to future generations. With his bottomless try and whippet's feet, Wolfman was a credit to his lineage and the men who'd bred him. To go further, this runty black dervish retold the story of a whole species each time he performed—a yarn of millennia in the wild, an uneasy bond with man, and a mythology that straddled the two.

Rodeo bull riding taps into ancient times and pagan faiths. From the cave paintings at Lascaux to Picasso's *Guernica,* that brutal wartime diagram, the bull has stood for sex and death, not necessarily in that order. Male warrior types liked bulls because they projected force, ruthlessness, and thank-you-ma'am virility—the virtues most prized by the warriors themselves.

"From sex to religion is only a step," as Allan Fraser wrote. In antiquity bulls served as supreme sacred animals—as the cult of choice—from Egypt to India to Greece. Then there was Crete, home to King Minos, son of Zeus and Europa. Minos was the sworn enemy of Theseus, himself the son of another Greek god who cross-dressed in horns and hooves, the powerhouse Poseidon. As painted by the historical novelist Mary Renault, Theseus would have hit it off with the bull riders in Las Vegas. Best known for slaying the bull-headed Minotaur, he was "light-weight; brave and aggressive, physically tough and quick; highly sexed and rather promiscuous; touchily proud, but with a feeling for the underdog; resembling Alexander in his precocious competence, gift of leadership, and romantic sense of destiny."

In Renault's *The King Must Die,* Theseus recalled his ride atop a Cretan bull into Athens much as a date between Tuff and the rank pen:

> I grasped the horn-tips and vaulted . . . to land upon his neck. I twisted round and straddled him, holding the horns low by the head and drumming my heels into his dewlap. . . . He charged on with me, as fast as a war char-

iot . . . though I felt shaken half to pieces, I could not leave him yet. "Open out!" I shouted. "Let me ride him!". . . He charged onward, tossing and bucketing till my very teeth seemed loosened in my jaws.

That woolly ride, in fact, was the noble Greek's final test to gain his kingdom. Like the gold-buckled champs who'd come later, Theseus proved himself by beating not merely a bull, but his own fear: "I had met and mastered the evil of my fate; I was King indeed."

Long after their divinity mostly faded, bulls held center stage in human commerce. In medieval times, a man counted his riches in cattle; *cattle* and *capital* were synonyms throughout Europe. Thanks to Columbus, who unloaded a number of bulls and cows on his second voyage to the New World, they would play a similar role in the American West. Before gold got rushed on the West Coast, cattle hides, known as "California banknotes," were legal tender. A few decades later, the great cattle drives would build nearly half a continent.

While bulls were always precious commodities, they were never domesticated like farm horses. They wouldn't evolve to pull a plow (unless gelded into oxen) or costar in *National Velvet*. The more spirited individuals—the ones that eventually found their way to the rodeo arenas and Mexican *corridas* — still reacted to man with the hard old options: flight or fight. They were not exactly wild, as lions or alligators were wild, but neither were they tame. They were "the other," a part of man's world but outside his control.

As bull riding surfaced in rodeo in the 1920s, "wild Brahma bulls" were billed like circus attractions. How bad were these brutes? "Vicious human-haters," claimed an impresario from those early days. "Among the meanest, most contemptible, and most easily riled animals on earth." Now as then, rodeo bulls were cast as crowd-pleasing villains. You'd have been hard-pressed to find a bull called Rose Garden, or Apple Sauce, or Gentleman Jim—three broncs who performed at the '91 Finals. The bulls that year had monikers like *Chainsaw* . . . *Viper* . . . *Terminator* . . . *Psycho*. (Sometimes a stock contractor goes too far in the red-eyed-killer vein. Several cowboys complained after drawing a bull named Body Bag; it just gave them the creeps.)

The rules of the game free bulls to vent their spleen. The rider has next to no equipment: no saddle, no reins, nothing at all to touch the bull's head or shoulders. And rodeo announcers do their part by hyping the sport's "wildest event" in cornball patter with the barrel men, clowns who hide in open-ended containers on the arena floor. Even the dumbest gags feed the bull riders' aura. For if bulls are truly untamed, so must be the men who would match them.

Announcer: "This bull has killed twenty-four rodeo clowns." (The barrel man springs up, in mock terror.) "Twenty-three *in* the barrel." (Alarmed, the clown makes haste to climb out.) "The other one running *away* from the barrel." (The clown faints as the fans yuk it up, safe in their seats.)

In real life, rodeo bulls offer a dozen different personalities. Some snort and bellow in the chute but melt after the gate flies open. Others are calm in the box but hell on hooves in the ring. Some are hit-and-run artists with fallen riders; others live to hit, and hit again. And still others, like the legendary, lovable Joe Cool, would buck to the moon with a cowboy on their backs, but grind into reverse to avoid mangling the same man on the ground.

What all bulls share, Ferdinand and Body Bag alike, is the outsize anatomy between their rear legs, their *raison d'être*. Ranchers prize bulls because they can impregnate up to one hundred cows apiece per year. And for souped-up masculinity, none can surpass the beasts that buck at rodeos.

The cowboys glory in the bulls' virile image, as though it stamps their own claims as major-league sex machines. (Never mind the joke that bull riders make lousy lovers who ride for but eight seconds.) In outlasting the baddest boys in town, they are slayers of dragons, masters of the Minotaur: men who are made by the force of their foes.

On the last Saturday night of the '91 Finals, as seventeen thousand fans settled in at the Thomas and Mack, as bull riders took aim at the big eliminator pen, a dozen men and women marched outside the arena with signs shouting: "Steer Clear of Cruelty!" They would not be cheering the brave boys on. Their hearts lay with the bulls—and the broncs and steers and calves that cowboys must humble to win.

For the animal-rights movement, rodeo is a savage throwback best thrown out, bull riding a criminal rite. In these partisans' eyes, the creakiest bull rider owns an unfair advantage over the mightiest bull. While the rider *chooses* to be hooked, flung, and trampled, the bull has no say in the matter.

Anti-rodeo agitprop takes two forms. At its outer fringes the movement attacks rodeo as hateful by definition. This camp insists that animals "exist for their own reasons"—a premise that, taken to its end, would kill rodeo, circuses, racetracks, dog shows, dolphin acts, and any remake of *Lassie Come Home* that cut in the collie for less than 10 percent of the gross. These purists will not so much as wear leather shoes, though they will don synthetic Nikes assembled by teenage girls in Indonesia for fourteen cents an hour.

Slightly less extreme are splinter groups like the Humane Society of the United States, whose goal is "to eliminate all rodeo events in which there is danger of injury, pain, torture, fear, or harassment" to the animals. These advocates abhor calf and steer roping in particular—the "running away" events. (More than a few roughstock cowboys agree about steer roping, which is sanctioned in only nine states.)

Bull riding also comes in for a battering. The animal rightists are unimpressed by a 1988 veterinary survey that counted zero injuries among more than a thousand rodeo bulls. They are unmoved by the blessing given the PRCA's livestock rules by the American Humane Association. The rules aren't strict enough, they'll tell you, and enforcement is lax.

In particular, they object to the flank strap, a sheepskin-lined leather belt cinched around the bull's hindquarters seconds before the chute opens. A bull bucks, they maintain, because the flank strap squeezes his genitals. And if that ploy fails, they go on, the contractor fries the crazed animal with an electric prod. This was torture by any other name, and the rightists wanted it stopped.

Not surprisingly, the cowboys and contractors sneer at these people as know-nothings—citified eastern folk whose animal sense is confined to their tabby cats. The bull men counter the best they know how, from experience:

1. The next time you pass a pasture on a cool spring morning, watch the baby calves. They will be running, romping—and bucking. Animals buck when they feel good.

2. Professional bucking bulls are exceptional, tautly strung athletes. They are born, not made. If a contractor could create a rank bull with a fifty-dollar strap, he wouldn't spend into five figures each year to cull prospects from duds. And if he damaged or neglected his goods, as Donnie Gay noted, he'd soon run himself out of business: "If the animals don't eat, I don't eat."

3. The flank strap is loosely fastened in front of a bull's scrotum and behind its rib cage. It produces a mild pressure, a foreign annoyance—like a rubber band over a dog's leg. When applied correctly, it enhances a bull's kicking action. But if pulled too tight, according to veterinarians, the strap hinders the flank and reduces that action.

4. Animals perform poorly in pain; like people, they yield to it instead. If a belt pinched your genitals, Ty Murray once lectured, would you jump up and down, or would you roll up into a docile, whimpering, pathetic little ball? Case closed.

5. Electric prods, known to cowboys as "hot shots," are tools for moving stubborn bulls into bucking chutes—and a sight more polite than using a whip or two-by-four. A standard, low-voltage hot shot runs on flashlight batteries and puts out next to no amperage, which means that it can't burn the bull. In fact, cowboys zap one another all the time at smaller rodeos, as a practical joke. They might jump at the shock, but they don't drop twitching to the ground. At the Finals, a contractor is bound to ask a bull rider's permission to "grill his steak" when the chute opens. The cowboys almost always refuse; they know that a bull dodging a hot shot often forgets to kick, or hips itself on the chute. "If they choose not to buck, there's no way you can force 'em," Cody Lambert said firmly.

6. Bulls are not like you and me. Their hides measure up to seven times thicker than human skin. They are large, tough animals that weather blizzards and the South Texas sun. They get branded by hot irons as babies, aren't covered by Blue Cross, and seem none the worse for wear. The only way he could possibly abuse a bull, Gay has asserted, is with "a forty-four magnum."

No doubt there are abuses at the thousands of semipro and amateur rodeos outside the PRCA's control, the worst of which show all the tender mercy of a cockfight. And rodeo life, with its heavy truck travel and unfamiliar food, can be stressful even for bulls in the top strings. But if you consider the alternatives, none are too pretty from a bull's-eye view. Start with a working ranch, where the livestock injury rate is thirty times higher than in rodeo. Young bulls are castrated (hold the anesthesia) into more manageable, tender-fleshed steers. Or if set aside for breeding, they become insemination machines, led to masturbate on a dummy with no regard for romance.

And those are the lucky ones. Most rodeo bulls have no special breeding value. If they won't or can't buck, they are headed to just one place—to become pet food or some cowboy's Big Mac. Which brings us to the central dilemma of the animal-rights movement. For better or worse, we live in a beef-eating culture, and no butcher will wait till a bull dies of old age. As long as cattle and capital mean essentially the same thing, bulls' liberation remains a long way off.

☆

John Growney has his own opinion about bucking bulls. "I believe that they come to us by their own choice," the stock contractor said. The day after wrapping up his last regular-season rodeo, six weeks before the '92 National Finals, Growney lounged in his double-wide mobile home on a forty-acre ranch in Red Bluff (population 12,434), an early-to-bed town 120 miles north of Sacramento. The bulls wind up with him, Growney continued, "because they don't conform—they don't get along with the other bulls, they don't get along with the rancher. If they didn't come to us they'd be eaten."

Slight and restless, with an easy charm and a gift for gab, Growney grew up as the pampered son of Red Bluff's Buick dealer. Voted "biggest flirt" by his high school's class of '66, he went to college for nine years, changed his major four times, got drafted into the army, and became a good enough bull rider to win the Cow Palace in San Francisco in 1976, a high he would never duplicate. Having peaked at the age of twenty-eight, he had no idea what to do next.

Three years later, with backing from local men of means, Growney became a professional stock contractor. Over time he built a three-hundred-thousand-dollar enterprise that numbered forty mature bulls and eighty-five broncs, and chewed up five hundred tons of hay a year. But even as his temples grayed and crow's-feet sprouted, Growney seemed uneasy with growing up. "We become what we are, and we stay what we are," he said, and at heart he would always be a rootless bull rider. His home, shared with junior partner Don

Kish and assorted rodeo roustabouts, was your classic bachelor pad: bunk beds without top sheets, wall-to-wall carpeting in the bathroom, a fridge filled with beer and Pop-Tarts.

Growney started out like every other contractor, buying stock at auction or private sales. He focused on the bulls, who'd thrilled and chilled him from early childhood. Early on he learned to seek out the nonconformists, the ones who shifted to the rear at inspection time, the suspicious types who locked eyes on your every move.

Then the contractor checked for the right physique: straight legs; a tight hide about the flank; a taut genital sheath ("If his dick hangs out, he's lazy"); a way of walking on the "toes"; and a short back, as longer bulls are injury prone. Most contractors favor husky buckers with big, showy horns. But Growney leans toward smaller, catty bulls built like defensive backs—big up front, slim in the waist and butt. He figures their joints will last longer, as less weight means less wear. Most of all, he knows the fans crave fast action. "We're going for the speed and the mind," he said. "We don't want them muscle-bound, we don't want them too fat—we want 'em lean and mean."

Like all the top outfits, Growney's uses cross-bred bulls. He favors the offspring of Brahma sires and either white-faced Hereford or Black Angus cows, known in the West as "red brahmer crosses" and "gray brahmer crosses," respectively. The Indian-bred Brahmas bring vigor, agility, heat resistance, and eye-catching humps to the gene pool, topped off by a surly attitude. The British strains, Growney believes, give his bulls brains and heart. (Purebred Brahmas tend to be stagestruck performers; they stall while being loaded or lie down in the chute, or give up halfway into a ride.) Growney's favorite mix is the Brangus, a gray brahmer cross. While nothing much to look at, compact and often hornless, Brangus bulls are quick and athletic; the best of them can kick over their heads.

Buying bulls green as grass is a tough way to make a living. An average animal costs a thousand dollars, based strictly on steak on the hoof, and it takes a full season to find out if he's really good. One of ten might have the heart and talent to last in rodeo. One of a hundred might make it to the A Team. Unfortunately, that leaves the contractor with a mess of bulls—a hundred or more per year at a Growney-sized operation—with no redeeming athletic value. After paying a sales commission, the contractor "cans" the rejects at a loss, getting nine hundred bucks apiece from a slaughterhouse.

A solid bucking bull, meanwhile, can be worth two thousand dollars and up. One good one out of ten will break you even on the deal. But it isn't rare for lots of ten or twenty or even thirty bulls to wash out without a single keeper, leaving a contractor deep in the red.

Bulls are shorter-lived than horses, and have briefer careers in the ring. A bronc might compete for fifteen years without flagging. But bulls aren't mature till they're five years old, and by eight or nine most are as gimpy as thirtysomething ballplayers, robbed of explosion by calcium deposits. "They get bad knees and bad feet and bad necks—they cripple up just like people do," Growney said. To stay afloat, a contractor needs to add five to ten competent buckers a year, a tough task without a big bankroll.

Growney's fortunes turned in 1984, when an amateur stock contractor summoned him to the small mountain town of Sisters, Oregon. The man was dying of cancer. He'd heard that Growney cared well for his animals, and he wanted to sell him a local legend named Red Rock, a bull never ridden to the horn. The price: ten thousand dollars, or four times as much as Growney had ever paid before. It was a make-or-break proposition, especially for an eight-year-old bull that Growney had never seen buck. But intuition pressed him forward, and Growney brought Red Rock home.

The history of bull riding resonates with the names of the greatest buckers. There was Tornado, a white-faced Braford who fought clowns and rolled barrels with unequaled flair, and went unbeaten till middle-aged Freckles Brown somehow lasted at the '67 Finals; V61, who soared six feet off the ground and onto the cover of *Life;* Mr. T, a belligerent spinner with classic form, who'd get stronger the longer he went.

But no bull was smarter than Red Rock, a reddish, tiger-striped brindle—a Brahma-Hereford mutt. While hardy and durable, brindles were deemed slow learners who bucked one set way, come hell or Tuff Hedeman. Red Rock was the exception. Every time the chute opened throughout his four-year pro career, *Red Rock would buck away from the rider's hand.* Whether right or left, he'd go the direction that most cowboys found most vexing—every single time. A bull who cased his riders; none had seen the like of it. "Did he feel it in the pull of the rope, or the knot, or the weight distribution on his back?" Growney wondered. "We're not sure, but he had to know it before they opened the gate. You'd swear there was a bull rider inside of him."

He seemed to smell show time coming. When Growney called for him, he'd respond like a German shepherd and trot inside the chute. As the rider got his wrap and wriggled into position, Red Rock tensed like a sprinter in the blocks, his flesh hard as a table. He wasn't the biggest bull, or the fastest. But he blew out of the chute with such trip-wire timing, and such seismic force, that most cowboys were chasing their rope from the start. With his rump in the air and his spine nigh-perpendicular to the earth, Red Rock would whack them in the butt with his back. Then he'd hit the earth so stiffly that those front hooves bounced three times—and any man not gone by then was surely in a heap of trouble. And the bull did not let up. As Red Rock spun he probed for openings like a grand master, tuned his speed to nudge his victim off the ledge.

The end would be sudden. Cowboys were slingshot over the bull's outside shoulder, slammed on their backs so hard they'd lose their wind. Bucking off Red Rock, said Ted Nuce, was like having an anvil fall off a cliff—with your arm tied to it.

Yet for all Red Rock's drop, he'd never jerk a man down to his head; by the time the man got there, the bull's head was gone. He might hurt your pride, but he'd save your bridgework.

Red Rock was, in fact, a pacifist; he'd been raised by a gentle milk cow after being orphaned by his mother. When a cowboy dumped in his path at St. Paul, Oregon, Red Rock fell to his side to keep from stepping on him. Where bull riders blanched as they nodded for Mr. T or Cowtown, serial slashers whose horns preceded them, they'd line up for the chance to draw Red Rock. They could put all their energy into the ride, take every extra chance. They knew Red Rock would spare them after they failed.

And fail they did, every one. Red Rock had thrown 180 consecutive men in the amateurs, and ran his streak to 309 in the pros. He took on all comers, besting as many as thirteen of the top fifteen bull riders in one season. The tougher the man, the more he put out. He threw Tuff and Lane, Ted Nuce and Charles Sampson. The cowboys, who got downright sentimental for bulls that fought fair and square, would never forget how Red Rock quit bucking the instant they were in the air, as though he knew the act was over and it was time for his bows. ("He was awesome," said Clint Branger. "He was *cool*.") Red Rock would trot round the arena in a victory lap, head and tail held high, lapping up the applause.

Growney wanted his star to go out on top after the '87 Finals, where Red Rock chucked Ted Nuce in the last go-round to clinch the title for Lane Frost. The brindle retired, undefeated, as bucking bull of the year. But at the age of eleven, Red Rock wasn't ready for easy street. He'd stop grazing in his field to watch cowboys practice at an adjacent ring. Whenever a rider hit the ground, Red Rock would buck in a circle for exactly eight seconds, as if to show the younger bulls how it was done. *He's asking for a comeback,* Growney thought.

On one of those lazy days in Red Bluff, the contractor hit upon how to give it to him: a best-of-seven "Challenge of the

Champions," Red Rock versus Lane Frost, two ultimate warriors in the definitive rodeo showdown. Lane jumped on the idea. He needed a change of pace; by early 1988 he'd been slumping. Lane had a shaky marriage he was struggling to put right, and an aching body not made for so much try. But he was the ideal matchup for Red Rock. When Lane was right, he rode with a supple precision, with a goalie's reactions and a prom king's poise. As a perfectionist student of the game, he would learn from his mistakes and exploit a series format. "If we're gonna ask who's going to ride the rankest bull between Tuff, Jim [Sharp], and Lane, I'm gonna say Lane," reasoned Cody Lambert.

The whole course of Lane's life had delivered him to this stage, from the time he was five months old and woke from his nap at San Antonio just in time to watch the bull riding—and then squalled when Clyde and Elsie Frost tried to beat the crowd by leaving a few bulls early. As Lane would say, "I think bull riding was bred into me, like this was all supposed to be."

Lane had it all, but on Red Rock he found himself wanting. The first tilt was set in April, as an exhibition to close Red Bluff's own rodeo. The arena sold out, as it would through the series. The crowd cheered Lane's name, then gave hometown hero Red Rock a standing ovation, and the favorite didn't disappoint them. Lane had ridden earlier in the rodeo proper and scored around ninety, but that was like a home run in batting practice before you stepped in against Roger Clemens. Belying his four-month layoff, Red Rock blasted off to the right, away from Lane's hand, and slammed him in roughly one second.

"Tuff, how'm I gonna *ride* this bull?" Lane moaned after the fact.

"If he bucks like that," said Tuff, never one to sugarcoat, "you ain't."

It went no better a week later in Clovis. Growney was proud of Red Rock, who'd run his knockout streak to 311, but he knew this was poor sport. If Lane kept losing, people would stop caring about the match. As Growney consoled the rider on their way out of the arena, Lambert caught up with them and said, "Should I tell him?"

"You better tell him," the contractor consented.

Wise owl that he was, Lambert had almost cracked Red Rock at a small rodeo in California. Knowing that the bull was most lethal at the start, when he dropped like a big red rock, Lambert tried an old saddle-bronc trick. Rather than jam his body up to the rope—and cue Red Rock's detonation—he sat back on the bull and relaxed. He nodded his head and only then jumped into position. Caught short, Red Rock left the chute like a normal bucking bull, instead of the latest test from Los Alamos. By the time he got cranking, Lambert had his own rhythm afoot. The cowboy lasted six seconds before his euphoria floored him.

Lambert had honored Red Rock by not revealing his scheme to anyone, and up to Clovis he hadn't thought to tell Lane; he'd have bet on Lane to ride any bull, anytime. But now was the time to share. By May 20, when Lane reached Redding, California, for the third match of the series, he was armed with Lambert's game plan.

Meanwhile, Red Rock was setting up for a fall. He spent the afternoon in a hot Safeway parking lot, helping Lane promote the match in "joint" interviews. (Growney interpreted for the bull.) The night stayed sultry for the season, sapping him further. As always, his great spirit was willing; when Lane paid a visit just before the match, Red Rock stood and bowed his neck stiffly, like a boxer staring down his foe at center ring. But the bull's body had to be weak.

That evening in the chute, Lane took his wrap and sat back like he'd ordered iced tea. To prevent Red Rock from smelling a rat, he'd looped the tail of his rope around the gate to keep it temporarily shut. No click of a latch would alert him. Lane called for the bull just like that and Red Rock emerged as advertised, another mortal creature having a bad hair day. As the bull shifted into third and gained altitude, Lane followed part two of Lambert's prescription. He swept out with his free arm, almost leaping into the well of the bull's clockwise spin. He overrode Red Rock as he had no other bull, and the gamble paid off. So hard and steep did Red Rock buck as he turned that a more rigidly centered cowboy would have whipped out to the concession stands. But Lane got lifted back to center with each jump. A simple adjustment—but one demanding high confidence. Lane was never completely *there,* but he stayed close enough to hear the sweetest horn of his life.

As the stands ignited, Growney felt a wash of guilt, as though he'd betrayed his best friend. "We took away the energy he should have had that night, and the first spring out of that chute," the contractor said. "I took something Red Rock could have gone to his grave with—never being ridden."

Lane rode the bull again at Livermore. By the fifth match, a June homecoming for Red Rock in Sisters, Oregon, the series was the biggest rodeo story of all time. *Sports Illustrated* hopped on board. Camera crews tracked man and bull. As it turned out, they were lucky to be there.

Feeling good in the place where he'd once sawed off many an amateur, Red Rock did something Growney had never seen before: he cut back to the left, *into* Lane's hand. When that didn't work the bull turned back to the right, then plowed straight ahead while twisting his belly to the crisp blue sky— another new move. Lane answered each time. There were days like these when he might have been the prettiest rider ever born—loose and free yet controlled, his long legs rolled so sleekly into the bull. But this was Red Rock's joint, and Red Rock's time. The bull would buck Lane off or bust, and so he did—just the slimmest instant after the whistle sounded.

No one else could have beaten Red Rock that day, Growney felt certain. If Wade Leslie's ride on Wolfman would be worth a hundred points, this one could have earned one-fifty.

When Lane prevailed in a tie-breaking seventh match at Spanish Fork, Utah, even Growney was smiling. Though rooting for his bull all the way, he'd grown so close to Lane that he knew there'd be no loser. As for Red Rock, he'd won more renown in three months of getting ridden than in a career of making men horizontal. Two years later he'd become the third bucking bull to be voted into the ProRodeo Hall of Fame, along with the lanky young man he couldn't quite shake.

By the time Red Rock returned to pasture, for good this time, Growney's pen had a national reputation. He and Don Kish, a no-nonsense sort known to friends as the Bull Lord, would get at least three bulls to the Finals every year. But they no longer had a superstar to help woo contracts from new rodeo committees, or dicker fatter fees from the old ones.

Enter Fonzie, son of the great Oscar, the skinny mixed-breed who once swirled Donnie Gay to ninety-seven points at the Cow Palace. Acquired by Growney in the early 1980s, Fonzie was a middling bucker, not quite good enough to make the Finals. But at stud the small gray bull was the second coming of Seattle Slew. Kish put Fonzie on twenty-two Red Rock daughters (the Great One had disappointed in the sack, producing seven heifers for every male), and the first crop was born to high anticipation in the spring of 1986. There were fourteen bull calves, fine-boned and lively; the Oscar strain was clearly dominant. As they matured, it looked like Growney had hit a genetic jackpot. Of those fourteen calves, six would develop into professional bucking bulls, an unheard-of proportion. Of the six, three would make the Finals. The cream of the crop was Wolfman, a worthy grandson of Red Rock and Oscar.

The calf got noticed early on. After Kish drove his fresh weanlings into the ranch's feedlot, two fields from their mothers' pasture, he found Wolfman back with mom the next day. Kish roped and dragged him out again. The next morning

Wolfman was back. By the fourth day Kish was put out. It was time to show this snuffy calf who was boss. The contractor roped the calf from his horse and roughly lugged him a ways at full tilt. Then Kish tossed the stocky Harvey Camacho his rope, to be tied to a trailer to finish the trip. Camacho never saw the little-bitty calf coming, never had a chance.

"He got Harvey down face first in the pasture—and this calf didn't weigh three hundred pounds; Harvey weighed more than the calf," Kish recalled over a doughnut breakfast in the bachelor pad. "And he hooked the *daylights* out of him, with these horns maybe three inches long."

After he managed to stop laughing, Kish told Camacho to mark down the calf's brand number. This one bore watching. "You don't see eight-month-old calves wanting to beat a person up in a big pasture," the Bull Lord explained. "Ninety-nine percent of the time, if they're wild, they leave—they're scared and they run. If an animal that age is willing to challenge you one-on-one, he has no fear of nothin'. When we walked off that day, I knew we had a bull that was going to be different."

A year and a half later, when Kish bucked the class of '86 for the first time out of Growney's practice chutes, his forecast proved out. Wolfman turned back so sharply that his back feet landed inside the chute, so close that Kish could have reached over and touched his narrow back at every round. "He was spinning right in his tracks, and you looked at him and said, 'God-*damn*,'" Kish said.

You can't train a bull to buck. You give him a chance and get out of his way, and then he either does it or not. Wolfman advanced through a patient apprenticeship: a few high school rodeos at age two and three, a couple of college contests at four. No rider could so much as warm him up, but one raw youth clung to the bull's side till he actually pulled him to the ground, bulldogger style. Wolfman fought back, of course, and his owners fibrillated at the thought of their prize specimen breaking his leg or back in the tussle. That did it for Wolfman's college education. He went to a few pro rodeos in 1990, as a four-year-old, but mostly he was turned out on the cows, till he grew a little bigger.

Wolfman learned his trade without resistance—"He was smart-wild," Kish said—so long as you gave him the express lane. When he got to the chutes, he loaded fast. When he came on to a cow, he bred fast. Most of all, he bucked fast. The hundred-point ride with Wade Leslie wasn't Wolfman's best trip; his hind legs trailed the rest of him, and twice he lost his footing. But it was a scrapbook display of killing speed. Wolfman made six full rounds that day. He spun like a cheerleader's baton, like a twelve-hundred-pound pinwheel. The old-timers hated the score—a *perfect* bull could never be ridden, they grumped—but no one said it came cheaply. An average rodeo bull might make two complete circles in eight seconds. A handful of all-stars made as many as four. Wolfman was three times faster than the norm.

Still, the little bull had his critics. Rival contractors dismissed him as a "flat," low-powered spinner who "couldn't kick over a Coke cup." Wolfman had been topped twice more in 1992, making five times for his career—all five with men who rode left-handed, like Cody Custer. The critics took note and shrugged. They knew Red Rock, and Wolfman was no Red Rock.

But the cowboys stayed crazy about the little bull. They loved knowing they'd win first if they rode him—with Wolfman, it was "either money or mud"—and they loved it that he always tried. Some rarely ridden bulls would weaken five seconds into a ride, flustered by alien experience. Others would dull after a few cowboys beat them. But Wolfman kept coming. He just wouldn't quit—much like Tuff, the match that Kish craved to certify Wolfman's right stuff.

The public, too, liked a bull that might get ridden every now and then for a show-stopping score. Bulls sold rodeos, and the industry thirsted for a star like Mr. T, who'd retired in 1991 with no heir apparent.

And that, for Kish and Growney, was the rub. After the "perfect ride" in Oregon and Wolfman's spectacular Finals debut, the bull was a celebrity. A headliner for local rodeo ads. A ticket seller. In 1992, every one of their thirty-one rodeo committees commanded a Wolfman performance—or two, if the rodeo had a short round. After limiting Wolfman to twenty-odd trips in 1991, the contractors used him thirty-five times the following year, four of them in one nine-day stretch. That run would have tested a two-thousand-pound veteran who'd learned how to coast and pace himself. For a Wolfman, who strained every fast-twitch muscle in his body whenever the gate opened, it invited disaster.

"We pushed him too hard," Kish conceded. "This summer he got to a point where his trips went backwards. It would be like asking a boxer to fight two days a week. You just can't do it; they put out too much energy."

Kish and Growney drew the line. They told one California committee that the bull needed a break. The committee retaliated by not renewing Growney's contract. The men from Red Bluff didn't blink; they could better lose the contract than the bull. Besides, Wolfman needed time away from the grind not just to rest, but to make little Wolfmans. After its initial success, Kish's breeding program had hit a wall. Fonzie was dead, Red Rock in his dotage. Kish was "about that close to saying, 'Get rid of the cows and let's just go to the sales.'"

Late in 1992 Kish tried out the first crop of inbred calves from Wolfman and his half brother, Outlaw. The two-year-olds were undersized and overbearing, in their sires' image, but the Bull Lord withheld judgment till they made two runs out of the practice chute. The watching restored his faith in Oscar's bloodline. Of the thirty-two young bulls, Kish reported, twelve were "just as good as you could want an animal to be," and twelve others would fetch nice prices at sale. "I think you'll see thirty percent of that crop at the Finals," Kish said. Wolfman, once again, had come through.

Whenever Growney wanted a peek at Red Rock, he had only to glance out the picture window of his living room. Just twenty yards away lay five fenced acres of lush, irrigated grass, shaded by oaks and English walnuts. This was Red Rock's own pasture, where the aging wonder was left to eat and loaf. An elderly neighbor man filled a shed there with fresh straw and alfalfa, and brought a lamb in to keep the gentle bull company. It cost three hundred dollars a year to keep Red Rock in feed, and his owner paid it gladly.

At forty-four, Growney had reached the age where a man strove to give something back. He tutored at a nearby grammar school, and invited bull-struck teenagers to use his bucking pen for practice. He hungered for approval even from his stock. While Kish had assumed day-to-day charge, Growney liked to spend "quality time" with the bulls. This autumn morning he slipped the gate latch and strolled into Red Rock's field. In summer the Sacramento Valley cooks under triple-digit heat, fit only for the olive and almond groves. But today the air was cool and sharp, with a hint of needed rain. At pasture's center a russet-toned brindle grazed contentedly. He raised his head as Growney approached, then ambled a few steps to nuzzle at the contractor's chest. It was hard to imagine that this was—

"Bucking bull of the year, 1987," Growney announced proudly. "Unridden his whole career. This one loves to be scratched, don't you?" The flies scattered from Red Rock's hollowed back as Growney scratched and patted him, then let a stranger take a turn. The bull grazed on. When Growney trucked him to local grammar schools, the bull got petted like a kitten.

Red Rock's ribs pressed against his graying, tiger-striped hide. "He's a little thin. At his age, it's hard to keep weight on," the contractor said, in a sorrowful tone.

As Growney propped his elbow to lean on Red Rock, a small charcoal bull with a lacy mask advanced to within ten yards. He stopped to stare at the intruders, neither backing off nor coming closer. Growney had put Wolfman in the field for his own protection, to curb him from fighting bigger bulls in the general population. "We used to walk out here and Wolfman would run to the farthest corner of the field, with his head up, not wanting to be bothered," Growney said. Of late the feisty one had grown more trusting, to the point where Kish could feed him by hand—with his other palm on the fence, just in case. Normally the two superstars hung out in seclusion, but today they shared the field with five other bulls likely headed for the Finals. In addition to twenty pounds of hay, each animal was getting a daily ration of fifteen pounds of top-grade oats, barley, and corn. Grain was "the ultimate high" for a bull, Growney explained. "We want to get 'em beefy, hard-fat, feeling as good as they have all year."

Soon Outlaw, Elvis, and Too Legit had circled near Growney and Red Rock, striking solemn poses with their sagging dewlaps and open gaze. "Horses are smarter, but bulls are more curious," the contractor observed. They were also more pugnacious. Though raised together since calfhood, the bulls in Red Rock's field still fought daily for dominance; they'd broken the fence twice in three days. Growney made sure that no cows wandered nearby: "One cow can create a bunch of teenagers out here. They go nuts—they'll cripple each other."

Only Red Rock was *hors de combat,* left alone by the younger bulls. In his day he'd reigned at the top of the pecking order, as brave as he was gifted. Once, shortly after Red Rock's retirement, a half dozen bulls snuck into his field and ganged up on him. By the time Growney got up that morning, Red Rock was cutting like a broken-field runner to evade the pack.

"I came running down there 'cause I knew he was in trouble, and he ran right to the other side of me," Growney recounted. "He took a deep breath and I swear he said, 'John, if you'll hold off the others, I'll take care of myself.' Right off the bat he went after the most dominant one and whipped him—they crashed horns and went *at* it, like two guys fist-fighting—and the other bull took off running. Then Red Rock whipped another one, and then another one, and the others just took off. They didn't want anything to do with him." Duty done, a worn-out Red Rock lay down and barely moved for three days.

A shower's first drops spattered the grass. Quality time was over. "That was his heart and his stamina," Growney said, with a parting scratch. "That's what made him what he was."

That afternoon Kish trucked his promising two-year-olds to an auction facility in nearby Cottonwood to get tipped. When bulls' horns get too sharp, they can injure one another while fighting or loading, not to mention shish-kebab a bull rider. Under PRCA rules, a horn's tip can be no smaller than the circumference of a fifty-cent piece. (The rule is sporadically enforced, to the cowboys' chagrin; some contractors figure they've complied with tips the size of five dimes in a pile.)

Growney used to tip his bulls in Red Bluff, in a bucking chute at his practice arena. Then he put himself in the bulls' place, and decided they might train better at home if it didn't double as the dentist's office. He had the bulls vaccinated in Cottonwood for the same reason.

With the bull held still in a hydraulic iron compartment, Kish wielded a circular saw with a slot in the middle. In two seconds he sliced through the top of the horn, leaving a blunted, bloody tip. As the bulls lowed amid the acrid smoke, Growney seemed grateful to wait outside and chat with a few of his thousand close friends. Insects hovered like low clouds. "One thing I've never gotten used to is flies," Growney said ruefully, "and they're everywhere around livestock."

The sun was setting as Growney pulled back up to the ranch in his red pickup, to find a slender youth pacing behind the practice chutes. Thirteen-year-old Shawn Hilliard, with a face full of freckles and a head of blond curls, was ready for his first steer ride.

If Shawn was antsy, his mother was positively bewildered. "He used to be hip, and all of a sudden he started wearing cowboy boots," Selma Hilliard sighed. Her two brothers rode bulls years ago, so she knew how boys went crazy for it. In her own youth she'd hung out at the rodeos, longing to marry a rich cowboy, not yet knowing they didn't exist. But Shawn was a town kid, raised in Red Bluff. Selma turned to Growney: "He needs a lot of learning."

Growney could judge that already by the look of Shawn's rope (seen better days) and the look on his face (terrified). But the boy was the right age to start and the right size for the sport, and he moved like he might be an athlete. "I wasn't raised on a ranch, either," Growney said, to begin his pep talk. "You just got to find something that you like doing, and do it really good—you chewing tobacco already?" He'd spotted the telltale white circle, the size of a Copenhagen/Skoal can, on the rear pocket of Shawn's black Wranglers.

"All my friends are doing it," Shawn said defensively. He mounted the low platform, peered down at the dappled black steer. He'd ridden calves before, but they were so small his feet had dragged the ground. This mother was *big*. "I got butterflies in my stomach," he said.

"You need a shot of whiskey," Selma suggested.

"I wish I was drunk right now," Shawn said. He adjusted his rope to Growney's instructions, then straddled the black. He couldn't stop picturing Nathan, a seventh-grade friend of his who'd landed in the hospital after a steer stuck a horn in his chest. They'd thought it was broken ribs, but Nathan was just bruised up. Still, it made a guy think. . . .

"I'm so nervous," Shawn said, and then, with his last bit of bravado: "I'm not really nervous-scared."

"I know you're not," Growney assured him. "That's just adrenaline, it's no big deal." He tousled the boy's curls. "What do you think?"

"I can't do it," Shawn said.

"Sure you can," said Growney, pulling the bull rope. "Tell me when it's tight. . . . I don't want you to worry about anything except screwing up your ride on this steer."

"I don't think I can do it," Shawn said, his voice shrinking, like a novice on his first steep ski slope.

"Just relax," Growney said. "Take your hand out of your rope. You ever ride a saddle horse?

"No."

"This is like riding a horse," Growney lied. "This steer has never been bucked before—all I do is bulldog this steer."

"So you're trying to tell me this steer isn't going to buck," Shawn said dubiously.

"If he does, he won't buck very hard."

"For some reason I don't believe you."

"Why would you care if he did or not?" Growney said. He was used to this exchange; lots of them had to go through it.

"Getting stepped on," Shawn said.

"What's he going to do if he steps on you? He only weighs four hundred pounds. He won't break anything in you."

Shawn paused to weigh this piece of information. "I really don't want to do it, but I'm going to do it," he said. There it was—that first spasm of blind will. A bull rider's baptism.

Growney's voice turned stern. "Remember, though, I want you to be tough. You don't want to be weak when you ride. It's like wrasslin'—you've got to be the aggressor, or the other guy is going to beat you. Don't just jump off. Put your hand in, bring that rope across . . . pull your thumb across. Get up there and just squeeze. . . ."

"I think he might not buck much when he comes out," Shawn wished aloud.

"Slide up there," Growney said, and then he flung open the chute to the clang of the bell.

"Come on, Shawn!" yelled Selma, moved in spite of herself. Her boy was riding—*riding!* Shawn stayed on for four hippety-hop jumps, then bailed when the steer turned back to the left. But for those four jumps he'd tried, and Growney was satisfied. "Now what do you think?" the contractor said.

Shawn's face was pink as the twilight. The butterflies had flown south. "I want to ride him again—the same one," he said loudly.

"Not tonight," Growney said. "We got a clinic here for high school kids on Saturday, and I'll run up some steers for you. But the thing you got to remember, Shawn, is there's always pain in this thing. Something always aches. I can teach you, but I can't change your attitude. You've got to decide that you want to do it, and by the time you're a freshman in high school, you're going to win some belt buckles."

Growney watched Selma's car spit gravel down the driveway. It would be some time before he'd know about the kid. "We'll see," he said, as the last dim light fled the scene. Shawn would get his chance, and in this life that was all one could ask.

CHAPTER 5

Roots

RODEO BREATHES OF ITS
vanished parent, the frontier. The sport thrives where the
West was hardest won—in Texas and California, the Southwest and the Great Plains. Where move-'em-in, cut-'em-out
cowboys once roamed a range worthy of the name.

The West—the true, wild West—is our favorite bedtime
story. Cowboys remain our ten-gallon passions, the cattle drives
our national epic. In our heads the saga plays out over vast
reaches of space and time. In fact, our storybook version of
the West lasted about as long as *Gunsmoke* galloped into our
living rooms: just one quarter century, a single generation.

Even before the big show closed, pulp fiction had recast it
for a hero-hungry readership. In his own day, the cowboy was
low man on the prairie totem pole—at worst a trigger-happy
desperado, at best a rowdy roughneck. But in the books of
Zane Grey, a New York dentist, the frog became prince. The
revisionist cowboy was strong and daring, fair and loyal, a
knight of the "high lonesome" he patrolled. As the United

States became a nation of multiracial immigrants, of tooth-and-nail class war at home and gunboat power plays abroad, the cowboy summoned a simpler age, a time when a man's hat was white or black. The cowboy came, he roped, he shot, he loved, and most often he left ("Who was that masked man?"), with no ties or expectations.

Real life was something different. In real life, cowboys were defined by cows. Like the Mexican *vaqueros* who preceded them (and who invented their tools and even their lingo), they were homeless herdsmen filling a need for cheap labor. In the late 1860s, the new cattle barons vied to round up and drive some five million longhorns, left wild to multiply during the Civil War. The trails wound north from Texas, through the vitamin-rich grasses of Oklahoma and Kansas, and on to railheads in Cheyenne and Kansas City, where they'd be shipped to either coast. A cow worth four dollars in Texas would bring ten times as much in New York or San Francisco, a bonanza that gave Cheyenne the nation's most millionaires per capita by 1880.

You didn't need a résumé to get a job on the Chisholm Trail. You needed muscle and stamina, and the moxie to sneer at chronic hardship. A good many cowboys were war-torn veterans from the South, young men in their early twenties, desperate for work and a fresh start. The work part was guaranteed. A trail drive could wind as long as four months and twelve hundred miles, over land so bleak and dry it made a man sad on principle. If the stampedes and rattlesnakes didn't get you, the saddle sores would. You'd go fourteen dusty hours a day on a rent-a-horse owned by your boss, keeping three thousand bawling cattle in a line. On night watch you'd throw sand in your eyes to stay awake. The food was mostly wretched, and the only women you'd meet were the boomtown hookers who'd help spend a month's pay in one night. It was a life to grind a man down; few lasted on the range more than seven years.

The cowboys shared nothing of the barons' wealth. They had one thing to show for their careers: the brotherhood of mounted men, one dating to Genghis Khan. A cowboy was marked by the slant of his boots and the rake of his brim, but his dress was just the shell of a code that clerks would never understand. In a place where laws were distant rumors, the code spoke to survival—of the man and the group. For starters, a cowboy always did his best. He would aid a buddy, a stranger, even an enemy in distress. He was cheerful when tired, a laugh riot when sick. And, most important, he never, ever complained. To "paw and beller" about wages (a dollar a day, give or take) or the weather was for lesser folk with softer lives. On the trail such gripes would spread like typhoid, infecting whole outfits with the notion of quitting, the cardinal disgrace. A cowboy saw a deal through. Period.

Any self-respecting wrangler was pure and passionate on these matters. He was guarding the cowboy's reward: to be his own man. No clock could time him, no marriage bind him. He was special because he was free—even if only to starve, or die young and alone.

Too soon the cowboys saw those free days fleeting, dwindling like the buffalo. The Dry-Up of 1886, with the great freeze that followed on the northern plains, bottlenecked the drives. Overcrowding choked the range. Beef prices crashed. Homesteaders and sheep men fenced off their ninety acres, checkering the domain like an Amish quilt. The cattle barons fought back by guarding their own pastures and water holes, stringing thousands of miles of a new invention called barbed wire. The old trails pinched and clogged. The railroads, meanwhile, tentacled deep into cow country, making the long drives redundant. The barons cut back on their herds, grew their own hay, and tinkered with beefier crossbreds to replace the tough and stringy longhorn. More docile and less mobile, these newcomers were best tended by men on foot; horses would only get in the way.

In 1890 the U.S. Census Bureau counted more than six people per square mile throughout the West, the threshold for a "settled" area. The frontier was written off by the frontier historian himself, Frederick Jackson Turner: old news to the cowpokes and punchers, who'd been laid off in droves. Some cowboys hung on by riding fence instead of trails. They fixed windmills, ran tractors, milked cows, gathered eggs, and told tales of a grander, emptier West.

But others bucked the fate of the hired hand, and clung to the code that lent their days meaning. These holdouts joined the Wild West shows. By 1885 more than fifty troupes threaded the roads, from low-budget dog-and-pony acts to the cast of thousands salaried by William Cody, the Cecil B. DeMille of live horse operas. The frontier might be done, but that wouldn't stop Cody from pitching it to the dudes, from Nebraska to Paris.

In Buffalo Bill's Wild West, the dull singsong of cattle herding became a ballad to individual freedom, to life without picket fences. Cody featured a stagecoach raid and a special guest appearance by Sitting Bull, but his star of stars was Buck Taylor, "King of the Cowboys," an Eagle Scout writ large: rugged, handsome, and courageous, a Galahad with the ladies and never in need of a bath.

As Cody played before presidents and princes, a different show surfaced, on a more human scale, back where it all began. The first rodeos were tests of skill among working cowboys at roundup time, on either side of the Rio Grande. The cowboys liked to bet on their games, but they needed no fans or prizes—just steers to rope, broncos to bust, pistols to shoot, and whiskey to swig.

The winners' feats would be toasted at many a cow-town bar. Interest pricked, the citizens of Deer Trail, Colorado, invited cowboys from three ranches to come play on Main Street back in 1869. Nineteen years later, as the last cattle lowed down the old trails, Prescott Frontier Days became the first commercial rodeo, complete with bleacher seats, admission fees, and silver medals for the winners. In 1897, Cheyenne Frontier Days, the "Daddy of 'Em All," opened its gates in a mission "to revive the thrilling incidents and pictures of life in the old days."

The West was dead; long live the West.

As the cow towns got slicked up and suburbanized, rodeo knitted them to their past. In the process, it stamped the cowboy—not the miner or trapper—as the main man of the West. As the range cowboys once broke and roped two time zones, the rodeo cowboy now tamed a single bronc or calf: the frontier in miniature.

By 1920 the Wild West shows were mostly history. Rodeo won out with lower overhead, but also by bringing home more of the range: skill and risk, chance and pain. Three of rodeo's seven standard events—saddle bronc, calf roping, and steer roping—came directly from ranch work. Three others—bareback, steer wrestling, and team roping—showed off skills that might come in handy in real-life animal control. The odd one out was bull riding, which was absolutely impractical, as pointless as milking a mare or yoking a hog. Here was a contrived test of courage, a calculated thrill.

No one knows exactly how it started. Maybe some hands were looking for laughs toward the end of a drive. Maybe they got bored with spurring horses that were tired and gentled. Maybe (most likely) the cowboys were drunk. And maybe Tex bet Slim that he couldn't stay on some unsuspecting steer as far as the next tumbleweed. A new game was born.

The first recorded cattle rides were cheered in Cheyenne, that trendsetting rail hub, on July 4, 1872, when a crew of Texas cowboys arrived to honor the holiday on steerback. By 1883, "Riding the Wild Texas Steers" headlined Buffalo Bill's Wild West. Novelty acts were all the rage in that period. But unlike mule racing or wild-cow milking, steer riding set mouths agape, and gradually it found its way into rodeo. In

1913 it was added to Prescott Frontier Days, with film star Tom Mix winning the first tilt.

But steer riding had one big drawback: the steers. For years the "wild and vicious human-haters" were longhorns (*Bos taurus*) who'd been shanghaied into showbiz while chewing their cud on a local pasture. Their horns spanned up to five feet tip to tip—but what are horns without hormones? Steers have been de-bulled, after all, to make them easier to handle in their brief life's passage from ranch to packinghouse. The people in the stands sought premeditated felonies. They needed a villain to the piece. By the late 1920s, Cheyenne had phased out the longhorn in favor of heavier Hereford steers, and then with the humped Brahma crosses that had flooded the meat industry. Brahma cattle (*Bos indicus*) had first been imported from India in 1849. Nothing bothered them—neither heat, nor drought, nor insects, nor the driest, coarsest grasses. When mixed with British Herefords or shorthorns, they produced the biggest, beefiest cattle ever seen in Texas. They were quick and prickly, good traits for rodeo. But the crossbreds were still steers, as inclined to scatter as buck. They could never match bulls for muscle mass or blood lust.

The next step was inevitable. In 1929, the Rodeo Association of America inserted bull riding among its seven championship events. Seven years later, Cheyenne left the steers to the ropers and wrestlers, and Brahma-bull riding became a full-fledged rodeo staple.

From the start the bulls made the crowd scream—especially when the stock forgot to stay in the arena. (As an old hand once noted, "People like blood, but very few want to give it up.") In bull riding it seemed no one was safe; therein lay its frontier charm.

While saddle bronc would always be rodeo's classic event, bull riding became the sport's purest abstraction, the stuff of instant myth. It satisfied people's yearnings *because* it was so strange. To work with livestock is to endure monotony and killing hours. Rewards, if they come, are measured by the year. Bull riding is just the opposite, all intensity and no practical substance. Within a few shallow breaths, a cowboy—and his fans—find relief and jubilation or life-threatening failure. By dwelling on such a far planet, bull riding gives rein to our romance with the West.

Which makes the bull rider, in turn, Buck Taylor incarnate—the range hand redux. Ropers are more apt to have grown up on ranches; bronc riders are by and large better horsemen. By contrast, many bull riders are city bred. Some hail from foreign countries like Australia or New York. But the bull riders' risk makes them especially western, and it leads them to a creed as harsh as any on the Chisholm Trail. Among their commandments:

Cowboy up. A bull rider's try is nonnegotiable. When it rains straight down and you haven't slept for two days, you hang tough. When you draw a bad bull that rearranged your face the month before, you keep your composure. As Cody Lambert, a leading keeper of the flame, will tell you, "You've got to get the job done, whatever it takes—that's the cowboy way."

Want to make a bull rider mad? Mention the latest quarterback holdout, or the hoop star who sat out a play out of pique. "Like to see one of them big-time, high-dollar, whinin' spoiled athletes walk away from *that* wreck," Bryan McDonald sniffed in his Finals tip sheet. Or as Donnie Gay put it, more succinctly: "If you want something soft, I'll shit in your hand."

No excuses. Life is not fair. When you make a living on the horns of a dilemma, and the dilemma weighs two thousand pounds, fairness goes out the window. But you better not complain. Once bull riders start crying about the odds against them, once they bow to the insanity of their job, the whole deal collapses like a house of soggy cards.

"A long time ago, if you were a farmer, your crop would tell the people how hard you worked," said Larry Mahan, who dominated rodeo in the late 1960s. "Now it's a different thing. It's a goddamn world of conning and hustling, and people jive-assing one another. But in this game here you can't do it. You can't blame it on anybody else but the person in the mirror."

Make your own breaks. Unbeholden to coaches or teammates, bull riders choose where they ride and accept the consequences. They win gold buckles by standing fast when others crack or back off. Gay won eight times by being more willful than anyone else: "Other guys say, 'I hope I win,' and I would say, 'I'm *gonna* win.' They're wishing on the one hand, and I'm *gettin'* mine." Call it a *High Noon* mentality: the dreamy frontier principle that a man carves his destiny and gets what he deserves.

Never play safe. Bull riding isn't a game of easy outs or half efforts. "I was raised to believe what's gonna happen is what's gonna happen," Ty Murray said. "Everyone's gonna die—that's one thing you can be goddamn sure of. I think you've got to live your life doin' what you want to do." And doing it *right.* Because there is no reride option in that big arena in the sky.

Honor the land of the free. As mavericks who march to their own rat-a-tat, bull riders aren't big on flag-waving. But don't get them wrong. They take dim views of any to the left of Rush Limbaugh; Jim Shoulders once owned a bull he called Khrushchev, "'cause he's big, fat, bald headed, red, and stupid." In a straw poll of thirteen bull riders at the '92 Finals, ten liked Ross Perot and three leaned toward George Bush. For the record, only two of the thirteen voted.

Fact is, these fellows aren't all that high on society in general. Like the old-time range hands, they've left the plow for lives of unfenced self-reliance. From the outside, bull riders might seem rootless, unstable, marginal. Indeed, they are all of the above—but they are also the final pioneers, the last free spirits in America.

The riders' creed wasn't etched in any rule book or handed from the sky. It was forged by generations of rodeo cowboys, smithed in the image of the best of them. Bull riding came of age in the 1940s, as cowboys started to realize there was more to it than hanging on for dear life. The first great "strength" rider was the flamboyant Dick Griffith, a former trick rider who'd arrive in formal wear, trade top hat for Stetson, and bust out still in his tuxedo. At the other pole was Ken Roberts, the last word in finesse—the rodeo equivalent to a junkballing control pitcher. Roberts rode so loose that he wouldn't lock his spurs' rowels for traction, as the rules allow. As quick as he got his wrap he'd nod his head, then flow into the bull's action like a Latin dancer, till it was hard to tell where animal ended and man began.

In the 1950s, rodeo's golden age, two men dominated bull riding like no two before or since: Jim Shoulders and Harry Tompkins. The self-taught son of a Tulsa auto mechanic, Shoulders was a Ruthian figure. Lean and limber, nerveless and unsinkable, he'd set the sport's most formidable record of sixteen world championships: seven bull riding, five all-around, four bareback. In 1954 he set an earnings record on the bulls, his favorite event. The record lasted twenty years, and but for inflation would stand today.

Though tall for a bull rider, a shade over six feet, Shoulders blended strength and finesse, talent and try. Homespun and country-blunt, he was also nobody's fool. He liked to say there was no science to riding—that you just "put one leg on each side of the bull and make an ugly face for eight seconds." If he was feeling talkative, he might tell you that he always watched the bull's head: "If his head goes to the right, his ass will follow. I've never seen one come in two." But Shoulders ran ahead of his time in using his free arm as counterweight, and his knack for judging the bull's next dive or spin verged on telepathy. A canny gamesman, he would tie four bells on a weak draw as a ploy to fool the scorers, who might confuse clatter for action.

In Shoulders's day the nation's cowboy darling was saddle-bronc marvel Casey Tibbs, he of the Hollywood looks and purple Cadillacs. While the acid-tongued Shoulders couldn't match Tibbs for flair, he cast a taller shadow within rodeo. When he spotted a group of young cowboys hustling rides to the next town, flat broke after losing their entry fees, he'd stoop to the ground and come up with a twenty-dollar bill. "Here," he'd say casually, "you dropped this." The gift would cover the cowboys' next meal or two, keep them going down the road.

Shoulders was a pro in the strictest sense. He gave everything to his job but sentiment. He went as hard as he could to win as fast as he could, all to pay off his five-thousand-acre cattle ranch in Henryetta, Oklahoma. "Bull ridin' was a business with me," he said from deep in a living-room BarcaLounger, watching his beloved Oklahoma Sooners beat up on some Big Eight also-ran. Shoulders had a gritty, emphatic way of talking, reminiscent of his old friend Slim Pickens. "How else could a country boy with just a high school education get his hands on thirty thousand dollars a year?"

His hilltop ranch house, full of windows, looked a sight more modern than its owner. Shoulders never cared much about appearances, and after a day of baling hay—"I'm the flunky"—he'd settled in baggy black dungarees and a half-open work shirt, gouty hands clasped over a broad, tanned chest. He'd kicked off his work boots to put up his stocking feet—one red, one blue.

"His socks don't ever match," apologized Sharon Shoulders, the comely charmer who'd married the big lug out of high school. After forty-five years of smoothing rough edges, she knew it was a life's work. "It would be an idiosyncrasy, but—"

"Neither one of them's got a hole in it," Shoulders growled, his blue eyes indignant behind wire-rim glasses. "Ain't nobody's business. . . . It's bad luck to wear socks that match." He coughed and cleared his throat. "After you get sixty years old, you get the goddamn asthma. . . ."

Shoulders had aged hard. His once-angular face was craggy and flushed, and it seemed like it ached him to stand up straight. But his silver hair was thick and his chin strong, and he still held by the old ways in rodeo. In Shoulders's time, a cowboy would mock a sorry bull by waving his hat to the fans or hollering some friendly abuse to the stock contractor, "just to clown and have a big time. It wasn't nothin' for Casey or Tompkins to jump on behind you and ride double, just to thrill the crowd," he recalled. "If you saw that nowadays they'd go nuts, maybe throw you out of the association. These boys today, first thing they do is jump off, then they go back and cuss everybody. They don't think anything about the people in the grandstand."

Shoulders left off riding gradually through the early 1960s. "I never did retire, I just quit winning," he said. "I never was thrilled just hearing my name called. When I got where I thought I couldn't win, I thought the best thing for me was to find something else to do." For a while he moved into stock contracting and the rodeo-school business. Lately he'd turned to producing a low-cholesterol crossbreed out of the old Texas longhorns.

With most of Shoulders's trophies lodged at the Cowboy Hall of Fame, the ranch house held few clues to a majestic career—two award statues from the Calgary Stampede, a single tarnished gold buckle. From one wall stared the mounted head of Buford T. Lite, the bar-hopping bull who worked with Shoulders in a series of memorable Miller Lite commercials. Nearby hung an oil painting of Tornado, the flagship of Shoulders's fleet in his contracting days. The red Braford bull looked like a chiropractic nightmare, rearing on his hind legs while twisting diagonally. It wasn't hard to believe he'd gone unridden for six straight seasons.

Shoulders walked over, slightly crick-backed, to peer at the painting. "There's never been one that would sell tickets like Tornado," he said. "He wasn't really mean, he'd never run you out of the pasture. He just bucked you hard enough to throw you off. But any bullfighter could get his attention, and he always fought. He'd roll that barrel around. . . ."

In 1968, a few months after Freckles Brown's historic Finals ride, Tornado came down with "hardware disease" from some nails in his feed. A magnet treatment failed. Surgery was ruled out. "We felt like he had already paid his way, so we turned him out," Shoulders said pensively. "He was fourteen when he died." The bull was buried by a flower garden at the Hall of Fame, but Shoulders kept his horns.

The Babe Ruth of bull riding saw his guest out. "Stay well, sir," the visitor said.

Shoulders squinted into the night and said, "It's a little late for that, don't you think?"

☆

Harry Tompkins had a restless mind. He was always thinking of a different way to do things. An amateur inventor, he created the sectional bucking chutes that cut installation time by 90 percent. When he put up a house in blistering Dublin, Texas, he had it built into the side of a hill for natural insulation. The house was roofed by a green pasture, and it was common to see three or four cows grazing atop it.

No less original in the arena, Tompkins won five bull-riding titles over a thirteen-year period, each one in high style. As Shoulders, his one true rival, summed it, "Harry's hard to beat because he can ride so damn good."

Like Shoulders, Tompkins was raised off the ranch, in the upstate New York town of Peekskill. He had an athlete's ease about him, and as a youth startled people by walking pipe fences. In 1945 he hired on with the nearby Cimarron Dude Ranch. It was a dream job for Tompkins, who loved to ride. Due to the wartime leather shortage he'd lead the dudes out without a saddle, six and eight hours a day, and on moonlit nights he'd go back for fun and jump bareback over stone walls and junked cars. On off days he'd load the white-faced steers used at Cimarron's weekly rodeos, rig up the chute, flank the animal, pull his own rope, lift the latch, and shove open the gate. He'd ride forty or more at a stretch; he couldn't get enough.

In 1946 the ranch tapped the nineteen-year-old Tompkins for its bull-riding entry at New York's monthlong rodeo at

Madison Square Garden, then the biggest, best-paying cowboy contest in the world. With only three practice bulls behind him, Tompkins managed to win three hundred dollars, which felt like easy money next to nine dollars per week of sixteen-hour days at the dude ranch. He'd found his niche.

Tompkins rode with Ken Roberts's finesse and added a dash of showmanship. He never wore chaps, the better to feel the animal under him. To buffer the bull's snapping jerk, Tompkins kept his rope loose, almost slack. For effect he'd ask a petite barrel racer to pull for him—"One of my girls is going to help me today"—or he'd do it himself, as though riding a steer back at Cimarron. One day he mixed up his schedule and found his bull loaded to go before he could change. He hopped on in his smooth, loose-tailored dress pants, and the ride was a revelation: he could *move*. From that day on, Tompkins bucked cowboy fashion by discarding his skintight Wranglers for jeans a size or two larger. When the good ol' boys muttered about "the damned Yankee" in baggy pants who kept stealing their entry fees, Tompkins laughed all the way to the bank.

His style had a sweet geometry, a buttery ease. Where other riders leaned over their bulls, Tompkins sat erect as a slide rule, his torso tracing the line of the bull's shoulders. He kept a constant distance between the bull's head and his own, and so rarely slid out of position. When the bull shifted direction, Tompkins was ready; he'd already felt the animal change leads through its shoulder blades. "I wouldn't just ride," he liked to say. "I'd ride and think at the same time." As that thinking was rooted in reflex, it never slowed Tompkins down.

There is a wonderful picture at the Cowboy Hall of Fame of a young Tompkins in action in 1949. His gray bull, with horns the size of rolling pins, has trampolined a good four feet into the air. Tompkins is sitting back to meet the spinner's kick, in about the same posture as Shoulders on his BarcaLounger. He is wearing a starched white shirt, a noncha-

To Jeff
Harry Tompkins
1992

lant smile, and a heavy-lidded gaze. Every part of him is limber and relaxed, to the half-curled fingers of his free hand. But what makes the photograph extraordinary is that Tompkins has turned sideways to face the lens; he is *posing*.

Indeed, the picture had been prearranged. With Tompkins's supernatural balance ("I could have been a trapeze artist real easy"), such high jinks were no big deal. He'd often kibitz like Charles Barkley in the midst of a fray, goading other cowboys,

"Why don't you ride like this?" Most knew better than to try. At a party in Phoenix, Tompkins showed off with a walk along a cable stretched over a swimming pool. Several cowboys went to follow, and soon the pool was filled with boots and big hats.

Tompkins was most vain about his two-point get-offs: "Yeah, I guess I could do that better than anybody, getting off and landing on my feet and not on my head." When he felt himself losing his balance—and it might not happen more than five times a year—he'd step off before trouble came. He saw no point in hanging helpless on the bull's side. A cowboy could get hurt that way, and besides, it made a shabby display. For Tompkins, to ride good was to look good.

He and Shoulders were comrades in arms who shared 10 percent of their winnings in case one of them drew cold. But they also rode for the same gold buckle. They never stopped looking to top one another, even decades after the fact.

"Jim rode just as well as I did, but he wasn't as ath-a-letic as I was when it came to getting off, or some of the moves I could do," Tompkins said.

"I always told Tompkins that if a man hit on his feet, he wasn't trying that hard," Shoulders countered. "He was pretty good about saving hisself, and fortunately for me he was, because if he had really tried that hard I wouldn't of won much. He could sure ride, *sure* ride."

In 1961 Tompkins was knocked down by a bull for the first time in a fifteen-year career. It was an unsightly melee—the rider rolling on the ground, the bull jabbing at him with its horns, the clown slapping the crazed beast's head with a cape—and when it was over Tompkins's elbow had torn out of joint. He couldn't straighten his arm for months, and though he got back to the Finals four years later, he'd never be the same.

But well into his fifties, when he was running a quiet dairy farm, Tompkins couldn't shake his bug to look *good* again. When an old-timers' circuit came calling in the early 1980s, Tompkins answered the bell, telling himself how strong his hands were from squeezing all those teats. That first season he ranked first in bull riding, though his timing was a fuzzy ghost of its old tuning-fork precision. The next year his foot lodged in a crack in the chute, and when the bull reared Tompkins ruptured a main artery by his groin. After surgery they told him he'd had one hour to live unattended. *That* was his last ride.

Back in Henryetta, Shoulders shook his head at his old friend's folly. He'd turned down a similar invite himself, with no regret. It was one thing for a grandpa to team-rope if he didn't like golf. It was another to risk your old age on a bull when go-rounds at the Senior Pro Rodeo Finals paid three hundred bucks a pop. "If I thought I could ride, I'd be enterin' Houston and Cheyenne, somewhere you could win something," Shoulders said. "Harry thought he was a kid. . . . They crippled a lot of guys in those things."

But not everyone sees himself through Shoulders's clear eyes. It eats at a cowboy to stay off the bulls, to play taps for the times that he's felt most alive. It can pain him even when he has no more to prove. Ronnie Rossen won two gold buckles in the 1960s, made the Finals nine times. They called him "Punch" for his hair-trigger temper, and he lived life the way he fought, jumping in on impulse. A Nebraska boyhood had taught him a healthy aversion to ranch work. Bull riding was his ticket out.

With his vests and bandannas, his lantern jaw and rebel glint, Rossen was as hard to dislike as he was to put up with. The last dancer on the floor, the last drinker at the bar, he made good times into religion. Wild and spur-happy out of the chute, he'd get pitched off bulls he might have placed on had he hooked in and stayed tight. He raised to the limit on every hand, and when he was hot very few could play with him.

But when he rode cold, Rossen was a bullfighter's nightmare. No one hung on to more lost causes with such a stout left arm. No one got dumped harder on his head or had more hell getting away. "That's probably why I have so many scars," he confessed. "I never let go when I should have." Those scars showed that Rossen was as true to the creed as Shoulders or Tuff. He looked for the edge of the envelope, and now and then he folded over.

"Money isn't the big part of riding bulls," Rossen once explained. "It's that inner feeling that you're going to ride a tornado, and by God you're going to conquer it, you hope." He could never cut that feeling loose. He went twelve rounds with booze and a few more in divorce court, but nothing dropped him to the canvas for the count.

For Rossen the old-timers' league was a governor's pardon, a reprieve from the pangs of a has-been. When he hitched on, it was almost unfair. The competition had paunches and pension plans—they'd grown up, at long last—but Rossen was rawboned and reckless as ever. By then he'd been sewn up and pieced together so often that his X rays looked like jigsaw puzzles, and still he rode like a young gunslinger, without nerves or second thoughts. He won seven senior titles while continuing to redecorate his face.

In July 1991, at the age of fifty-four, Rossen notched another winning ride at Rocky Ford, Colorado. He heard the horn and the cheers—*yeah, this old man still had it*—and then he got flung underneath, one last time, down to the hooves that planted square in his chest. Rossen died two hours later of massive internal bleeding around the heart. He was a bull rider, and he never let go when he should have.

CHAPTER 6

On the Road

*T*UFF SMILED AT THE SIGHT of a short cowboy with a skinned forehead and an outlandish shiner shuffling his way by the baggage claim in Denver. "How ya doin', little Roscoe?"

"Had a mean bull in Reno," Branger replied. "It's a good story. It was real . . . excitin'." Up close, his right eye was a revolting study in rose and pea green. A line of rough stitches curved up like a second brow. "Miss me?"

"I been missin' you real bad," Tuff said, and you could see it was true beneath the banter. Cowboy Christmas, the spate of rich rodeos around July 4, scattered travel teams all over the map.

"I missed you," Branger said. "Feelin' good today, aren't you?" And Tuff surely was, by comparison. Branger had been sitting second at Reno—"a *payin'* sucker"—going into the short round on Sunday. He'd drawn a headhunter, "only weighed a thousand pounds, but he's the meanest little thing I ever saw in my life." The bull reared back at him in the chute, and matters got worse from there. Early on Branger tipped into the well, the last place he wanted to be, "because if I go down in there he's going to tromp me and hook me—he's *mean*. Finally he gets me in such a bad spot where I just took my head and tucked it down, and he smacked me above the eye with his head." Branger toppled to the ground, stunned and bleeding, and saw the bull make a beeline to finish the job. He counted himself lucky to escape to the rail.

After that came the hard part—a solo, eight-hundred-mile drive from Reno back to Montana with an eye that was pounding, draining, and refusing to focus. It took seventeen hours, with a four-hour sleep break in the backseat. "It wasn't real fun," Branger said, "but it was either sell the car in Reno and fly home, or drive home and fly here." Twice before he'd left cars he owned for dead on the side of the road, but this one was a '91 Cutlass Supreme, worth too much to write off. It took a second Bloody Mary on the flight down to Denver for Branger to feel human again. After Greeley he'd have five rodeos over three days, which was the good thing about Cowboy Christmas: no time to get discouraged.

It was six o'clock when Mike Gaffney, a slick-riding young Texan, piled into their rental car. Greeley lay an hour off—plenty of time to make the rodeo, which wouldn't load the bulls till past nine. On the way, the cowboys traded shoptalk.

Gaffney said, "I fell off in Big Spring, a piece of shit."

"They're all a piece of shit when you get bucked off," Tuff remarked.

"He didn't fit my style, either," said Gaffney, who was known to skip a rodeo when he missed his wife too much.

They reached town just after seven. Strung over a deserted Main Street, a banner clued you to the people's whereabouts: "Greeley Independence Day Stampede." A minute later Tuff swerved into the parking lot, lying to the guard that he'd unload and come right back out, the only way he could get a good space. At times the indignities wore on him. Did Troy

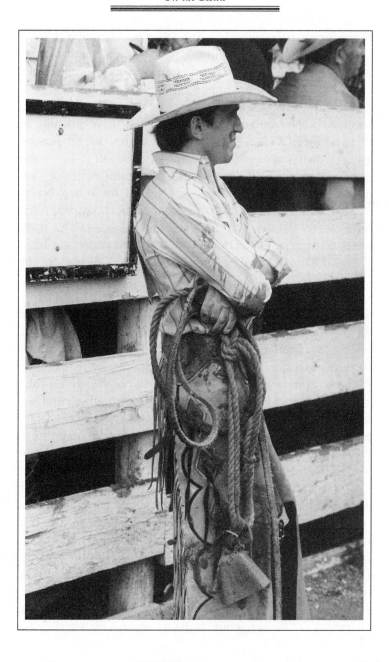

Aikman have to haggle when he docked his Mercedes at Texas Stadium? "We're the pilgrims," Tuff groused. "Got to park out in the cheap seats so that these fat, drunk committeemen can park here. *We're* not important."

To the jounce of a brass band inside the arena, the bull riders heaved their bulging canvas bags from the trunk and set them on the blacktop. As at many summer rodeos, the parking lot was their dressing room. They stripped off T-shirts and donned carefully folded, showy numbers from Roper or Panhandle Slim. Running shoes were traded for riding boots. Straw hats—the vogue from Easter to Labor Day, when felt returned to fashion—were tugged and adjusted. The three were still zipping and tucking as a line of red-white-and-blue-spangled women loped by on horseback, locals headed for the Grand Entry.

The cowboys stopped first with the rodeo secretary to write checks for $285: one-fifty toward the purse, a hundred for day money (to be split among all who made the whistle), twenty-five for the final round's pot, and ten to pay for their medical insurance and the computerized entry system.

Dusk came and cooled the ninety-degree day with a John Ford backdrop, clouds of slate scudding through a coral sky. Like fireworks, the bulls were saved for after dark. The heavy animals paced in their pens, flies speckling their humps, just yards from the men who would mount them. Outdoor rodeos were different from the Finals, more open yet more intimate.

Twilight flickered out. A few naked bulbs half lit the ready area. The bull riders stopped talking. As the barrel racers ran their cloverleaf patterns, the cowboys whipped into pre-ride gyrations, genuflections. A young one slapped both of his cheeks, as if daring himself to a duel. Then it was time. Gaffney—*"the G-Man from Lubbock!"*—was belly-rolled to the dirt and scraped by a horn below the rib cage. Branger survived a jerking bull for a seventy-seven and no new colors on his face. Tuff sat pretty up to the six-second mark, when his handle jerked from his hand. He clutched to his rope's tail the last four jumps, and was startled to hear he'd earned an eighty-three, second best of the night to Ted Nuce. After a spatter of applause the families filed their retreat, into the dark of the crickets' song.

Back in the ready area, almost empty now, a tiny figure sat alone on a bench, peeling off manure-stained jeans in the cool night air. At thirty-five, elderly in this game, Charles Sampson had burst out to a grand start in 1992. He'd grabbed fat checks—more than seven thousand apiece—in Kansas City and San Antonio, and jumped to second in the standings. But in May he'd gotten hurt, and badly, one more time.

In the trade, Sampson was notorious for leaning way out over the bull's neck, and for the deep hold he took with his legs and feet round the animal's belly. The lean kept him centered and the hold kept him stable, and he finished fun-house rides that would unravel most anyone else. But on a draw with lots of drop, a wrong move could jerk Sampson down with terrible force, to the barely padded basalt of the bull's skull. A taller cowboy might slam his chest or shoulder, but Sampson's short upper body made for a more lethal trigonometry: a literal meeting of minds.

In their gallows humor the cowboys called this a "kiss," and nine years earlier Sampson nearly died from one. The damage wasn't so grave when he got brung again in May, on the bull called Body Bag, but Sampson still broke both jaws and lost seven teeth.

Injury is the great leveler, the universal truth about bull riding. Yet Sampson stood out. He was Job in Justins, the one who skated closest to ground zero. Every top rider had a horror story, but only Sampson had crushed his entire face, or broken his leg *five* times, or had an ear sliced clean away by a knifing hoof. As Gary Leffew once remarked, "He reminds me of that old guy in the medicine show in *Little Big Man*—'God-*damn*, every time I see you they just keep whittling you down.'"

Just four weeks after Sampson's tête-à-tête with Body Bag, the fat cash in Reno drew him back to the one life he knew. Spurning doc's orders to wear a helmet, he fought off the jitters and rode his first bull, then bucked off a second "because I was acting like a wimp—I wasn't sure, I was a little timid."

His friends looked on and shuddered. Back in Houston, Myrtis Dightman, Sampson's gritty mentor and the first black cowboy to make the Finals back in 1964, voiced the general sentiment: "I'd quit. Once you're a champion, there's nothing else for you to do—you're always number one."

Sampson was in a bad mood at Greeley, where he'd bucked off a bull he could ride like a Shetland pony when he was right. As he methodically changed his socks, he puffed up in anger when Dightman's message was passed to him. Charles Sampson would bow out on *his* terms, not because he got clocked by some damn droppy bull.

"Why not just continue to do what you want to do?" he said defiantly, in the sputtering rhythm he fell into when excited. He stared out to the middle distance; his new dentures glowed dully under the lights. "No matter how many championships I've got, no matter how many times I get hit, all that matters is: Do I want to *do* it?

"People always criticize. They can say, 'Charlie gets a hold too much.' It doesn't really matter. It matters how I do, so *fuck* what they say, as long as I get by with the way that I ride. The bottom line is, let 'em *last* as long as I have.

"Pain is a frame of mind," Sampson said. "Most people couldn't probably stand the pain like I do." He swung his eyes toward his questioner. They were round, nearly black, soft as calfskin. They told you that those who were wounded the most didn't always harden to it. "When you're hurt it ain't no fun—it's hard enough to ride when you're healthy. But at the same time, if I want to do it, you got to praise me, not discourage me. . . . I see more of the big picture than they do. I know *me*."

It was as Dightman had predicted: "A man won't quit till he gets ready."

Though Sampson was still in the top fifteen, his layoff had dragged him far out of the lead. He could no longer rodeo as hard as younger, sounder men. Was he really mining for another gold buckle? The round eyes snapped back: "I've been trying to win the world championship again since 1982. Why *shouldn't* I get one more run at it?" Sampson would not go to the Finals for some nostalgic last hurrah; he would go as a contender, or not at all.

By 11:15 Tuff and company were back in Denver, at a bustling Denny's. Tuff hadn't eaten since a one o'clock sandwich, and he joined Branger and Gaffney in ordering with gusto from a "Moonlight Menu": burgers, eggs, hash browns, onion rings. Young men's food. In rising spirits, Tuff sang along with Chris LeDoux's "Cowboys Just Got to Be Free."

"He's not afraid to beller out," Branger observed.

"Riding taaalll . . . ," Tuff crooned, something like Wayne Newton with a sinus condition. "I *am* a good singer."

At 1:20 in the morning the bull riders reached a Hampton Inn near the airport and fell in, two to a bed. Less than three hours later, showered and dressed, Tuff nudged Gaffney, who started awake and bumped his head on a hanging lamp. It was time for their flight to Dallas; Tuff would be winging home for a few free hours with his family. In the elevator Tuff chirped, "A good night's sleep and ready to roll." Sipping a lemon-lime Slice for breakfast, he was at the rental-car wheel by four, in the plane for takeoff by 4:40.

Tuff had piled enough frequent-flier miles for two tickets to Bora Bora on any of five airlines. He knew every flight crew going, and this morning he chatted into the dawn with a blond flight attendant who happened to be a stock contractor's daughter-in-law. A few minutes later he and Gaffney moved up to first class, "to sit with the pretty people" into Dallas–Fort Worth. Rodeo folk take care of their own.

At 8:15 Central, Tuff was revving his Chrysler Euro out of the airport for the seventy-mile drive to Bowie. With his left hand more or less on the wheel, he extracted his three-ring-binder date book, its flaps packed with plane receipts and Canadian money. He worked his car phone the whole way, confirming rodeo dates and rousting friends from sleep.

As Bowie neared, Tuff was champing at the bit. Earlier in his career, "when I was a little freer and a little wilder," he'd be gone more than half the year. Now he averaged twelve days away per month, and still it was too much. He was moving a smooth fifty-five on a two-lane road, his hair glinting reddish in the low sun, when he got stuck behind a watermelon truck. "Need to practice my race-car skills," Tuff said. He passed the truck while roaring uphill: driving ugly. By the time he squealed a right over some railroad ties and onto a dirt road, he was doing seventy.

Home was a modest brick ranch house, ringed by oaks and set on fifteen acres of grass. Three cows and their calves formed a welcome committee. Inside Tuff dropped straight-away to the living-room rug, to join his son and a toy pig on wheels. A pie-faced towhead, young Lane favored his mother, except for the way his tongue stuck out when he was thinking extra-hard. "What does a pig say?" Tuff prompted.

"Moooo," cooed Lane, eager to please.

Tracy laughed and said, "Doncha know, Daddy? Everything says moo."

Tuff's trophies were outgrowing his living room. Seven tooled championship saddles bloomed on a metal tree. Eight framed photographs of the top fifteen, one for each of Tuff's Finals, packed one paneled wall. Two other pictures remembered Lane Frost on Red Rock, the rider stylish even in a still, his free arm a smooth curve ascending.

"I go home more than probably most anybody," Tuff said, as he laid off a roping game—with his son as the calf—to sit down to a burger lunch. "It costs me a lot to come home the way I do, but it's worth it to me."

At 1:45, four quicksilver hours after he'd walked through the door, Tuff waved his good-byes and headed back to the airport. He made his plane six minutes ahead—"That's early for me, that's real calm"—and arrived in Midland, Texas, at five o'clock. Tuff dozed in his seat as a line formed to exit. He allowed himself a flash of weakness. "I'm tired," he said. "I'm *real* tired."

At the airport Tuff cadged a ride to the next rodeo in Pecos with Bobby Harris, the defending cochampion team roper, and squeezed into a Rambler pickup with seven other timed-event cowboys, few of whom could pose for the "after" part of a Slim-Fast ad. "You can't be too picky in this business," Tuff would remark. "I went from flying first-class and a suite at the Golden Nugget in Reno to driving with eight guys in a pickup truck. You got to take it as it comes."

Soon they were barreling through sand-dune and sagebrush country, scrub and shrub, all browned in the blast furnace of West Texas. It was the kind of flat, parched scenery that left you indifferent to the layers of ex-bugs on the windshield. Oil derricks spoiled the horizon, and the heady, burnt-rubber stink of petroleum filled the truck's cab. Tuff had fled the desert clime of El Paso for the green of greater Dallas, and every trip to Pecos made him gladder he'd left.

The affable Harris wanted to know about the Carrillo brothers, bull-riding phenoms from Tuff's hometown: "Do those little twin midgets from El Paso ride pretty good?"

"Yeah, they do," Tuff said.

Harris, who went five-eleven and 245, said, "They're just so cute, a guy would want to buy 'em and just have 'em around."

Ropers were cut from a different cloth. Their shirts were plainer, their jeans looser, their joking gentler. They had a special affection for Okie and Arkie riddles, rodeo's favorite ethnic humor.

Q: How do you keep an Arkie from biting his nails?
A: Make him put on his shoes.

After a pit stop at a red-sauce Mexican restaurant, the pickup made the arena at 7:30. Pecos contended with Prescott for the title of "the World's First Rodeo," and its facilities backed the claim. The bomb-shelter decor of the cowboys' dressing room made Greeley seem luxurious. The only chair was bogarted by a PRCA official, and a single toilet—one more than many rodeos provide, in fairness—sat in a doorless stall. But Tuff had a soft spot for Pecos. He'd earned one of his first checks there, a hundred and some dollars in day money, "and I thought I was really chasing the title."

Out in the grandstand, five thousand fans applauded a steel-guitar national anthem. From that point on suspense centered on when the storm would come. There are no rainouts in rodeo, though bulls are slippery when wet. "It's like hanging on to a bit of steak stew," said Mike Gaffney, but Tuff took the weather in stride. He rode a choppy, scooting bull with enough snap to it for an eighty-six, which Tuff guessed would rate at least second. Post-downpour, when Pecos felt like an unvented bathroom after a hot shower, he stuck around to give autographs to a gaggle of locals.

In slumbering towns like these, rodeo week was more than a sporting event. The cowboys crowned a festival that included a high school beauty pageant, a "Fiesta Night" in Old Pecos, a downtown parade and barbecue, a western art show, and a dance that still swung at the adjacent civic center. But bull riders rarely had time to linger, and by midnight Tuff was on the road again, sharing a sedan with a garrulous bareback rider named Ken Lensegrav. Their destination was Window

Rock, Arizona, home to the Navajo Nation Rodeo, five hundred miles away.

After zonking out at a New Mexico motel, the pair turned west on Route 66 toward the Continental Divide. The land turned with them, to a moonscape of ore-rich mesas and sculpted orange outcroppings. Tuff was getting pumped: "Going to the res!" Window Rock was the tribal capital of the sprawling Navajo Reservation, a breadth of cliffs and canyons larger than Connecticut. The four most popular sports among the Navajo, so they say, are rodeo, rodeo, rodeo, and basketball. Bull riding has a special following there, dating to the '50s, when the Indians used to mount Hereford cows with no time limit. If the cow went over the hill, the ride might last an hour.

Most Navajo bull riders compete within their own leagues; few have the confidence and backing to take on the PRCA. But their people adopt the vagrant cowboys as their own each July. "They're the world's greatest rodeo fans," Tuff said. "They don't get that excited in the stands, but I guarantee you there'll be a crowd out there after the rodeo, and they'll want you to sign their hat, their programs, their babies. They really go all out." The evening sky at Window Rock was a cobalt splendor, the air clean and dry. It was a glorious night to be a bull rider, and doubly so for two young men the size of eighth graders who stood gabbing in the open-air ready area as they rosined their ropes. They were mimeographed copies: the same pink cheeks and trim black hair; the same crooked noses and dimples and faint traces of acne; the same favorite chewing gum—Dentyne red—working their jaws.

Meet Adam and Gilbert Carrillo, twenty-year-old cowboys extraordinaire. Ty Murray called them "the Munchkins," and they tickled him so much that he'd shortly take them into his home. "They're two little boys that get to live men's lives," said Murray, now the grizzled veteran going on twenty-three. "They want to cuss real bad but they're not sure how to do it yet. They'll say, 'No, I damn didn't!'"

The Carrillos speak by habit in the first person plural. They finish each other's thoughts, like Donald Duck's nephews, giggling by turns at the punch lines. "Me and Gilbert, we make a living out of this. We don't come to these things—"

"for the experience."

"We come to these things to make—"

"money."

In their time on earth the longest they'd been apart was one week, when Gilbert went off to the college finals in Bozeman the summer before. It was a long week. "It didn't feel right," Gilbert said. "I did terrible on my first bull. I hung out with my friends but it wasn't the same."

"I went to North Platte, Nebraska, and got thrown off," Adam said. "I was fallin' off more bulls than I ever have."

"I had to rely on other people, and I didn't like doing that," Gilbert said.

"You ask any of the top fifteen guys," Adam said, "and they'll tell you if you see one, you'll see the other."

Back in El Paso, where they'd hunt rabbits bareback through the mesquite, the twins had been tutored by Tuff's big brother, Roach. They entered their first jackpots in their early teens, still inches shy of five feet. They'd crawl up on the bad, hooky bulls that scared off local cowboys twice their age, and they'd ride and fall off and learn to do better.

Now the Carrillos were up against the names they'd watched for years on the Nashville Network. Ted Nuce—*the* Ted Nuce—had fallen in with them that spring and took care of their entering. The twins pinched one another and tried to stay cool, but it wasn't easy. "Now me and Gilbert tell each other we're *doin'* it—this is it, don't worry," Adam said. "You don't need to get all huffy and puffy now. We know how to ride. Shoot, in college me and Gilbert hung on to everything, and they're the same bulls here."

For the Carrillos bull riding is a team sport. They pool their winnings and share the cost of a van. At each stop they figure they have two shots to win, and when one gets bucked off, the other bears down even harder. Once a bull flipped over in the chute with Adam on its back and tore off the heel of his boot. Gilbert didn't think twice. He pulled off his own boot—a ladies' size six—and gave it to his twin, along with a spur. Adam slipped it on and rode the bull for an eighty-nine, just knocked the brute out. Because Dodge Trucks had placed a promotional "bounty" on the bull, the ride was worth seven thousand dollars.

That kind of togetherness, the Carrillos were convinced, would propel them to their private wing in the Hall of Fame. In this, their first season, they aimed to finish one-two for rookie of the year. But that was just for warm-ups.

"There's a great goal in our lives," Gilbert said earnestly. "Donnie Gay, he has eight world titles under his belt. I have the most respect for him, but we'd like to break his record—each of us. If we rodeoed for twenty years, I could win one year and Adam could win the next, and we could keep going back and forth."

Their dream didn't end with a score of gold buckles. The twins had already formed a corporation. "We plan on investing our money in real estate, not just piddling around," Gilbert said. "We'll get a good ranch, say a hundred acres, with a big pond and stock it with bass."

Their houses would sit side by side, Adam said, "and in between we'll have a swimming pool, 'cause me and Gilbert love the water."

There they'd be, men of leisure by the time they turned forty, sipping pastel drinks and perfecting their swan dives if they felt like it. It was a perfect picture, but for one detail. They would still be too short. They would still be five-foot-three.

"I'd like a couple extra inches," Gilbert admitted. "We have to wear size twenty-eight 'students' in jeans—no men's size fits us. Everything's kind of baggy."

"Everyone's taller than us—even the girls," Adam said sadly.

Had they stopped growing? "I hope not," Gilbert said. He turned to his brother: "Are we gonna grow any more?"

"I hope so," his twin said.

Adam, who'd been pressing of late, fell off his bull that night. But he jumped up behind the chutes to pull his brother's rope, as always, to clap him on the back and urge him on. Gilbert got beat around the corner, scrambled back, and got beat again off to the outside. He was riding sideways three jumps before the whistle, but somehow hung on—to the high delight of the man who looked just like him. "Gilbert, way to go!" Adam cheered, as his red-faced twin clambered back over the rail. They exchanged victory taps to the chest. Then Adam winked at a friend and said, confidentially, "See what I mean about us trying harder?"

Sammy Andrews had brought his vaunted bulls to Window Rock, and they made the stock at Pecos and Greeley look like practice pens. In Andrews's sixth year in pro rodeo, he would send twelve of his bulls to the Finals that December, four more than any other contractor. But success hadn't spoiled him. He still rooted for the top guys to ride his stars for big scores, rather than get bucked off. It was better publicity, and besides, the cowboys had to eat, too. "Got to watch him," he told Tuff about his draw that night, a gray Brahma named Killer Bee with a medicine ball for a hump. "I seen him go all the way out to the calf-roping chute before he turned. Might want to put a clown out in front to turn him."

"Thanks, pard, I appreciate that," Tuff said. Like many near purebreds, this one was chute-funny. Tuff tried to gentle him, resting his knees on the bull's back before lowering his legs, but it didn't help. Killer Bee squatted to the dirt like a cranky camel.

The announcer droned on: ". . . illustrious rodeo career . . . three-time world champion. . . . This bull is a bad dude. Last week he jumped so high that he ended up inside the barrel, squashed the barrel man so bad he put him in the hospital. You know where he is today? Rooms twenty, twenty-one, and twenty-two."

Most riders wouldn't nod their head till a bull stood up, but Tuff had a different view. It took a lot of trouble to get a new wrap and repull the rope and fight for the bull, and Killer Bee probably wouldn't stand much better if he did. Tuff also knew that no bull in the history of the world had jumped out of a box without first standing up—"It's like you laying flat on your back and in one leap trying to jump to the television set." Besides, Tuff was a cowboy, and a cowboy makes the best of it. When the going got mean and nasty and absolutely rotten, Tuff liked to get going. He called for the bull.

But cowboy virtue isn't always rewarded. On the second jump out Killer Bee went sunfishing and tipped Tuff to the left, into his hand. "Hell," the rider said afterward, "he just bucked me off." Back of the chutes, Tuff leaned heavily against a pole, weak with disappointment, and exhaled a small oath. A teenage girl approached him to inscribe her hat. Tuff almost put her off, then smiled and relented, but you could tell that failure still killed him after all these years.

The scene reminded Claryce Hedeman, who'd driven eight hours from El Paso to watch her boy ride, of the time she threw away the family's Monopoly set. She'd wearied of watching Tuff and Roach and Cody Lambert come to blows over lost fortunes. "Tuff thought it was real money," his mother related. "These kids haven't changed since they've been in third grade. You wanted to haul them off by the neck with baling wire. None of them were any good losers. That's why they did good—they hated to lose."

The sting faded a few minutes later, as Tuff sat inside a striped tent to sign for a calm and endless line. The fans still adored him, and Tuff knew that Killer Bee was but a speed bump in his drive toward another Finals, and perhaps a fourth gold buckle. He'd move on the next day to Prescott, then back to the short round at Greeley, where he'd place second in the average and ride a bounty bull for eleven thousand dollars. By week's end he'd surge to fourth in the world, and he'd recall how the road once felt like home to him. As Tuff noted, "You can go on no sleep, you can be sore, you can be hurt, and it doesn't bother you—if you're winning."

CHAPTER 7

Buddies

THE FOLLOWING NIGHT AT Window Rock, Ty Murray and Cody "Cletus" Lambert needed to make a quicker getaway. They had a plane to catch the next morning in Denver, six hundred miles down the road. But they also had their fans, and after stowing their ropes and saddles and Ty's bareback rigging into the back of a silver Dodge Ram, they made small talk. They scrawled their names on shirts and plaster casts. A small boy reached out and grabbed Ty's hand and said, "I want to be just like you." Ty would have liked to drop everything then, to kneel down and truly talk to this kid who'd touched him, but it was pushing nine o'clock. He sidled his way through the five-deep horde and made for the truck's open door: "We got to go!" Lambert popped the emergency brake and the truck groaned off.

"Good luck to you!"

"God bless!"

As the crowd receded, Ty leaned back into the rear upholstery and yelled out the worst word he knew. He inspected his hat for dirt and ran his fingers through his sandy, razor-cut hair. He repeated the word more quietly, resignedly.

"Good bronc ride, though," Lambert said. In the rodeo's first section of bulls, Ty had bucked off Sammy Andrews's Super Dave a second from the horn. A half hour later he'd ripped the lips off a run-of-the-mill saddle bronc, then vaulted from its back like Mary Lou Retton after her second bowl of Wheaties. Ty landed on his feet routinely, that was no big deal for him, but he'd put some extra spunk into this one.

"I can ride them easy ones that don't hardly do much. I can ride them all the way," muttered the greatest rodeo cowboy in the world. Ty would wind up fifteen hundred dollars to the good at Window Rock, placing third in saddle bronc and seventh in bareback, but none of that mattered at the moment. When he bucked off a juicy bull like Super Dave, Ty felt like his head would explode: "That was just a good old-fashioned, no-heart, givin'-up, quit-tryin', thought-I-had-him piece of junk. Clete, please remind me to try tomorrow."

"Remind me to spur my horse, will you?" Lambert said. He'd been disqualified in the saddle bronc for failing to spur above the bronc's shoulders coming out of the chute.

"I did, three times," Ty teased.

"It's Cowboy Christmas!" Lambert shouted in mock merriment.

"Merry Christmas!" Ty shouted back. "Clete, I'm tired of bein' a loser. I want to be a winner."

"Me, too. You got some altitude off that bronc tonight. You were pissed, weren't you?"

"Yeah, I was a-pissed," Ty said. "He spun and spun, and then he made like to jump out of it." That bull again. "Did you ever feel that you had a bull rode? I thought I had it for six seconds, then—" At the parking lot's perimeter, two squat Navajo cops stopped the van for some autographed pictures.

"Remember when we signed that kid's forehead on either side?" Ty said when they were off again.

"I kind of tattooed him," said Lambert, whose humor ran to extra-dry. "I asked him if anyone had a match so I could burn it in."

"If everybody in the world was as good rodeo fans as Indians—"

"We'd be very rich men," Lambert said.

Ty stared out into the dark as the pickup rolled back onto Route 66. "If I'd of won the bull riding I'd be real happy," he said. As he mulled Super Dave some more, he decided that he had tried, after all. It rained more often in this desert than Ty Murray quit trying: he went for the chili every time. It was more that he'd quit *riding*, that he'd waited on the whistle and held what he had, instead of hanging loose to make one last move with the bull. "The stupidest thing you can do," he grumbled.

Ty had lived eight seconds at a gulp for most of his young life, but time could still surprise him. "When you're on a scatterin' hunk-a-shit, that whistle takes a long time," he said. "But if you're makin' a good ride on a good bull, sometimes the whistle seems like it comes too fast. That bull tonight, that's the kind of bull I live for—that's what I love. If I'd of finished the ride good and stepped off, and wouldn't of won a dime, I'd of been happy—I'd of done what I was supposed to do." He smiled, tight and hard. "You can bet your ass tomorrow if I do get bucked off, it ain't gonna be for lack of tryin'."

He had a young-old voice: flat toned, tenor pitched, unmistakably Texan. It matched his face, which was smooth but somehow finished, like it wouldn't change much over the next thirty years. When the Dust Bowl wasted Oklahoma, Walker Evans took pictures of faces like this, of burnished cheekbones and stubborn chins.

Among those who didn't know him, Ty had a rep for being colorless, even humorless: a windup rodeo automaton. They'd missed the big, dimpling, wolfish grin that could split his mug, the evil gleam that lit his green eyes when raising hell among friends. He was that odd celebrity who came to life after the cameras shut down.

Lately Ty was grinning more often. That spring he'd slumped in his bull riding, to where he "couldn't ride in a wagon with the flaps down." Aside from driving Ty crazy, the dry spell renewed a popular debate in the rodeo world: Should he pull back to one or two roughstock events, instead of working all three?

Back in Jim Shoulders's day, it was common to try both bulls and broncs. But Ty rode in an era of specialists. With so many talented, rodeo-schooled *hombres* out there, a cowboy had better bring all his skill and energy to the table if he planned to win something, and few could afford to spread themselves thinner. By the late 1980s, few even tried. Aside from Ty, Lambert was the only cowboy at an NFR level in two roughstock events. Ty was the first to reach the Finals in all three in nearly twenty years, since Larry Mahan became "the Legend" by winning six all-around titles.

Doing it Ty's way calls for more than simple stamina, as each event makes its own strict demands. Saddle bronc is all about technique. With no rope or rigging to secure him, with only a rein for the gripping, a rider is freed from the horse's power and less beholden to his own. Your chest may be sunken and your limbs thin as pipe cleaners, but you can win in the saddle if your spurring's sharp and timing's right.

Bareback is a horse of a different holler. To stay on, a cowboy needs control; to score high he must expose himself, like a human jack-in-the-box, to the bronc's every jar and jolt. And even when a ride goes picture-perfect, you feel like you've been mugged by ten angry mountain men. "You just can't be scared," Ty said. "The guys who win ain't afraid to let it all hang out. When things get wild they just get a little wilder."

Then there's bull riding, which calls for strength of body but something more—a capacity, as Mahan put it, to handle the "mental weirdness . . . to do something that is so off-the-wall." Now in his late forties, a prospering businessman with a signature line of western wear, Mahan recollected bull riding as "definitely the toughest event, because you have to control that element of danger. It makes no sense for us to ride bulls. Does it to you? To go get on one? At my age now, it's hard to imagine that I did it."

Like Mahan before him, Ty owned a special equilibrium, of brute aggression and bedrock discipline. He could ride three times a night without looking forward or back. He could reset himself after a mishap or (tougher still) a ninety-point ride, and minutes later start fresh. His success hinged on those transitions, as horses and bulls bucked in different ways. A bronc funnels its power into its kick, and so a rider needs to stay back if he's not to pitch over the steed's head. But bulls are strongest when they lurch to jump *away* from you. If you aren't perched forward you get jerked down, and out.

When Ty came a cropper with his bull riding, as he had that spring, there was no mystery to it. He was raising his torso, throwing his free hand behind the plane of his body, stringing back to the end of his rope. He'd look to be in per-fect form—but for bareback, not bulls. Ty could ride a nice spinner that way, but a rank one would fling him into the next performance.

For all of Ty's dominance as the all-around champ—he was working on his fourth straight gold buckle in 1992, with no end in sight—he had yet to win the world in any one event. The very greatest rodeo stars, like Shoulders and Casey Tibbs, had done both. Mahan, by his own admission not quite in Ty's league, had added two bull-riding titles to his string of all-arounds, the first when he was twenty-one. For the cracker-barrel critics, it wasn't enough that Ty had been the most versatile cowboy in memory since before he took a legal drink. Or that he tried like a sailor in a bar brawl; every time the gate opened, he aimed to make the crowd scream. Perfec-tion was boring, and people stalked some flaw to pick at.

Some insiders felt sure that Ty would become a champion bull rider—might be one already—if he dropped bareback, the most punishing event, the one that made elbows look like knees. What with the rigors of the season, followed by thirty rough rides at the Finals, it asked a lot of Ty to beat Tuff or Jim Sharp at their own game. Then, too, Ty rarely hedged by double-entering two conflicting rodeos, then turning out the weaker draw. He simply went to the best shows and took his chances; he figured he had three shots to win each night.

Ty had heard the arguments a hundred times. None had made a dent. "I'd love to win a championship in an event," he said, "but I ain't gonna back off." A practical man, Ty was setting his rodeo income aside for a cattle ranch. By working three events he'd become the first rodeo cowboy to earn more than two hundred thousand dollars in a year. Dropping one event would clip a third of that ranch.

Not that money drove him, deep down. Ty was a throwback to a younger West, when men were jacks-of-all-trades by necessity. He got bored fast when there was nothing to do. He'd raise a sweat by enlisting as a pickup man, to help bronc riders off their mounts or rope horses out of the ring.

Ty wouldn't say which event he liked most. He took pride in keeping them "equal" in the standings: "When I get done, I don't want 'em to say he was a damn good bull rider and he rode bareback horses okay. I want 'em to say he was a *cowboy*." Ty used the term with more than a little reverence. And if you were piecing together the perfect roughstock android, his was the build you'd arrive at. At five-eight and 150 pounds, with minus-two percent body fat, Ty was poured into Jack LaLanne's classic "V": bull neck, massive shoulders, wasp waist. His legs were long and slightly bowed—the better to squeeze a bull—and his hands large and strong, with thick, squared-off fingers that wouldn't lose a grip lightly. It was a body made for endurance. Ty never seemed to get hurt, or even sored up.

When his spring drought on the bulls persisted, Ty took to fiddling. He scrapped the pad under his rope's handle. No help. Slumps are toughest on the naturals; they *know* what to do— why aren't they doing it? Then one day in Sacramento, as Ty was getting on his bull, Lambert jumped up behind his chute.

Hey! Ty glanced up. *Just go out there and be a cowboy.* Something clicked. Ty stopped thinking and simply rode as best he could, which was as well as anyone living. "I just loosened up like I did when I was a kid," Ty said. "I was back to my old self. That's a big part of being a cowboy: don't make stuff more complicated than it really is." By June he was back to mashing his bulls like Idaho potatoes.

And for those who still doubted Ty could do it, could have his broncs and his bulls and a gold buckle, too, the people who knew him best were ready to give fair warning. His family and friends, and the men he rode against, had three words for the skeptics.

Hide and watch.

It was a good time of year to hit a hot streak—money time. The day before, Ty and Cody had motored from Ponoka, Alberta, down to Great Falls, Montana. Leaving the pickup to a driver friend, they flew to Midland for the rodeo in Pecos, then caught a ride to Window Rock. Now they'd be stashing the truck in Denver to fly to Oregon for the Fourth, return at dawn the next day for the short go at Greeley Sunday afternoon, then drive a thousand miles to get to Calgary Monday morning. From there they'd motor twelve hundred miles to Santa Fe for a Wednesday-night performance, followed by shorter hops to Pretty Prairie, Kansas, and Vernal, Utah. By the next Saturday they'd be heading up to Calgary again for the short go and the fifty-thousand-dollar showdown.

"Me and Cody travel smart, but we've been damn sure busy," Ty said. "There's lots of times when you're tired, so tired that you can't even believe how tired you are." There were afternoons when they'd left the chutes on the run with their chaps on, gassed a car hell-for-leather to the airport, and dashed into their plane as the door was closing—only to do it again in reverse at the other end, like silent-movie comedians.

It was enough to make Lambert regret he'd quit jogging, and to ache for his wife and five-year-old son back in Henrietta, Texas. "July is the best month for rodeo but it's the worst month for people with a family," Lambert said, steering east past dark mesa silhouettes. "You just feel so helpless when things go wrong and you're not there."

To make the miles go easier, there was the best-in-class, fully loaded Ram 350, leased free by Dodge to the champion all-around cowboy. They'd installed a double-sized foam mattress in the back. "It's cool and dark, like sleepin' in a motel," Lambert said.

"Only thing it lacks," Ty reminded, "is a bidet."

"Yeah, we have to wipe ourselves."

Both partners liked sleeping more than driving, and before their friend hired on they tried to limit their shifts to two hundred miles, "depending on how far we're going," Ty said.

"If we're going a hundred and sixty miles, I'll drive eighty, not eighty-one," Lambert said.

"If he drives eighty-one, he'll back up a mile."

Tonight Lambert went five miles before stopping to replace a spent headlight. Looking for diversion, he bet Ty he could change the light in less than ten minutes. He finished in four, and eyed with disdain the bill Ty pushed at his nose: "When have we ever bet a dollar about anything?"

Two hours later, after Ty had crawled in back to stretch out, he called out the magic words: "Road piss!"

"No!" Lambert said defiantly.

"Now!" Ty demanded, and bounced a pillow off the back of his partner's head. "I've got to road piss *bad*." Lambert pulled over, then went on without further incident.

They say that traveling partners are like married couples, and it's true, except that no pro cowboy spends that much time with his wife. The average pairing lasts as long as a Hollywood affair. Some bull riders never find a compatible buddy. Others think they have, then grow apart. Any number of things can capsize a partnership. One man might stop winning and get swallowed by debt. One might want to rodeo harder, or sleep later, or hum the Canadian national anthem whenever he damn well feels like it. There are a thousand reasons to break up and try someone new, if only to see a fresh face in the morning.

But while the wrong match spells misery, going alone can be worse. Your partner is your coach and your dinner companion, your confidant and confessor. He helps celebrate the good rides and laugh off the bad, and if you get broken he'll be right there next to you in the ambulance. With bull riders, the danger boys, the bond wraps especially tight, as among foxholed soldiers who can't count on tomorrow.

It was Cody Lambert's fate to be known best for the Hall of Fame cowboys he sidekicked: first Tuff, then Lane Frost, then Ty. Less well understood was his role in their success, for it wasn't Lambert's way to primp his image. He could be dour and grumpy, and his haircut belonged in San Quentin. He talked slower than he walked, in a fuzzy drawl, and he walked pretty slow. For all that, Lambert was probably the smartest cowboy in the business, both clever and country-sly: Brer Bull Rider. In a land of impulse he was that remarkable figure, the thoughtful man. "Sometimes when you visit with Cody, you don't think he's too bright," John Growney said. "But he figures it all out. He *thinks* about stuff."

No one knew more about riding than Lambert, or could talk about it more astutely when in the mood. And no one cared more about being a cowboy—about doing it right. If Tuff was the rooster of this coop, Lambert was the mother hen, the compulsive helpmate. In a tent where all performed without a net, his hand was always there, outstretched.

"You've never won a gold buckle because you're so good at playing second fiddle," Donnie Gay once told him, and Lambert couldn't deny it. He'd always taken pleasure in helping his partners. Then, too, he'd married Leanne when he was twenty years old, and Riley came along five years later, and so he knew early on he'd found success, even on nights when the bull finished first. When a man's eyes were opened, he stopped shoving blindly to the top.

"I know that Donnie Gay had to pay the price," Lambert said, as a stream of Red Man found a plastic cup. "Maybe he had to get on some bulls he didn't really like, or maybe he suffered by having to be away from his family more. Maybe I wouldn't pay that price.

"My family life is so great that . . ." and here Lambert halted, stymied to find a phrase grand enough. "Some people might say I wasn't as good as all the people I hung out with, but I've tried to do the best I can. I'm not finished by any means, and I'm not saying I won't ever win a championship. But if I don't ever win one, I have no other option but to live with it."

Lambert met Ty when the future champ was a baby. The Murrays were based in Phoenix and the Lamberts in El Paso, but both families summered at Ruidoso in New Mexico, where the dads worked at the racetrack. When Ty was two years old, Lambert and his brother caught a wild baby burro and plopped the toddler on its back. "We held the little burro by the neck and it was jumping, and Ty thought that was really something," Lambert recounted. "He wanted to ride. We held on to him, but he wasn't one bit scared. He's never showed any fear in his life—of anything."

Many years later, Ty mounted a turned-out bronc for fun at a pro rodeo in Phoenix, and rode well enough to win. Lambert was there, and told the high school junior that "whenever he decided to go [pro], I could help him enter." The opportunity came in 1988, when Ty was eighteen—perfect timing for Lambert, who'd drifted away from saddle bronc while traveling with Tuff and Lane, and pined to come back to it.

After eight years on the road, Lambert had refined entering into an art form. He knew the habits of every committee, the quirks of each contractor. When two rodeos ran the same weekend, he might choose the one adding less money if he knew the bulls were tougher; the stronger the stock, the better a top cowboy's chances. Then he'd ask to get up for Saturday, the night they'd use the rank ones, since most contractors sought to wow their biggest crowd and close the rodeo with a bang.

From the start Ty had the tools and the head to compete against grown men, and it seemed clear he'd make it big in the PRCA. But no one doubted—least of all Ty himself—that Lambert helped him make it quicker. The first season was tough on both sides. They were eight years apart, which meant a lot at the time. "It felt like I was raising him," Lambert said. "I'd get mad having to tell him what to do all the time." For his part, Ty had no idea of how to pace himself, just wanted to *go* till they dropped. When Lambert confessed to some dog-day weariness, or hankered to be home with his baby, Ty would pin him with those wide eyes and demand, "How come you hate rodeoin' so much?" The kid couldn't imagine wanting anything beyond this life of adventure.

A few thousand hours of travel will either weld a bond or push two people to divorce. By their second year together Ty and Lambert were as brothers—closer, maybe, for the lack of rivalry. Lambert found himself learning as well as teaching. By living rodeo through more than one event again, he refired his zest for bull riding. "It's more of a challenge, no doubt, than any other event," he said. "The feeling you get from riding a rank bull that seldom gets ridden, you can't match that with anything else."

And while Lambert was never a slouch in the try department, watching Ty kept him inspired. "I don't know anybody that has more try than he has," Lambert said. "He's a rodeo fiend—like a dope fiend or a sex fiend. He tries so hard in all three of his events."

With time the two found they staked common ground on the basics: politics, religion, the National Football League.

They shared a twisted sense of humor, took joy in putting others on. "We both like dogs," Lambert ticked off. "We both like kids."

"And we both like to go home," needled Ty, who'd finished his nap and was set to take his shift.

"We both like to go home," Lambert agreed.

"We're perfect for each other," Ty said sincerely. "I only wish that he was my age. I'll rodeo with Cody till he doesn't want to rodeo with me anymore."

Lambert had one more for the list: "We both want to be cowboys every day, not just when we're at the rodeo."

Had Ty not come along, Lambert would have been the top multi-event roughstock cowboy of his era, might even have snagged a gold buckle in the all-around. In every town they went, reporters hunting for friction would ask him, "How's it feel always being second?" And Lambert always answered: "It really makes me feel *good*." When you were second to the best, you'd done something.

"I've drove up this road many a time," said Ty, who took the wheel near Las Vegas, New Mexico, and steered north. Not so many years ago, his mother carted him most every weekend from their summer home in New Mexico to junior rodeos in Colorado and Kansas, even Iowa and Nebraska. Other twelve-year-olds might have mooned to be a drag racer one week, a baseball star the next. Young Ty never wavered. "My parents dedicated a lot to me rodeoin'," he said, "because they knew it wasn't a passing thing. Rodeo wasn't ever a passing deal for me."

It was two in the morning, but Ty seemed fresh, in stride. "We live a whole different kind of life," he said. "We're not on a schedule. I can wake up in the middle of the night and drive, or I can eat breakfast at four o'clock in the afternoon—when I get some breakfast." More than once he'd stopped to call his girlfriend and couldn't tell her what state he was in. That didn't bother Ty. He felt sorry for the nine-to-fivers who always knew their place, who counted down all week toward Friday evening, when their real life began. "That's one good thing about rodeo—we don't live one weekend at a time," he said. "I ain't a robot all week long. And it just gets funner to me all the time."

The wandering life did have one drawback, however: the cuisine. Ty liked to eat well. On the road he looked for cafeterias with fresh fruits and vegetables, but he also grabbed what he could get. At the moment he picked through a bag of pretzels and Reese's peanut butter cups, then dipped into a cheddar cheese and cracker sampler. Ty held out for three hours, till a Colorado dawn pinked the sky and the Ram's thirty-three-gallon tank got thirsty. At a Quick Stoppe he surveyed yesterday's burrito under glass and an assortment of freeze-dried delectables. "Hard to make up your mind, isn't it?" he said. Ty resisted the burrito, but at Stapleton International Airport gave in to a nacho cheese dog—a "gut bomb," in cowboy talk.

By noon the pair's station wagon was plowing through a pelting rain to St. Paul, Oregon, thirty miles inland. The asphalt was so slick that Ty and Lambert actually fastened their seat belts. They'd traded desert and mountains for thick green woods and hop farms. Lambert followed some tiny signs to St. Paul, a hamlet of three hundred people that had somehow supported a big-time rodeo for fifty-seven years.

Outside the arena, an Independence Day crowd thronged a Ferris wheel and a booth hawking "Coney Island Sandwich Hamburgers." Ty and Lambert were up on their broncs that afternoon and their bulls in the evening perf. They settled in for a long siege in the cramped ready area, exposed to the day's chill drizzle. As water dripped from their straw hats, "A Cowboy's Prayer" echoed over the outdoor speakers:

Oh, Lord, I've never lived where churches grow;
I've loved creation better as it stood

That day you finished it so long ago,
And looked upon your work and called it good.
Just let me live my life as I've begun!
And give me work that's open to the sky;
Make me a partner of the wind and sun,
And I won't ask a life that's soft or high.
Make me as big and open as the plains;
As honest as the horse between my knees;
Clean as the wind that blows behind the rains;
Free as the hawk that circles down the breeze.
Just keep an eye on all that's done and said;
Just right me sometimes when I turn aside;
And guide me on the long, dim trail ahead—
That stretches upward toward the Great Divide.

That afternoon the cowboys would take any help from Upstairs they could get. The footing was perilous, especially after several antique cars rutted the ground in the Model T Ford and Pig Race. After riding his bronc, Ty paused with a grateful high school cowboy. He stopped again in the parking lot when he spied a small collie taking shelter under a van. A few seconds later the dog was in belly-scratch heaven and licking Ty's face. "I love animals—I grew up with them," Ty said. The kinship served him well in the chutes. He'd had the gift to gentle a scared one ever since he was eight years old, when he helped his father gate-train colts at Ruidoso.

"It's amazing how many guys ride broncs for a livin' don't know how to treat a horse in the chute," Ty observed. "Animals are like people—there's a million different personalities. Some horses are scared, some are bad, some are really just nervous. A lot of younger horses, you run 'em in a coliseum and there's bands playing and people screaming and other horses acting up. They're going, 'Jesus *Christ*, what's going on in there?'

"I know the difference between a horse that's scared and a horse that's bein' a prick. I get down in there with him, and the way I touch him, the way I sit on him—I let him know that everything's going to be all right, and I have less trouble in the chute than most guys."

In Ty's view bulls are not so complicated. Less sensitive than horses, they might get riled and antsy, but never fearful or skittish. "Bulls have got an overdose of testosterone. They're just swelled up and mean," Ty said. "The reason they act up in the chutes is that they're mad they can't hook you. With bulls you got to get in there and take charge."

When the partners reached downtown, a single intersection, they ducked in from the chill at the St. Paul Country Inn and ordered a "cup of Joe," black. While awaiting his coffee, Lambert fixed a piece of bubble gum in the middle of his chew—a trick he'd gleaned from Catfish Hunter to keep the tobacco moist—and stuck it under his lip, content.

"When I started rodeoin', Clete told me how nasty this stuff was," Ty said.

"I was driving all night from Florida once," Lambert said, "chewin' all the way, and I stopped somewhere for a men's room. I looked in the mirror and I had it between my teeth, and on the corners of my mouth, and I brushed my teeth and didn't chew again for two years." He started up again on the road, to give himself something to do besides watching the white lines. "I really like to spit, too," he admitted.

"That's the fun part," Ty agreed.

Two coffees later the rain kept falling, with three hours to kill till the evening show. Lambert knew he had nine more days of this glamorous existence without a break, and sometimes it got to him. He started clapping his forehead with his hand while groaning to the beat, "I—want—to—go—home."

Ty looked at him with clinical interest: "I hope we can get you there before we have to check you in someplace."

As usual, Ty got on that night without prior introduction to the bull. Unique among the top riders, he never called to check what he'd drawn, never "sweated" a bull's past form or pumped the contractor to guess what it would do that night. Oftentimes he'd hop behind the chutes without knowing the animal's name. Ty trusted his body; information could only get in its way. For the record, he topped a dipping, droppy bull named Gambler, stayed out over its front end—chin tucked, shoulders squared—and rode it into the ground. While the score was nothing special, Ty was satisfied. He'd needed to ride in St. Paul to put Window Rock behind him.

As he and Lambert wheeled back to Portland through a foggy night, Ty said, "The hardest thing for me—and it's real hard to put it into words—is that you got to try your guts out, but you can't try too hard."

Lambert lent a hand: "You can beat yourself sometimes— you can make a dumb mistake if you're too tense."

"It's kind of like a distance runner," Ty went on. "He's got to try as hard as he can, but he's got to stay real fluid and keep his pace. Me and Cody, we know *everything* about riding bulls. It's easy to sit here and know exactly what you did wrong yesterday. But when you're doing something that scares you and thrills you—the fastness and the power and the fear—it's a lot harder to stay focused on what you need to do."

Which was all about becoming a cowboy to the nth degree. A bull rider's life is a crapshoot, a random draw. He can't hope to control the world out there; he may sit atop a bull, but he knows the condition is temporary. Cowboy buddies are so close because they know they aren't at odds with one another or even with the bulls. The real war lies inside, between their courage and their doubt, and they troop to the front every day.

"A cowboy ain't how you dress, or how you look," Ty considered. "Like when that bull laid down with Tuff the night before and he called for him—that's cowboy stuff there. Guys that ain't cowboys don't do that."

"Whatever situation comes along, a cowboy will handle it," Lambert said. "He'll take care of it."

Ty picked it up. "It's pouring-ass rain, muddier than hell, other guys are sitting around crying, but me and Cody get out in it and just like it. Because you ain't got no other choice—you might as well like it."

"Bein' a pickup man, that's really cowboy stuff," Lambert said dreamily. "Riding a horse and ropin', and catchin' the broncs. . . . Spending time in a stock saddle, gatherin' cattle on ranches and brandin', that's cowboy stuff. If I didn't rodeo, that's what I'd be doing every day."

Instead they'd be rising at 5:30 the next morning for their flight back to Denver. For Ty and Lambert that was cowboy stuff, too, at least for now. Ty thought about the bed before him and the wake-up call soon to follow, and with a violent yawn he predicted, "It's going to feel really good and then really bad."

Lambert looked on the sunny side, as all good cowboys must. "It'll feel good before it feels bad," he said.

CHAPTER 8

Big Daddy

*I*F ED SULLIVAN HAD PRO-
duced a rodeo, it would have been Cheyenne Frontier Days,
the place where all roads lead the last week of July. Two thousand volunteers—led by a businessmen's group called the
Heels—put on the "Daddy of 'Em All," and any one of them
can reel off its glories. Cheyenne is the biggest outdoor rodeo
in the world. It bucks out the most head of stock each day,
into the largest rodeo arena, and it takes the most entries: 160
in the bull riding alone.

What the numbers can't capture is Frontier Days' special
atmosphere, how the air feels charged here as in Saratoga in
August or Louisville at Derby week. For fifty-one weeks out of
the year, Cheyenne is a staid state capital justly honored as
"the Most Polite Community in the Nation." The city has no
boardwalks or hitching racks, no gaslit Old Town. The lone
stampede to watch for is of quake-weary Californians. But
then comes the rodeo, an unbuttoned bow to the richest,
rowdiest cow town of the late 1800s. For nine days merchants

wear Resistols and cops teeter on horses, and every good citizen—by mayoral edict—greets you with "Howdy!" rather than hello. For nine days a community retrieves its history . . . plus $20 million worth of tourists.

People come here with certain expectations. They want theme-park perfection, and get miffed at the smallest false note. One day, minutes before the traditional "bomb" opened the show, a bucktoothed man rushed between the Outlet Sales Building—turquoise bolas, rattlesnake belts, teriyaki beef jerky—and the arena. His jacket was fuzzy blue, his zippered cowboy boots at half-mast. As a disco version of Tchaikovsky's *Romeo and Juliet* boomed over the lot, he muttered to himself, "What kind of damned music is *that?*"

Everyone gets with the program at Cheyenne, even the working press. At the entry to the cowboys' ready area, fenced by chicken wire beneath the steel-girdered grandstand, a large guard stood ready to enforce the posted dress code: "Cowboy HATS, LONG Sleeve Shirts, Cowboy Boots Required."

There is even tradition in Cheyenne's wild weather, which shifts from sun shower to downpour ("liquid sunshine") to dry heat to hail in the space of two hours. After months in the desert and semitropics of Arizona and Texas, cool breezes off the pine groves are welcomed by man and beast alike.

Just one glitch intrudes in this place where bigger is better and things never change: it puts on a second-rate bull riding. From the riders' point of view, Cheyenne's size is the enemy. There is so much stock on hand that it has to be self-fed, so the bulls overeat. There's such commotion around the pens that they miss their normal rest. Once in action, many get seduced by too much "air"—the arena is the infield of a half-mile racetrack—and run off as if to pasture. In a similar setting, St. Paul erects a barrier to make its bulls turn back and spin. But that just isn't done at Cheyenne.

Then there's the rodeo's thrill-a-minute pace, which comes at a price. The next chute is opened before the last bull is roped and dragged out—a mighty distraction to the one to be bucking. "They don't ever want it to stop," sighed Harry Vold, the beefy contractor who stocks Frontier Days. "It's like a three-ring circus."

Vold is a patriarch of the sport, the best bronc man in the business, but his bulls are humdrum. He hires subcontractors to plug the gap, and they have just so many good bulls to offer, far short of the 160 required. The remainder are "fillers," which makes Frontier Days, for all its charm, the ultimate drawing contest: a cowboy lottery. No one dares turn out—coming home to Daddy is like church on Easter Sunday—but riders best enjoy the free pancake breakfasts and not count on much more.

Cheyenne is famous for scores in the fifties, and a man won't earn a reride 'less his bull stops with insulin shock. You can get on two Purina Specials, ride them both, and be shut out of the short go while some weekend dilettante wins the whole shooting match on three middling bulls. It costs $275 to enter here, and many's the cowboy who gets less than his money's worth.

Meanwhile, the show goes on. Attendance soared 20 percent in 1992, and no one was wanting a rebate. The fans come to Frontier Days on vacation, in a spirit to go with its flow. They treasure the yearly Cinderella stories—like the one about Randy Thornton, an obscure Texan who'd win eight thousand dollars and Cheyenne's bull-riding buckle this year.

The top riders are less enchanted. Their plaints are nothing new; in 1979, when Cheyenne took 343 entries and trucked bulls from Florida that moved like Brahma-crocodile crosses, Donnie Gay blasted Frontier Days as "the largest amateur bull riding in the world." The Heels didn't like to hear that, but they knew Gay was right. They halved the entries and improved the stock, and now the event was up to semipro.

On the sixth day of the rodeo Clint Branger sat hunched amid a clutter of saddles and riggings in the ready area, pondering why his bull had just finked out on him. Despite a new black eye (from a barroom sucker punch this time) and a groin strain, Branger was holding second in the season standings, just two thousand dollars behind Cody Custer. After a seventy-eight on his first bull here, he'd had hopes for a big payday. He'd seen his second bull loop the loop in Prescott just three weeks before, but that was then. This time the big oaf crow-hopped to sixty-five points. Branger wouldn't make the short round. "It's frustrating," he said. "But that's just the way it is—that's just Cheyenne."

Tuff was feeling less tolerant. He'd never won squat at Frontier Days, and stopped looking forward to it after Lane Frost met his death here in 1989. An exhibit on Lane graced the Old West Museum, and by next year a fifteen-foot bronze statue would rise at the entrance to Frontier Park: more ghosts. There were places, many places, that made Tuff remember Lane in a soft light, but Cheyenne wasn't one of them.

The Texan had been stuck in a drawing slump, anyway, and when a *Wyoming Eagle* reporter asked some harmless question before his first bull, Tuff popped off: "I just don't think the bulls are as good as they should be. It's like putting a great jockey on a slow horse. . . . It happens to me year after year."

Then Tuff opened with a seventy—"a good practice bull"—and came up swinging. "There's two sure things about Cheyenne—you know you're gonna get wet and you know you're gonna get on a sorry bull." Sheepish about complaining, he added: "Kind of a bad attitude, I guess."

Six days later, his second bull bucked hard for four seconds, "but then it felt like somebody shot him between the eyes," Tuff said. "I thought he was going to stop and I'd get a reride, but he slowed down just enough to kill my score: 'Here, let me crap in your cornflakes.' He just quit." Tuff returned the favor by skipping out the next morning, hours before the short go. He'd take what remained of his good humor and ship it on home.

It was a shame he felt that way, for bull riders would be the last ones to begrudge Cheyenne its sepia-toned history. They'd found their profession, after all, out of a soft spot for the West and what it meant. Cheyenne was the first big show they'd heard tell of growing up. They liked it for its quirks, the way it set apart from all the cookie-cutter contests, and they lusted for the prestige of a Frontier Days sterling buckle. When you got a check from Cheyenne, even a small one, you photocopied a souvenir. When you won the Daddy of 'Em All, it felt like the greatest rodeo in the world.

In fairness, the issue was bigger than Cheyenne. What made some cowboys sore was that you could get killed in this game, but you couldn't make a living at it. Back in the 1970s, Larry Mahan had called rodeo cowboys "the most underpaid athletes" in the country. Fifteen years later, he'd seen little to change his mind: "It needs to be better than it is. As far as I'm concerned, everybody in the top fifteen should make a million a year."

As the business stands, there are only two active rodeo heroes—Tuff and Ty—who can sell a product by linking their face to it. As royalty of their sport, they rope in sponsor bonuses and endorsement deals into the low six figures, or roughly 1 percent of Michael Jordan's off-court income. When their riding is done, they'll walk away with futures assured.

Among the bull riders, another handful win enough to pay their bills and salt a few bucks away for when their arms and backs give out. At the third tier are thirty or so full-time pros who may make the Finals in a given year but have nothing to show for it, apart from joints that creak like the Tin Man's. They risk their lives and livelihoods a hundred times a season, and at the end they'll be penniless—less able to buy a small piece of ranchland than a comparably ranked bull rider in Jim Shoulders's day.

These cowboys are as solvent as their last performance. When busted up or sore unto death, they have nothing to fall back on: no sick leave, no disability, no workers' compensation. When they can't co-pay the 20 percent on their meager group insurance, they stop seeing doctors and pull the tape a little tighter. They're among the freest agents in this oh-so-free land, and they're especially free to go bankrupt.

A good example is Wacey Cathey. Everyone liked good old Wacey. At a geriatric thirty-nine, he was beating men he could have fathered. In 1991, his hair shot with gray, Cathey made his fourteenth National Finals, breaking Donnie Gay's record for their event. He'd never finished higher than fifth in the world, never quite challenged for a title, but Cathey was a fixture, a twenty-four-carat bull rider in or out of the ring.

In Cheyenne you know Frontier Days has arrived when they raise the lights in the Hitching Post, summer home to Ricky and the Redstreaks. Back in the mid-'70s, before they'd taken that precaution, Cathey was feeling so frisky one night that he leaped from his table and grabbed a chandelier, then swung upside down from his knees, spurring to the beat. "He's not as boring as he appears to a lot of people," noted Karen Cathey, his second or third wife, if anyone was counting. "He's quite entertaining at times."

These days he was also quite desperate. Cathey had lasted so long because he'd stayed healthy, but in 1992 his body began to chip apart. After ranking second early on, he broke two ribs in April. Cathey came back before he healed, but he wasn't staying on much. In June he got thrown onto a bull's head and boxed around, breaking his free arm. He was back again a few weeks later, riding with a removable cast.

Cathey knew he wasn't ready, but felt he had no choice. "Right now I'm pretty broke," he admitted, just before mounting a juicy brindle named Slammer at Cheyenne. "Either I'm going to win something or I am going back to work—whatever I have to do."

It was a pivot point in his life. For twenty years Cathey had been running from the tractor at his dad's ranch in Big Spring, Texas, but he'd never quite lost it in his rearview mirror. Now it was gaining on him. Cathey had won close to a million dollars in his career, but a million sliced thin over eighteen years once you took away the entry fees and plane fares and what it took to raise three kids. He'd finally crept back into the top fifteen that week, and he needed to make the Finals again to balance his checkbook. He couldn't win much riding a couch, so Cathey traded his cast for a flimsy splint and hoped for the best.

It was the hottest, bluest afternoon of this Frontier Days, and Cathey was up early, the second man in the first of three bull-riding sections. At about two o'clock he mounted Slammer, who stood calm in the chute; just another ride, like some three thousand before it. The reddish brindle burst out high and twisting. His hurt free arm lagging, Cathey dumped off to the side, too close for comfort, his white hat skimming off like a Frisbee. As he scrambled to get away, the first pass of Slammer's hind hooves whizzed a few inches from his face. Cathey was up now, but slow out of the blocks, and the bull spun round for a second shot. This time the hooves blindsided the middle-aged rider. Cathey dropped like a rock and lay there unblinking. The medics clasped an oxygen mask over his head and carted him out on a stretcher. As if on cue, a gothic thunderstorm drenched the grandstand.

Later that day, Memorial Hospital released this report on Wacey Cathey: four broken ribs, a bruised lung (later found to be punctured), a broken wrist, a broken left arm (same one, same place), and a concussion. Two months later, after cracking yet another rib, Cathey would give up on the season and his string of eleven straight Finals. A few months after that, he and Karen would split up. And two years after that, he'd be raising some scratch as a laborer for a Las Vegas road-paving company, which made that tractor look good.

What happened to Cathey seems criminal, but it happens all the time. The PRCA made much of the fact that total prize money would exceed $20 million in 1992 (up fivefold from 1970), but forgot to note that most of it came out of the cowboys' own wallets in entry fees. Put aside the National Finals and rodeo's overall economy is about as healthy as Brazil's. After the local committees and promoters and contractors take their cuts, the cowboys are left with the crumbs—as little as 10 percent of a show's revenues. Most purses have lagged behind inflation, not to mention galloping travel costs; as a group, according to a PRCA director, the cowboys spent

$30 million to win the $20 million. No wonder, then, that so many go bust. As Donnie Gay once said, "The best thing about rodeo is it's recession-proof. You're broke all the time anyway, so it don't really matter."

The Finals itself is a bittersweet bonanza. "Anybody can have a bad week, or a bad two weeks," Tuff noted. "I figure if you're in the best fifteen in the world, out of a membership of more than five thousand people, you shouldn't have to win something at the National Finals to be able to pay your credit-card bills next month. That's a very, very sad part of rodeo."

What irks Tuff and the rest is that they know there is a better way. They have seen the future in Houston, and it works. That winter the Houston Livestock Show & Rodeo had set a hidebound culture on its ear by limiting entries in the riding events to fifty-seven top qualifiers. Three go-rounds were stocked by a clutch of powerhouse contractors, and anyone good enough to ride three times was sure to make the short go.

The top cowboys thought they'd gone to roughstock heaven. In return for a five-hundred-dollar entry fee, Houston added more than fifty-five thousand dollars to the purse in each event—about two-thirds of the total prize money. (By contrast, Cheyenne added only 31 percent of the total money in bull riding; more than two-thirds came from entry fees.) Ty Murray declared that Houston might be "the only rodeo that gives a fair share of the pie back to the cowboys."

But if Houston is the future, Cheyenne is the unvarnished past, and the past still holds sway in this sport. Frontier Days billed itself as "an absolutely open contest" back in 1913, just as the cattle drives once welcomed any man with the grit to survive them. Cheyenne is all about "fairness" and "democracy." Like the twelve-handicap duffer who longs to play in the Pebble Beach Pro-Am at least once before he dies, thousands of weekend cowboys scrape up their entry fees for Frontier Days. Cheyenne is their festival, and they won't let it go lightly. As Bryan McDonald acknowledged, "A lot of people belong to the PRCA just to come to this rodeo. It's one of the pieces of the puzzle that makes it all work."

The Daddy of 'Em All doesn't cater to Tuff Hedeman. It's there for all the wanna-bes who live out of vans and sleep under the stars at the Cowboy Campground. For men like Mike Goforth, a nearsighted truck driver from Casper, Wyoming, who was all grins after getting hung up and head-thumped in the chest more times than he could count. Back in 1988 Goforth had cleared about thirty thousand dollars on the bulls. He'd kept trying to repeat that year, to break through to the Finals—and what better way than to win at Cheyenne? There were thousands of weekend warriors out there like him, men who fanned their fantasy—to crack out full-time—by investing their paychecks in entry fees. Few ever grubbed a big enough stake to do it, but the striving kept them happy.

"People on the outside think it's crazy," Goforth said, lifting a bottle of Coors to his chipped front teeth. "But this is my life. This is the place I fit in. Whether I make money or not, it doesn't really matter because I love it so much. . . . It's the last part of the American dream that I see."

On the evening of July 23, a few hours after Wacey Cathey touched base with the angels, a devil-may-care eighteen-year-old named Tyler Sprague gunned for a national high school championship in Shawnee, Oklahoma. Square jawed and barely bearded, the youth known as "T. R." appeared to have a big future in the sport. No question that he owned a bull rider's resilience; after getting stepped on at the Colorado state finals in June, he limped out of the hospital for the awards ceremony that same night. His friends bowed to his courage and his straight-backed style. No one could remember T. R. Sprague getting whipped down over a bull.

Then he drew Sammy Andrews's Blue Bonnett Palace, a double-rank spinner headed for the National Finals that December. Blue Bonnett Palace threw off better than 90 percent of the professionals who tried him. In a press release put out that season by Bull Riders Only, an independent circuit, the dark red Braford was said to use "all eighteen hundred pounds to thrash and pummel his riders. Cowboys who stay on him win buckles and beaver hats. Those who don't get doctor bills." Even if you sifted out the hype, the bull figured to over-match any high school hopeful. As Gary Leffew saw it, "That's like sending a Little Leaguer up against Nolan Ryan—he don't have a chance, and if he gets beaned he's going to be killed."

Leffew offered this with some hindsight, as T. R. Sprague never made the short go in Shawnee. Jerked down by Blue Bonnett Palace, his temple butting the bull's head, Sprague bounced and crumpled like a crash dummy without a seat belt. He was out before he hit the dirt, and dead by Saturday morning.

In the aftermath people spouted clichés for comfort. The arena director held that Sprague had died "doing the thing he loved more than anything in the world. Bull riding is the most dangerous athletic event in America. This was just one of those freak situations."

Freak or not, the incident told much about the laissez-faire state of rodeo. While the best cowboys in the world were damning Harry Vold's high-school-caliber bulls, a bunch of teenagers grappled with the cream of Sammy Andrews, one of the toughest strings ever assembled.

When you're still a teenager, and some kid you were goofing with behind the chutes lies comatose ten minutes later, it makes an impression. Three nights after Sprague's death, nineteen-year-old Kevin Martinez came to new terms with his sport. Martinez looked like the perfect math nerd: black horn-rimmed glasses, meager physique. But his looks deceived. He'd ridden bulls to an engineering scholarship at the University of Wyoming. The previous fall he'd sustained his second collapsed lung and a surgical hole in his side that had to be patched each time he showered. The injury "played with my mind a little bit," Martinez said. "I wasn't that eager to get back on too fast."

He finally came back that spring, traveling with Sprague to Little Britches contests around Colorado. Tonight he'd come again, to an open show a few miles outside Cheyenne, his hometown. Martinez's mother had "about fainted" when she heard about T. R. Her son was less emotional, but still he struggled to block out his friend as he huffed and jerked through his warm-ups. "He had so much going for him," Martinez said. "He was just excellent. All the kids would look up to him, ask him how to do stuff. He would help anybody— just an easygoing type of guy.

"He has a bunch of rope tricks that he shows people," the skinny youth went on, lapsing into the present tense. "He's a good kid." It hadn't been easy to come out to this rodeo, to his first bull since the news from Shawnee, but waiting wouldn't bring T. R. back. Martinez had some steel in him. "You just got to go on," he said.

Martinez hauled himself up to the platform behind the chutes, to join a chattering set of amateur bull riders in the half-light. Most looked like poorer kids, the kind who don't get much dental care. Some jitterbugged their nerves away as they waited their turn. Others perched on the top rail, to spit from time to time on a bull's back. As Martinez gingerly sat to take his wrap, a self-assured young man gave him the low-down. "He's not real strong coming out of there—he's not going to run you off your rope," Chris Stoddard said. "He was out there like two [jumps] with me, then right around the corner. He got up in the air and has a lot of drop."

Martinez licked his lips and nodded. "If I get up on my legs, he'll pack me," he said.

"As long as you're up on your legs when you come around that corner, you got him whipped," Stoddard agreed. "I had a seventy-three on him. You do good—just try."

Stoddard was twenty-three years old and already had a full plate: a job on his family's wheat and pig farm, and now a wife and baby daughter. But his heart belonged to the bulls. "I raced motorcycles, I pole-vaulted in track—the most dangerous thing in track I could find—but there ain't *nothing* like bull riding," he said. "I was looking for something that might scare the hell out of me, but I was also looking for someplace to set my spurs, so to speak, and I found it. This is my niche in life."

"Martinez!" hollered the chute boss. "You're next now, Kev."

Justin Lovelett, a husky carpenter with a blond Fu Manchu mustache, leaned over the chute, all business. As Martinez's tightest pal and the one who pulled his rope, he made sure the rider was ready. "Just be aggressive, buddy—do you hear me?"

Martinez nodded as he tightened the thong of his riding glove in his mouth. A chorus of "Hustle up!" rose from behind. He nodded again, for real this time, and the gate loosed the bull into the shadowy space.

"Come on, buddy, come on!"

"Lots of reach, lots of gas!"

The ride didn't proceed quite as planned. The bull hipped itself, then skipped on its front end and turned back to the left. Martinez slid off, hung up for an instant . . . and dropped clear. The hundred people in the stands sent up a puff of applause.

"It felt like he stumbled and it got me out of time," Martinez reported back to the clan.

"You were makin' some *moves* on him, though!" Lovelett said, and the two slapped hands. Martinez would be back the next night, with grounds for encouragement. He'd really tried out there, despite the outcome. As he'd sat down on the bull, T. R.'s face had finally quit his mind. Not least, Martinez had walked away when it was over, which he no longer took for granted.

CHAPTER 9

Love with the Perfect Bull Rider

O<small>N</small> O<small>CTOBER</small> 3, 1992, twenty-five master bull riders gathered in Denver for their richest one-night stand ever, the second annual Bull Riders Only World Championship. Total added purse: thirty thousand dollars, with half going to the winner.

Bull ridings have a built-in appeal. Since so many rodeo fans come out mainly for the bulls, why make them wait to the end of the program—why not give them what they want from the get-go? A few annual events, like Bullnanza in Guthrie, Oklahoma, and the George Paul Memorial in Del Rio, Texas, are major-league productions with top-drawer fields. Bull Riders Only was the most ambitious enterprise to date: nine regular-season shows, four corporate sponsors, and coverage by Prime Cable Network.

"We sell bull riding as an *event,* not just as a sport," explained Shaw Sullivan, the chief executive, en route to McNichols Arena in his Chevy pickup. "You don't go watch tennis to see the ball go over the net. You watch tennis to see if Agassi can beat Becker. It's the same with us. We give our fans the best performers on the best stock, head-to-head."

Behind his burnt-orange sunglasses and two-day-old beard and fleeting smile, Sullivan was always selling. A few years before, he'd sold stocks as an investment banker for Stuart-James in Denver, making "six or seven hundred thousand a year" at the age of twenty-four. He drove a Mercedes; he was a card-carrying Master of the Universe. He was doing so well that it bored him. Now, at thirty-one, Sullivan was selling a sport, and a vision: that bull riding could win a national following if only it were packaged right.

A professed "adrenaline junkie," Sullivan had ridden bulls in college. Though charged by the game's speed and power, he deduced early on that rodeo was a poor man's sport. Sullivan swerved into high finance—"I was poor all my life, and I didn't want to stay poor"—but continued to ride as a hobby. He watched big talents drop out with empty pockets, and he wondered: Why couldn't bull riding cross over to a broader fan base? Why couldn't a Tuff Hedeman become as big as Richard Petty?

Sullivan bounced his idea off Eric Dickson, his old Stuart-James auditor, a city boy who thought cows had horns and who channel-surfed past rodeo on TV—except when bull riding filled the screen and made him loiter. They sold the concept in turn to Tony Lama Boots and Chevy Trucks, to Roper Shirts and Bailey Hats. By 1991, well ahead of schedule, they'd raised $2 million, quit their jobs, and opened for business. They caught a break with their timing; as the economy slumped and threw old colleagues on the street, the latest western craze was cresting. The fans packed arenas in rodeo towns like Phoenix and Salt Lake City, but they also came out in Long Beach and St. Louis. Ratings were strong and the phone response huge. Fifteen shows and more than three hundred thousand dollars in prize money later, Bull Riders Only was inching toward the black.

Contestants came strictly by invitation. They paid no entry fees, and vied for a top prize of ten thousand dollars at each stop. One of three contestants would take home a check, about three times the ratio at Cheyenne.

In Denver there would be four rounds of bulls, each tougher than the last, with the highest scorers in each round advancing. The top score in the fourth round, against the "Amazon" pen, would win the jackpot. A rider couldn't back into a payday; in that last round, stocked mostly by Sammy Andrews and Dan Russell, the top two bull men in the country, there were no easy draws. With its underdog plot lines and sudden-death finish, Sullivan's show was made to order for a one-hour TV time slot.

It was also a solar system removed from tradition. The PRCA sanctioned close to eight hundred rodeos in 1992, run in a crazy quilt of formats, entered by more than eight thousand contestants. More than 17 million people would attend—not as fans of a top-fifteen cowboy, but because rodeo was woven into their lives, and their parents' before them. Who needed stars? Not the PRCA, Ty Murray notwithstanding. Stars were trouble. Stars made demands—for more money, or better working conditions, or special treatment—that the industry wanted no part of.

But Bull Riders Only aimed to *make* stars. It wasn't enough to hire the best announcers (including Bob Tallman, dubbed by Sullivan "the Dick Vitale of bull riding"), or the ablest clowns, or even the best stock. To build couch-potato loyalty in the big urban markets, you needed all-star power. You needed glossy programs with photos and capsule bios of both riders and bulls. You needed jokey interviews with the cowboys for a segment called "Choose Your Own Poison," where riders picked their draws—"some of the baddest animals in the world," Sullivan would cackle to the crowd—from an aluminum bucket. Most of all, you needed bull riders who did their job very, very well, and who could beam their luster to the second deck.

So Sullivan was tickled to have Clint Branger as Bull Riders Only's top seed in Denver. Branger had closed to within three hundred dollars of Cody Custer in the gold buckle race, and seemed ready to shift into turbodrive. "I'm convinced right now," Sullivan said, "that Clint is riding better than anybody in the world."

He was happier yet to see Branger's cheering section, a passel of young women in up-close twenty-five-dollar seats, stamping their feet in anticipation. The women called themselves Roscoe's Rangers, and they were sweetly crazy about the guy. The dour Montanan was a cult object in spite of himself.

Why Branger? "Because he's the best," said Roni, in western-wear sales.

"Oh, *yeah*," said Pat, a beauty-supplies buyer. "He's just a great athlete. And he's not totally cocky—he's humble."

Other women in the stands, and there were lots of them, were less subtle. The operative word was *hot*. Tuff was hot. Bull riders were "more hot," not to mention "better-looking" and "more tough than those cattle guys," the ropers. They were also "cute" and "brave," especially when you considered how "mean" the bulls were.

Bull ridings could be habit-forming. For Dee Anderson, a prim credit-union manager from Colorado Springs, it was her fourth time. "I prefer it to rodeo, because this is what it's all about," she said. "This is the main action—this is *it*. These guys are *great*. There's just something about the bull riding that makes it happen." Anderson's voice fluttered and her face flushed beneath her makeup, and now it grew clear that Sullivan was selling, more than anything, the oldest, most market-tested commodity in the book: sex appeal.

With show time approaching, Sullivan scanned the paying customers. Most were bareheaded, *sans* Stetsons: the cross-over crowd. The house lights dimmed save for a double spot, which pinned a gray brindle bull trotting tentatively across the arena floor. To the lilting theme from *The Pink Panther,* one of the spotlights swung back in front of the chutes, and there was Branger, arms across chest: Spartacus primed for glory.

An irate man in a white T-shirt, already three Bud Lights to the wind, stood at the mezzanine rail to log a complaint. "That's bullshit!" he shrieked. "I come here to see bull ridin'. I didn't come here to see *tor*-ment to an animal. The lights, the music—that ain't bull ridin'!" After a muscular usher warned him to move on, the fan turned meekly toward his seat: "I'm goin', I'm goin'—I can't believe they do this to animals, man!"

No one else seemed to mind. As Tallman spieled the contestants' credentials like a ring announcer on No-Doz, they strode out one by one to form two facing lines on the field of battle. Their reception was loud and raucous, more rock concert than rodeo. Branger was introduced last, out of deference to his seeding, but Tuff got the loudest screams.

Both Branger and Cody Custer made it to the fourth and final round that night, with two other cowboys. Branger reached into the bucket and drew Blue Bonnett Palace. He lasted seven seconds before falling hard on his shoulder and snatching angrily at his grounded rope. "He got his horns up in my face and I guess I weenied out," he told Sullivan and the world minutes later, to chuckles all around. Branger got a reprieve when the other three riders also bucked off—the first shutout in the league's brief history. Sullivan gave the signal to Tallman: overtime.

"Should they all get on another one?" cried the brass-voiced announcer. The crowd shouted its approval. "Four more?" Whistles, hoots, a few banshee screams. "We're going to have to get a *lot* more excitement than that." A beery storm rained down, a standing, stomping, screeching ovation. When bull riding was this good, you could never get enough of it.

In the extra round, Cody Custer wrestled Copenhagen High Five to ninety-five points—a high but not unbeatable mark, as Sullivan's judges weren't afraid to score great rides accordingly. As the Diamond Vision scoreboard played him back in slow motion, and Custer knelt to pay his heavenward respects, the tension wound tighter. It was a one-run game, bottom of the ninth.

"You want to see Clint Branger be around ninety-seven points tonight?" Tallman prodded. Roscoe's Rangers darn-tootin' did, but Skoal's Dagger lacked the gas to send them home exalted. A pursed-lipped Branger settled for an eighty-nine, third place, and three thousand dollars.

Back in the visitors' dressing room, the smell of liniment hung heavy. Tuff brushed a few spots of greenish "guacamole" off the crown of his thousand-dollar, 100X hat, a perk from Resistol. His up-and-down year was down again. Three weeks before, he'd strained his groin muscles—an occupational hazard for bull riders, as men aren't built to straddle so broad a back, but the first time for Tuff. A week after that he lost his '91 gold buckle, his credit cards, a brand-new hat, and his bull rope in a car break-in at a Dallas mall. Everything was replaceable—even the buckle—except for the rope, his lifeline.

Tuff had ridden two bulls since the crime, with two different borrowed ropes, and both times the handle yanked out of his hand. In Denver he'd opted to break in a new model, a virgin, and it was like jumping into a new Porsche on the day of the race. Between the rope and his groins, now heavily taped, Tuff didn't feel quite his aggressive self. When Super Dave, Tuff's third-round draw and one of the best bulls in the world, snapped away from his hand, he couldn't catch up.

"They're good excuses, but they're still goddamn excuses," Tuff blustered. "The bottom line is I didn't deliver."

"Your bells are too damn shiny and your rope is too damn clean," burly Marty Staneart crooned from the next locker.

"And my balls are too small," Tuff said, with a loser's slap at his manhood. He flung down the white rope, set those shiny bells to clanging. He was mad but it was a clean mad, without the bitterness of Cheyenne. "This is the deal," Tuff said, as he unwound his taped thighs. "This is a competition here, not a circus. I love rodeo, and I'm a rodeo fan, but this is an *event*. I didn't win because I got bucked off; Cody Custer was the champion because he rode better than anyone else. I had the opportunity and I can't complain." A bull rider lived for such occasions, when he carved his own fate with a bundle in the balance. Even when he lost he reclaimed something. For a while, a short while, his life seemed to make sense.

☆

Winners and losers alike found solace at the Stampede, Denver's country-and-western, come-hither capital. A corral-sized rectangular bar sprawled at the center of the dance floor; each bartender juggled under big-screen highlights of the evening's bull-riding action, the violence disorienting without audio. A crush of couples two-stepped to Clint Black round the perimeter, clutching shoulders and backs and whatever else they could get away with.

Steam was rising all around, thickest in the vicinity of any rider fresh from the wars. The cowboys generally drank with two or three lithe young things at a time—he taking long pulls from a foamy bottle, they (generally blond) sipping clear liquids from plastic cups. Within an hour Clint Branger had been propositioned three times. He turned all of them down, even the woman who promised, "I'll ride you, and I know I can ride you for more than eight seconds."

While a sensitive man of the '90s, Branger was no threat to Mel Gibson in the hunk department. A star bull rider didn't need leading-man looks or snappy patter. He could be dumb and pug ugly, a Cro-Magnon in a clinch, and still he'd be the prize in the Cracker Jack. Bull riding and sex were like eggs and grits, rope and rosin, Ricky and the Redstreaks. In both, according to David Fournier, a loquacious Cajun cowboy, a man was "riding a feeling. You feel the bull do a certain thing, and your body does another thing. Just like a woman—she does one thing, you do another thing. You get in rhythm and you ride the motion."

(Some riders took this farm-animal analogy a step further, according to Doug "Scruffty" Vold, prodigal son of contractor Harry Vold. Any cowboy who denied a sexual past with livestock, Scruffty claimed, was "either a liar or a piss-poor roper.")

When Fournier and his cohorts were growing up, bull riders were the toughest, coolest guys in their towns, like bikers without cycles, living fast for as long as they lasted. They were, said Donnie Gay, "the ones who always had all the girls." Granted, they weren't for everyone. Some women hadn't the heart to get hooked on these western demolition experts. Some were annoyed by small men with big egos. But there were plenty who craved these cowboys, who'd follow them anywhere for fun on the run. They were known as buckle bunnies, the groupies of rodeo.

The bunnies subscribed to the *ProRodeo Sports News* and kept avid track of the top fifteen. They knew who was winning and who'd been down on his luck, who were uppercase Christians (sometimes, but not always, off-limits) or devoted family men (ditto). They circled and clipped the mug shots that most moved them, and counted the days for the rodeo to return to their town—to Las Vegas or Pretty Prairie, it made no difference. When the big night arrived, they tracked their quarry like so many private eyes. The first blushing encounter might come at the arena or later, at the bar, but the setup never much varied. Shrink-wrapped in halter top and black jeans, the bunny would spot her mark and saunter over—her flaxen hair tumbling, her silver cactus earrings a-tremble—and pay some pointed compliment, the fruit of her research. If sparks flew they'd be an item for the evening, or till the cowboy moved on. Another year might pass without contact, till the rodeo came back and the lovebirds resumed without a hitch.

"They'll come up and act as if it was just yesterday that you left," said Branger, who'd played the game well until lately. "And it don't really seem that long when you see their face. Everything's the same—the place, the smell, *everything*—and you go right along with it. The only reason you wouldn't go along was if she had a friend who was prettier. Then you might hang back to see if you had a chance. If not, you'd go for the sure thing."

And so the trade was made, of sex for fame or its proximity, with a pinch of companionship thrown in before sodden sleep. The same deal worked for bronc riders and ropers, of course, but bull riders supplied that extra death-wish magnetism. The danger cut both ways for them, as for GIs flitting through wartime London—as both a turn-on and a wedge against the mess of expectations. Why ask for tomorrow from a man who might not make it that far?

And if the hooves didn't get him the calendar would, for age doomed both bunny and bull rider, robbing one of her looks and the other of reaction time. A couple might have five or six "anniversaries" with no hopes of a long haul; once a lover lost exchange value, the affair was sure to founder. On the other hand, there were always new riders goin' down the road, and new girls to greet them—girls like Marilyn the ambulance technician and Kim the nurse, who'd driven sixteen hours to Denver from their small town near Houston to meet the men they held most dear. The Stampede marked their farthest field trip yet, and they weren't here to restrain themselves.

Did they go to a lot of rodeos?

"Yes, *sir!*" said Kim, chubby and twenty-two, her bare midriff peeking between a fringed blouse and matching skirt.

And they liked bull riders in particular?

"Yes, *sir!*" Marilyn said. "You never know what to expect, they're on the go all the time. But they got a real good personality. The guys are a bunch of sweethearts."

"Agree, one hundred percent," Kim said hoarsely, straining to be heard above George Strait. She seemed unfazed by the prospect of a sweetheart torn in half as she gazed raptly on. "I'm a nurse—I'll take care of them," she said brightly. It *was* sometimes hard for Kim to watch: "It's like heartbreaking, but at the same time it's, oh, my god. . . . You don't want 'em to get hurt bad, but it's *exciting*." She clinked beer bottles with a middle-aged businessman in a pricey Resistol, one of the deal makers the bull riders had drawn to them of late: a toast to all forms of desire.

"You nasty bitch!" The businessman was incensed that Kim had cracked the neck of his bottle. "You're a nasty bitch!"

Kim giggled; she wasn't easily offended. It was true, she allowed, that she liked the way bull riders were put together: "You know, 'Wrangler butts drive everybody nuts!'" But she insisted that they were latter-day Galahads all. "They just wine you and dine you, that's it," she said.

"They're really sociable," Marilyn said. "They're gentlemen, they really are."

"They know how to treat a lady," Kim said. "Calf ropers, they just know how to treat their horse."

The catch came when a bunny took stock and decided she was Mrs. Rabbit material. The odds stacked against her—if a bull rider settled down at all, it was usually with a Nice Girl, preferably a rich one—but she might make it if she was pretty and pert enough. She might just become a trophy bride, a rodeo wife . . . and then wonder why she'd gone to so much trouble.

A rodeo wife's home address sat between the sixth and seventh circles of hell. She made do with a spotty household income, hostage to bad draws and torn muscles. She endured her husband's slumps and gloomy silence, and the griping he'd hide from his friends. She watched him ride with held breath and white knuckles, or faint prayers to any power above. When he got hung up or run down, she'd dash to the medics' room, hoping her hardest that the bull hadn't laid him off for three months, or worse. And when her rider was going strong and chasing a title, she coped with the gray strain of separation. "It's two forces pulling," said Cody Custer, whose wife was pregnant with their first child. "I want to be home, but I want to be out here, too."

Larry Bastian set the dilemma to music with his lyrics to "Rodeo," sung by Garth Brooks that night on the Diamond Vision screen:

> *She does her best to hold him*
> *When his love comes to call*
> *But his need for it controls him*
> *And her back's against the wall*
> *And it's 'So long girl, I'll see you'*
> *When it's time for him to go*
> *You know the woman wants her cowboy*
> *Like he wants his rodeo.*

A wife might join her cowboy on the trail, but it was hard to sustain. She'd be derailed by a baby, or fatigue, or the odd notion that she had a life to lead back home. Or she might come to realize that the road was no place for women, mainly because bull riders liked it that way. It suited them to be with other men, to laugh and drink to all hours and cast a wandering eye if so inclined. "Being gone a lot," one rider proposed, was "the best way to get along with a woman, ain't it?"

In fact, it was the best way to get divorced. There were lots of good excuses for a cowboy to indulge his cheatin' heart—loneliness and opportunity, to name two—and the stray rate among bull riders was right up there with major-league ballplayers and traveling salesmen.

Even the faithful ones lived at an inner distance from their spouses. They couldn't share what made them tick, because you could never truly share bull riding with a civilian, and when, after all, had you last seen someone's wife on a red-eyed, spinning killer? *If it was easy, women and children would be doing it.* That was unthinkable. Bull riding was all about physical risk, and in these parts women didn't take those risks—their men protected them.

But the West held a contradiction here, a tradition of women who'd jimmied their way into a rough man's world. Back when free land was a chance for the self-reliant, thousands of widows and single women proved up under the Homestead Act, in some places filing one of six claims. They put up hay and mended fences, broke horses, and calved cows. They were bona fide players in their era's great game.

So it was natural for women to get equal time in early cowboy competitions, both on broncs and on the "wild steers" used at Cheyenne. Tad Lucas, the greatest cowgirl ever and the flashiest trick rider since Lady Godiva, took it to the next level. Not quite five feet tall, Lucas rode smaller Jersey bulls as a teenager at county fairs in her native Nebraska. By the 1920s she was entering all the big pro rodeos, generally in "ladies'" riding events. Lucas conquered fighting bulls in Mexico City and the jumbo steers called stags at Madison Square Garden. Like Annie Oakley, the crack shot of the Wild West shows, she routinely outshone the men. At a time when rodeo cowboys did well to earn five thousand dollars a season, she'd win twice that or more.

Lucas was so good—and so valuable to rodeo producers—that she could dodge her day's conventions. She was the first cowgirl to cut her hair short, flapper style, and the first to trade in bloomers and silk stockings for more sensible bell-bottom pants. Everywhere she went, with her angora chaps and glossy lipsticked smile, she created a sensation.

But in the 1930s, with funds drying up in the Great Depression, local rodeo committees cut costs by scuttling the women's riding events and their special strings of stock. At a time when female workers all over were nudged back home to ease pressure for jobs, a female bull rider—and one getting top billing to boot—was a dubious role model. The men in charge "said it was too dangerous," wrote Tom Robbins in *Even Cowgirls Get the Blues*. "Well, it was dangerous. Tad Lucas broke every bone in her body. The Brahma bulls almost made chop suey of her. But the men got hurt, too. They were wired together like birdcages, most of them."

With trick riding now a specialty act, women like Lucas and Alice Greenough were shunted to the margins. In the 1940s, their vacancy was filled by silk-and-satin "glamour girls" who'd preen in the Grand Entry and canter around barrels. Some could barely stay upright in the saddle, but they sure filled out those purty blouses, and fans were always suckers for a horse race. The riders and ropers, the ones left out, formed the Girls Rodeo Association. Now officially segregated, roughstock cowgirls performed at second-rate venues for third-rate pay. The gap steadily widened, and by 1990 the world champion barrel racer earned thirty times as much as the all-around world champion cowgirl.

At that point, a young woman bent on rodeo had two choices. She could become a barrel racer and go first-class, with a shot at real money and a berth at the National Finals. Or she could pursue bull riding as a hobby, with maybe half a dozen sanctioned rodeos per year. Few took the lower, harder road. Those who kept at it, who chose the bulls with no money or sponsors to tempt them, were a proud, defiant bunch. Anyone could be a barrel racer or cowboy chaser, they liked to say, but only the tough could ride bulls. These women gashed their livers and broke their backs, and came back because they loved it. When they talked about riding, their passion compared to any man's.

Tami George (hairdresser; Brentwood, California): "You're on an animal that's unpredictable—it's you against him and he's got the advantage, the power. To make a great ride is to say that you've conquered him."

Kathy Stroud (secretary; Owosso, Oklahoma): "Knowing you can compete with a beast, it's just a massive, natural high."

Deb Christensen (hairdresser; Henderson, Nevada): "It's the most tremendous adrenaline rush you'll ever feel. Inside you're just bubblin'. . . . And it's a challenge, it's fear, it's about every emotion you have all rolled up into the biggest bomb, just ready to explode."

By September 1992, when the Women's National Finals opened at the Lazy E Arena in Guthrie, Oklahoma, six of the sixteen bull riders had yet to win a dollar in competition. At least five couldn't set their gear without help. There were also half a dozen competent riders, and among them one star: Jonnie Jonckowski.

Jonnie would be making the last rides of a fourteen-year career in Guthrie. Now thirty-eight, she still had days when she felt like a world beater. She had others when her body was a time machine, whisking her back to old wounds. Of late she'd been stalled in 1988, when her riding arm shattered so bad they thought she'd never write her name with it again. As Jonnie stepped up her training for the women's finals, the elbow flared with tendinitis.

"You can only take so many cortisone injections and so many anti-inflammatories before you go, 'Man, this ain't worth it,'" Jonnie said, as she stretched a half hour before the first round's grand entry. Her broad shoulders strained a pink shirt with little black broncos printed on it.

"The guys can do this as a business, but most of the women are weekend warriors," she went on. "They go home and they're forklift drivers, or secretaries. They're not professional bull riders. It's different for me. This has catapulted me into a very visible limelight, and I want to go into the movies and TV. I use the finals as a grand commercial."

Jonnie had made a career—more, a saga—out of being different. Among a group of normally proportioned women behind the chutes, she stood out every time she stood up. At five-nine and 143 pounds, Jonnie wore a size-fourteen jacket and size-eight pants, a figure that cost four hours a day in the gym.

Her face told another story. Thirty minutes from mounting the back of a bull, Jonnie was wearing dime-sized silver earrings, a rich-hued lipstick and nail polish (Elizabeth Arden's New Red), and enough blush and mascara to make Tad Lucas proud. As her press kit made clear, she was not a cowgirl but *a country lady,* down to the long-stemmed-rose logo on Jonnie's pink business cards.

There were other women who'd been riding bulls as well or better, but only Jonnie understood how to parlay her act into guest shots on *David Letterman* or *American Gladiators.* "Why walk around and strut and be tough?" she said. She could be "down and dirty" on a bull, but "when it's over I'm a woman. I want the chair pulled out. I'm a marshmallow at heart—I cry easy, I break."

When Jonnie was twenty-one she enrolled in a roughstock school in Colorado, the only woman out of more than a hundred students. At that time female bull riders all gripped their rope with two hands—under the assumption they weren't strong enough to use one—"and they all had no teeth and scars on their chin" from getting jerked forward. Jonnie would be different. She would ride like the men.

She wound up second for the school buckle in bull riding, but her last draw flipped her to the ground. The next thing Jonnie saw was a hoof closing in on her face, "and my neck snapped back and I saw the hoof go away . . . and I'm thinking, 'He missed me.' I jumped up and I felt this warm rush on my face and all these people are screaming and running at me, with these foghorn voices. . . . I could hear one guy out of the crowd, and he goes, 'Geez, her nose is torn off!' "

Wasn't quite as bad as that, but close. A convention of plastic surgeons in nearby Colorado Springs sewed up Jonnie's face with 160 stitches. "I went in lookin' like Michelle Pfeiffer," she'd tell you, "and came out like the Elephant

Man." She was joking—she'd gotten a Beverly Hills face-lift—but Jonnie did have some nerve damage and a permanently crooked grin. As she mended she decided, "I *got* to go back to ride bulls. I'm a freak now—what else am I going to do?"

It took a decade of trying, a bushel of injuries, and precious little reward—less than a thousand dollars per year, on average—before Jonnie won her first of two world championships in 1986. She was irresistible, like Hurricane Agnes, and in 1991 she was inducted into the National Cowgirl Hall of Fame in Hereford, Texas.

Her peers weren't so starstruck, not with so few crumbs at their table and one person sweeping off most of them. There were bull riders actively rooting for Jonnie to lose in Guthrie. "It's gotten kind of old that she gets all the attention," said the stern-faced Tami George, Jonckowski's main rival. "I don't believe she could be a true friend. She's all out for herself."

But nothing could spoil Jonnie's good humor in Guthrie. Not even the women's two-round finals format—"dumb luck if you win and dumb luck if you lose"—or the green, uneven stock. The previous year's champion was a coed who'd covered all of three bulls in her life.

After riding a limp one to sixty-six points in the first go ("Not enough bull for me"), which just about killed her chances, Jonnie talked about Scottsdale, where she'd entered Justin Boots' big-time bull riding that spring with CBS News as entourage. For Jonnie it was P.R. heaven. But the top cowboys noted her draw was hand-picked—the bull was big and humpy, but gentle—and quite a few were ticked off by the intrusion. They weren't impressed when Jonnie fell off five seconds in; Ty Murray still steamed when asked about it months later. Women, he burned, could never compete against men on bulls: "Not ever, no way, *impossible*. They're not strong enough, they're not tough enough—until they prove me wrong, there never has been one."

But Jonnie hadn't been out to beat the men. "Cowboys shut you down when you compete against them," she said sagely. She had no illusions that she could handle the strongest, double-rank bulls. "All I wanted to do," she said, "was stay on long enough to look like I'd been there before and that I knew what I was doing." When it was over she'd won a line in the *Guinness Book of World Records*—plus three small nods, four masculine handshakes, and a comradely pat on the butt.

As his friends cavorted at the Denver bull riding, Ty Murray sat with a troubled mind and a bulky black brace on his knee. On August 16, he and Jim Sharp were headed home when they pulled off at Odessa, Texas, their old college town, to visit with friends. By coincidence, a little jackpot bull riding was getting under way. It was easy money, Sharp said, and each of them threw their sixty bucks into the pot. Sharp won first and five hundred dollars; Ty tied for second and cleared about three hundred. It was like rolling downhill till Ty left his bull in the loose, sandy soil. He didn't jump off like he often did. He just stepped off real easy . . . and that's when he heard his left knee pop, felt the burn inside. Soon it calmed down and Ty figured he'd just turned the joint. He walked out of the arena and forgot about it.

The next morning he woke up with a Florida grapefruit in the middle of his leg. After X rays Ty heard the two most depressing words of his young life: *torn ligaments*. The medial collateral would heal on its own; the anterior cruciate would not. In the best case, according to J. Pat Evans, Ty's knee would function almost normally again after a seven-week layoff with exercise.

In the worst case, if the knee played out or locked up when Ty rode, he'd need reconstructive surgery.

An operation would mean five months without rodeo, and for Ty that would be living death. He never forgot that he loved the game, but all those pinball weeks down the road might have led him to mislay just how much. Now he remembered. Ty missed rodeo like a sailor missed the sea. He longed most for the riding, the quick trips that recharged him. But he also missed the highways and road signs, the sense of getting somewhere all the time. And he sorely missed Cody Lambert and the rest, the ones who spoke his language. The lonely Lambert called him almost every day—"Get your ass *out* here," he'd command—but those cornball jokes weren't quite the same over a phone wire.

Five weeks after the accident, grounded at his four-bedroom ranch house, Ty was still dragging the brace around, his animal grace a memory. "It's the shits, any way you look at it," Ty said glumly, as he sat in his pine-paneled kitchen, his leg stiff and straight. "It's a bad deal, 'cause them ligaments don't heal. Once you tear one, it's torn. It'll probably never be like it was." The layoff would likely cost him forty thousand dollars and any chance he might have had for that elusive one-event gold buckle, but Ty could live with that. What got him down was something more spectral, the stuff of bad dreams and the blues. This wasn't a bronc mashing him in the chute, or a bull drumming his rib cage. When his knee buckled in Odessa, it was the first time his body gave way for no apparent reason. It was Ty's first glimpse of his athlete's mortality; he was no longer the charmed, untouchable golden boy. It got to him so bad that morning that he'd left the room when a housemate slid a National Finals tape into the VCR.

After a week with his folks in New Mexico, Ty had come back to his house and ten acres outside Stephenville, Texas, ninety miles southwest of Dallas. With more than fifty active PRCA members out of fifteen thousand inhabitants, Stephenville was the Cowboy Capital of Texas, and therefore the world. Its most famous institution was Jake and Dorothy's Restaurant—"Since 1948," with the vintage Formica to prove it. If Larry Mahan and Roger Staubach were to walk into Jake and Dorothy's, Mahan would sign all the autographs. "I love this town," Ty said.

The house was sunny and functional, but no lifestyle for the rich and famous. Ty shared it with a fluctuating number of young cowboys, plus Sparky the dog, a mottle-faced mutt saved from death row. ("I went to the animal shelter and I couldn't decide, so I asked which one they were gonna kill next," Ty said. "And they pointed her out and, boy, I couldn't have picked a better dog.") The place had a breezy dormitory atmosphere, except it was far too tidy. Ty was a bug about neatness. "He yells at you if you don't make your bed," Adam Carrillo reported.

These were lazy days for Ty. He had no deadlines or routines apart from his two-hour workout in a converted trailer by the house. He ate when he was hungry and worked the ranch ten hours or none: "I get up and do whatever I want to do." At the moment he wanted some of the crawfish étouffée rustled up by Charles "Meathead" Soileau, a saddle bronc rider from Louisiana whose family raised its own crustaceans. As the smell of garlic and onion wafted from the stove, someone asked Soileau if he was cooking Minute Rice, and the chef made plain he'd been insulted. "He'll make someone a fine wife someday," Ty observed.

As the housemates chowed down, one beetle-browed guest took to complaining about some woman at a dance who'd spurned his advances. "Well, damn, you wear your mustache on your forehead," Ty said, to much hilarity. "Whenever you shave you should run it right down the middle there, break it up. . . . Gary gave him a nickname—what was it, Gary?"

"Ya-te-hoo-te-hay."

"That means, 'He Who Wears Mustache on Forehead.' "

After lunch Ty went out back to feed his animals. First came Count, the bay quarter horse he liked to ride through the near hills. Next the four ostriches by the barn. Not yet full grown, the birds' bizarre pinheads bobbed eight feet from

their hooflike feet. "Goofy-looking things," Ty muttered, as he filled their trough with fresh water. "They're the dumbest animals I've been around. When they're young they're *real* spooky. One day me and Charles was in here buildin' a feeder, and we'd walk around the corner and they'd go—*whaa!*—flyin' backwards, spookin' from us. Two minutes later we'd come walkin' around the corner and—'Goddamn, there they are again!' They did it about ten times, like they'd forget we was in there.

"I've been around animals all my life, and I can pretty much tell what they're thinkin'. But it's really, really hard to tell what's goin' through ostriches' minds."

The birds had a saving grace, though. Bought young and sold a year or so later, a breeding pair gained value by a thousand bucks a month—unless one of them ran into a wall and dropped dead. Ty had funneled the proceeds into a cow and calf operation, which now numbered three hundred head. The ostriches also had a mysterious fringe benefit: their droppings disappeared, with no shoveling required. Ty guessed that the mounds "just kind of turned back into dirt or something."

Feeding done, Ty joined his housemates for the big chore: clearing the land for a sturdier wire fence, with cedar stays to keep Count from running into it. Today's business was to strip some old wire and bulldoze the scrub oaks invading the fence line. Ty deftly handled a heavy fence cutter, then laid it aside to wrestle with a thorny shrub. There were rodeos out there that balmy mid-September day, broncs to ride and bulls to be bucked, but for the moment the world's greatest cowboy seemed utterly content. He wiped the sweat from his forehead and soaked in the view, the rolling grasses that stretched cross the road to the horizon. All he could hear were the crickets and the crows. All he could smell was the land and the animals.

"This ranch is a small scale of what I'd want one of these days," Ty said. "To me it would be fun to look across there and own all the land I could see." There would come a time when Ty would lay aside his bull rope. He'd be ready for it. But he wasn't there yet.

CHAPTER 10

The Wrong Paint Job

*C*HARLES SAMPSON SOLVED his own leading question—*Do you want to do it?*—that summer. He rode lucky and good for weeks at a stretch; he was Finals-bound. He felt great, he told any who asked, which meant he could wince his way out of bed without crying out loud. And then in late September he got spilled at a rodeo in Yakima, Washington, just a poor night at the office till the bull trod on Sampson's left leg. The cowboy was a connoisseur of pain, and he knew it was bad before looking—at the bone poking through his shin, at his ankle dangling, disconnected. There were five distinct fractures. The surgeons would need three hours, two steel plates, and seventeen screws to set the splintered limb.

By that time Sampson had earned enough to eke his way into the NFR. But Las Vegas loomed less than ten weeks away, and the doctors figured he'd need twice that time to recover. The news winged through the rodeo grapevine. Sampson was through—for the season, for sure, if not for good.

As he hopped about on crutches that October, Sampson wasn't arguing the point. He'd been craving to quit for two years; Yakima was just the clincher. The NFR was out: "I ain't riding another bull, nobody's gonna talk me into it. I've just been *abused* by the bull, by my sport. I don't care, I'm retired—I'm done."

The first of November, when Finals lineups were set, came and went with Sampson sitting thirteenth. Meanwhile, back at his ranch in Casa Grande, Arizona, he bore out his reputation as the fastest healer in the West. Four days after surgery, Sampson shed his cast and limped about his house unaided. Ten days after that he laid down his crutches for good. He walked miles each morning and punished the stair machine, pushing through pain to save his calf muscle from atrophy.

And now, a day before the Finals' first go-round, Sampson sprawled on a bed at the Gold Coast, all 130 pounds of him, a subcultural legend in red sweat shorts and a black T-shirt reading "RIDE." You could trace the metal's contour inside his left leg, which squared off instead of tapering at the shin. At the moment the leg twitched as if palsied, pulsing to the beat of a twenty-volt stimulator. To mend a little faster, Sampson plugged himself into the toaster-sized box two hours a day, or as long as he could stand it.

Without his black hat and monogrammed spurs and gold buckle at his belt, Sampson looked very breakable. He has a lightweight's sinewy body, with big hands and long limbs for the rest of him. Strong features crowd his round face. A broad mouth strains to show more than Sampson allows to outsiders; the smile checks itself, turns quizzical, and fades, like the Cheshire Cat in reverse.

It is, unmistakably, a bull rider's face. A slanting scar mars the bridge of Sampson's nose. A second one mimes the line of his left eyelid; a third hovers over his mustache. The prosthetic left ear is a rough puttied facsimile of the original. It is a face that has seen the wrong side of too many panicked hooves.

"Take a look at these X rays; they ain't pretty," Sampson said, pulling the gray plastic sheets from a manila envelope. They were, in fact, gruesome—snapshots of a living erector set. He counted the breaks with pride and fascination, for they told what he'd withstood: "That's five different places . . . eleven screws in the tibia, six in the fibula." The hardware would remain in his leg for at least three years. "See how the bone's still lined up?" he pointed out. "See how dark it is in there? That's healing up great—the spaces are closing."

Yes, he'd been ready to pass this Finals by, up till a trip to his doctor in November. As his brother-in-law drove, Sampson confessed his leaning: to hit Vegas for the parties and his official Finals jacket, but to save his face for his grandchildren—to turn out. It was the only sane choice. What else could he do?

"I don't know, Chuck," the in-law said slowly. "I'd try."

"What?" Sampson exclaimed.

"You rode sore before. You ought to try at least once— you ought to see if you can do it. If this is your last time, you go out swinging."

"That's right!" yelled Sampson, finally hearing what he'd wanted.

As the doctor pored over his pictures, Sampson popped the question. Could he—hypothetically, now—ride two weeks later in Las Vegas? The surgeon couldn't say for sure, but then he couldn't read try off an X ray. Sampson was his own trainer. The decision, as always, would be his.

It would be nice to leave it at that, to hail a minor miracle and applaud this "cult hero for fallen bull riders," along with the rodeo press. But the hard fact was something else: Charles Sampson would ride the next night because he was broke.

"That's the reason I ride bulls. I have to face that, and that's the sad part," Sampson said. "Not that I don't know where my money went. It went to airplane tickets, to entry fees, to meet my bills. I got land, I got a family, I got taxes. And if I didn't win on the bull. . . ."

Sampson grabbed the ringing phone and a grin creased his face. It was Tom Chambers, star forward for the Phoenix Suns and a Sampson associate in Bull Riders International, Shaw Sullivan's competition. "I'm stimming my leg right now," the rider reported. "They drew the first two bulls and I got two good ones, just what I needed."

Sampson confirmed he'd found Chambers some tickets—precious items at the Finals—and signed off. He tinkered with the electrodes on his leg and said softly, "You never want to break your body, Jeff." The leg resumed twitching. Sampson grew reflective. Over the last three years he'd turned to religion to make sense of the chaos of his life. He'd struggled to "not rebel against Him, because I have faults. I'm no drug addict or alcoholic, but sometimes I commit adultery, sometimes I go out and get boozed up, and that's not a God thing.

"What changed my mind about the NFR was I had some bills to pay, and I ain't had no money comin' in. And as I started feeling better and walking around, I just started talking to myself, to get in a good frame of mind: 'Aw, shucks, Charles, God took it from you and he gave it back. Don't worry about it, you can do it—you're a bull-riding son of a bitch.'

"The devil told me, 'I broke your leg, you can't ride bulls no more. Now I got you where I want you.' So I dealt with that, I dealt with that"—and Sampson slid into gospel singsong—"and I just let go, and started asking God for guidance: 'What do I do?' And He reassured me that it's okay to go back out there and ride bulls."

Sampson had reached this revelation with the aid of one Reverend Alfred Craig of Coolidge, Arizona. Still feeling shaky, he'd packed a cassette tape of his favorite sermon to play each day in Vegas. The sermon's title was "Overcoming Discouragement," and Sampson slipped it into a portable player. Then he lay back, hands clasped behind neck, and with the first tinny words he visibly unclenched, as if releasing all worry.

"The Lord spaketh to Joshua, the son of Nun, Moses' minister, saying, Moses, my servant, is dead. Now therefore arise, go over this Jordan, and to the land. Every place that the sole of your foot shall tread upon, I have given to you. . . ." Pastor Craig preached up-tempo and treble-cleffed, like a bebop trumpet.

"In this discouraging moment, God said, 'I will not fail thee. *Be strong, and of a good courage!*' See, God is encouraging us. Be strong! And of a what?"

"Good courage," the congregation droned.

"So many times things happen in our lives," Craig went on, "and God gives us the vision, and Satan comes along to discourage us, to take the vision out of us." Sampson murmured assent from his bed. "But here God says be strong."

"Be *strong!*" Sampson echoed.

"And what?" the pastor called. "*And have good courage!*"

"I was there in the church that day," Sampson cut in, "and you know there's some days you go there and they're talking right to you? He was talking right to me!" The cowboy's face flickered a glimpse of the young, exuberant Charlie Sampson, the ghetto son who once charmed Jim Crow country in spite of itself.

The preacher had warmed to his subject: "I want to *encourage* you today. See, life is a series of battles. The greater the battle, the greater the victory. As Paul said, 'When we were come into Macedonia, our flesh had no rest. We were troubled on every side.' Every which way you look there's trouble—trouble with the finances, with your marriage, with the kids, with the house. Here was Paul, a man of God, doing the things that was right, and every which way he went there was trouble!"

Sampson said slyly, "There'll be a lot on these bulls."

Reverend Craig had entered that climax known as *the whoop,* when a preacher is most open to both text and congregation. "Thank you, Jesus!" he shouted, with fraying voice and quickened beat. "I am overcoming discouragement!" The congregation clapped and shouted back at him. "Don't let them take your courage out!"

"That's right!" Sampson cried.

"Hallelujah!" the preacher sounded.

"Hallelujah!" the flock replied.

And while no one could say what the next ten days might bring, the tiny man with the twitching leg, it was clear, would not go gently from the game that made his name.

The eleventh of thirteen children, Sampson was born in Watts ten years before the rebellion there. His early life was shaped by two events: his family's move a mile or two down the freeway, toward Gardenia, and his father's flight to points north. Seattle, Alaska—it might as well have been Mars. Sampson was six years old at the rupture, and over time his image of the man lapsed into shadow.

Never a street kid himself, too small to shine at basketball, Sampson passed through childhood unremarkably—until his Cub Scout troop took a field trip to a ramshackle carnival by the neighborhood junkyard. Under a tent sat the usual suspects: monkeys and bears to be taunted, mummies of vague pedigree. But for Sampson there was only one attraction, a ride on a shaggy pony. It was his first time aboard an animal, and it fired him to feel the heavy flesh shifting beneath his own. Five lazy circles and it was over, too soon. Sampson was captured as only ten-year-olds can be. He took to haunting the grassy edge of the freeway with a gunnysack, scavenging for bottles he'd redeem at the liquor store. Each quarter paid for a trip round the pony's littered ring.

Within a year he'd moved on to a nearby stable called the Hill. There he struck a deal with a fun-loving bulldogger named Gene Smith: in return for mucking out Smith's stalls and feeding the horses, Sampson could ride for free. As he worked he listened to the other black cowboys who gathered

there. Weathered transplants from Texas and Oklahoma, they regaled the sixth-grader with rodeo tales. They taught him rope tricks, gave him a niche and a nickname: Peewee.

Sampson became infatuated by all things western. At home he'd rope dogs and chickens, and any toddler within range.

On Sundays he would serve as Smith's jockey in ten-dollar match races; Friday nights he'd ride ponies at an auction arena east of town. The sale animals were often unbroken, and bucked to throw the wild child clinging to their back. For his efforts Sampson earned two dollars a night.

You have to go back twenty years to find out why I keep coming back. That's when I first fell in love with riding bulls. . . . Sampson was twelve when he rode his first steer. Steers are not bulls, true enough; once gelded, they lose both muscle mass and the will to maim. At the same time, steers are not ponies. "I had a little fear of getting on, but the fear made me excited," Sampson said. "It was, 'I'm gonna bear down and I ain't gonna let go!'"

The virus found its host. Soon Sampson couldn't pass a barrel or a bale of hay without scooting aboard and slicking up his moves. He entered steer-riding jackpots against grown men in Long Beach, risking three bucks to win fifty, and won more than his share. He hitched his way to every rodeo he could reach in southern California, where he'd fidget till the bull riding. Sampson would hang around afterward to meet the top riders—dandies and lady-killers, local heroes every one. *That's what I want to do,* he told himself. *That's who I want to be.*

His chance came in 1972, the summer he turned fifteen, when Gene Smith took his stable hands home to Oklahoma. Sampson had to beg his mother to let him go. Days later he found himself at an open rodeo in Tishomingo, happy just to tend his friends' horses. Then Smith declared, "You can ride these bulls," and the youth they still called Peewee agreed to give it a shot.

When Sampson went back to check out his draw, the bull was drowsing in the dead heat. Kicked and jumped real strong, the locals reported—a guy placed fourth on him last week. This wasn't some flighty, skittering steer, Sampson thought, pumping himself up. *This was the real deal—and I can ride him.*

Then the bull unfolded and stood up . . . and up . . . till it towered over every other in the pen, a big, black seventeen-hundred-pounder with horns to spare. There was no turning back, and Sampson, who weighed a hundred pounds after breakfast, rosined his rope and waited. "I went behind the chutes, and a guy shouted, 'Get down, kid, you're gonna get hurt!' I said, 'I'm in the bull riding—I'm with Gene Smith.' The guy knew Gene, and he couldn't believe it. He thought Gene had entered this little kid in the rodeo just to get him killed."

Sampson took his wrap and nodded for the gate to open, and he felt a surge beneath him, and inside him, that he'd never felt before. He rode two jumps in a blur—left or right, he couldn't say—and all he'd recollect was hitting the ground and scrambling back to the chutes.

"What did you do that for?" one of his buddies demanded. "You jumped off—you was riding good!" But Sampson was satisfied. *All right, I rode a bull! I'm a bull rider now!*

He tried a few practice bulls in California that season, then laid off in 1973 with rheumatic fever. The following year, at the age of sixteen, Sampson borrowed an entry fee and placed fourth his first time out. He won $147. A week later he paid his own way and won two hundred more. He felt swelled by his wealth and his future: "I thought there would never be a sad day, a poor day."

Sampson looked to two potent role models in those years. The first was Myrtis Dightman, the gentle, strapping Texan who'd pass time at the Hill whenever a rodeo brought him through Los Angeles. Gene Smith and the rest catered to him without stint, for Dightman was the Man. The other cowboys Sampson knew were amateurs, or weekend pros at best, carpenters or blacksmiths in real life. But Dightman was in the sport for keeps. The one truly professional black cowboy of his day, he widened Sampson's sights.

"When you're young, you've got to identify with someone, and he was the only guy to participate on a full scale, the way I do now," Sampson explained. "He never insinuated that rodeo wasn't good for him. . . . I didn't know till later on how he was treated."

When Sampson first met his hero in 1969, he was twelve years old and had yet to venture farther than Fresno. He was sick with wanderlust. The boy couldn't decide which he found more appealing: Dightman's record at the Finals (the first black man to make it there, he'd climbed as high as third in the world), or his life on the road, to go wherever the spirit and a fat purse moved him.

When Sampson fessed up his ambition, Dightman pushed the long view. A man couldn't ride bulls forever, said the Texan, himself a barely literate seventh-grade dropout. You needed an education, something to fall back on. If Sampson cut class for the Hill and ran into the Man, there was no horseback riding that day. "You finish school," Dightman bargained, "and when I come back to California, I'll help you." Sampson would graduate, and Dightman kept his word.

Sampson's second mentor was Gary "Stinky" Leffew, the ex-hippie bull rider who'd won the gold buckle in 1970. The average cowboy would tell you that Leffew was . . . well, *different*. Before he crashed the pro scene, bull-riding theory could be summed in five words: shut up and do it. But Leffew trusted in positive thinking, even read books about it. A *hot* man could do anything, he claimed—could even make himself a champion.

In 1975, Sampson copped a sixty-mile ride to Leffew's weekend clinic. "We didn't even have any bulls—all we had was bucking machines and video machines," Sampson recalled. "Gary showed us the bull-riding tapes, how the top guys ride. I got on that bucking machine and he was gung-ho praising me. I'd never had any help on mental preparation before—the guys at the stable would just tell me, 'Ride, ride, ride!'"

A fast study, Sampson learned his trade's basics: how to ride with his knees, whip his free arm forward, get off without harm, "all the stuff I didn't know." When the two days were up, he had made a quantum leap. Soon he would enter a far larger arena—and, against odds, make it yield to him.

There were always black cowboys, ever since there was a West to win. Not that you would find them in Zane Grey or John Wayne shoot-'em-downs—or, for that matter, in the sober tomes of Frederick Jackson Turner. It took a new wave of research, prodded by the civil rights movement of the 1960s, to recall that black people helped build the Frontier.

In the great cattle drives along the Chisholm and Shawnee Trails, one of five cowboys was black. In Texas alone, four thousand black wranglers rode the range. What with the Mexican *vaqueros* recruited across the border, and thousands of Indians hired for their horsemanship, white wranglers were a minority throughout much of South Texas.

Most black cowboys were ex-slaves born on Texas ranches, while others had fled the Deep South. The West made no promises to them. Once new towns were settled and white women imported, racist "black laws" and terror were quick to follow. But as long as they kept pushing westward, black cowboys shared the trail's grind and its poverty as rough equals. They ate and slept side by side with the white hands, got paid the going wage (though few became foremen), and even drank at the same saloons—if often, by custom, at the far end of the bar.

The most skilled of these men came to star in the Wild West shows and the earliest rodeos. In the loose-change days of the sport, rodeo was often mixed. But segregation advanced with the new century, and by the 1920s—as rodeo became a national craze with real prize money, and the Ku Klux Klan surged through the land—black cowboys found arena gates slammed in their noses.

As in Protestant churches and bowling leagues, exile gave birth to separate, less-than-equal rodeos, often held at local fairs. Black riders and ropers, some hauntingly talented, would strut their stuff in tiny black hamlets like Okmulgee, Oklahoma. They'd risk all for thirty-dollar purses and a few dozen fans, a far cry from Denver or San Antonio. In 1947, as Jackie Robinson stole his first bases for the Brooklyn Dodgers, a group of black Texas ranchers went the other way and founded the Negro Cowboys Rodeo Association. From that day on, a good many black cowboys never saw a white face in competition.

But a few balked at the status quo. Marvel Rogers was a massive yet agile man with unreasonable appetites: for tall stories, aged Scotch, fair fights, and the finest, longest Cuban cigars he could lay his huge hands on. Rogers began his rodeo career as an exhibition "hat rider" on rank bulls and broncs after the white cowboys had finished. Since his earnings came from a passed hat, it paid to be flamboyant. Billed as "the Bronze Flash," Rogers wore a white Stetson, starched white shirt, and pressed black jeans tucked inside high-top, spit-polished black boots.

Eventually Rogers chafed at his sideshow status. In the early 1950s, with the backing of Beutler Brothers, a mammoth Oklahoma stock contractor and Rogers's longtime employer, he became one of the first black cowboys to be carded into the theretofore lily-white Rodeo Cowboys Association, precursor to the PRCA. Where other black cowboys had skirted the color line by passing as Indians or "gauchos," Rogers punched a hole and swaggered on through.

Cracker rodeo officials might rig the draw against him, or cook down his score, or make him ride in the "slack," the morning sessions where weaker stock got dumped. Rogers was both sensitive and square-fisted, and he'd take names at each slight. After one bloody fracas, he had to be stolen out of town under a truckload of hay.

In years to follow, black cowboys would channel in one of two directions: into the ranch-rooted timed events, or toward the derring-do of bull riding. Rogers was one of the last black saddle bronc riders, and the reason had everything to do with racism. Saddle bronc is the ultimate *judging* contest, where a clumsy ride might score twenty points less than a pretty one for the same trip. In Rogers's time, all sorts of extraneous factors— from bribes to the cast of a cowboy's skin—could alter a score. Discouraged, black cowboys turned away from the event, until it came to be deleted at black rodeos large and small.

But bull riding was a *riding* contest, and it wasn't rare to see just two or three cowboys make the whistle. A black man might still be cheated out of first, but he'd likely leave with some money if he made eight. In bull riding, as Myrtis Dightman noted, "the bull be the judge."

The hanging kind of judge, at that—a point that made Dightman bull-shy his whole career. A standout rodeo bull-fighter when he needed sure income, Dightman felt safer when the beast was in front of him, not under him. "The thing I don't like about this bull riding," he'd lament, "is that first you have to get on that damned bull."

Dightman had a second reason to hesitate, for rodeo clung to its traditions, including the bad ones. Even as the Freedom Rides shocked Alabama, and the Boston Celtics played four black men out of five, only a handful of black cowboys had cracked the PRCA. There was no shortage of brilliant black bull riders: J. D. Gibson, Buck Wyatt, Willie Thomas. But like Marvel Rogers, they were labor-list men, tied to their jobs and tethered to a contractor's home turf. They'd given up on the white-run game, shaved their dreams to size.

Only Dightman took the plunge, in 1964, as a twenty-nine-year-old rookie. He liked punching an eight-second time clock, and he had this stubborn idea about making the Finals. Forget that, his friends warned—it wasn't allowed. But each time they played that give-up tune he'd dig in a little deeper. "If you try, you can do it," he'd insist, "and if you *really* try, people will help you do it." With his brawny style—he had four men pull his rope, tight as a noose—Dightman reached the old Oklahoma City Finals six times in seven years.

An impact player everywhere he went, Dightman was the first black cowboy to win at Cheyenne and Pendleton, the most storied shows in the country. He did that and more while certain judges routinely chopped him half a dozen points, or whatever it took to keep a man with "the wrong paint job" from a victory lap. It got so bad at times that the crowd would moan its protest. When Dightman broke the race bar in his hometown of Houston in 1971, he rode one that bucked much the best. The judges were Harry Tompkins and Ken Roberts, bull-riding giants who'd won the world eight times between them. At the end of the round, Tompkins asked his colleague whom he'd scored highest.

"And Ken said, 'No goddamn nigger's gonna win it, not while I'm judgin' it, that's for sure,'" Tompkins revealed, years after Roberts's death. "And I said, 'Well, I got him win-nin' it, and however you post your markings I'm gonna change mine so he wins first.' I was going to go to the limit, and Myrtis did win first at that go-round."

The endings weren't always so happy. In 1967 Dightman led the standings for much of the year, only to be passed in the stretch by Mahan and Bill Stanton. As his chance slid away, he confronted his friend Freckles Brown and exclaimed, "Man, what can I do to win the world?"

The plainspoken Brown replied, "I'll tell you what, you just keep riding bulls like you do—and turn white."

Years after he closed his career, Dightman reminisced on a worn brown armchair in his steaming shoebox of a Houston apartment. He was home from his clerk's shift at the American Hat Company, just the eight-to-four humdrum he'd always dreaded. "I try not to think of things that happened to me, 'cause you can't go backwards," he said.

Tacked in a spot of honor by the hallway, stained and faded in the gauzy light, was a set of red-white-and-blue crests with "NFR" in big letters. Those were Dightman's finest hours, when he'd worn those cloth badges. Twenty years after his last appearance, he kept this message on his machine: "Hello, you have reached the seven-time National Finals cowboy." He'd gone further than the folks back in Crockett, Texas, had ever hoped for him. But he'd never quite reached his destination.

Dightman broke off his gold buckle quest when he was forty years old. It took that long to resign himself; maybe it took a little longer. "I thought one day it would be me," said the Jackie Robinson of rodeo, more wistful than bitter, "but that day ain't come."

After losing a year to his first broken leg, Sampson came to Central Arizona College on a rodeo scholarship in the fall of 1976. He'd left the city lights for a patch in the desert, one way in and one way out. In that patch he became a star. He rode bareback horses and team-roped, and even wrestled steers, an outlandish event for one so small. But bull riding stayed Sampson's bread and jam, the event that put cash in his pocket. He rode every chance he got, from his school circuit to weekend amateur affairs to the odd pro event that fit his calendar. In 1978, college completed, he placed high enough at two PRCA rodeos to earn a membership card. That winter he quit his job branding cows and jumped into the life he'd long envied.

Sampson saw every town with wide eyes, every bull as a peak to scale without landmarks. "When I first started out, it was all subconscious, all reaction," he said. "I'd get on a bull, and I didn't care which way he went—I was like glue on him. And I would get off and somebody would say, 'God-*dawg*, you really rode that sucker!' And I'd say, 'What did he do?' And they'd say, 'He turned a flip!' And I'd say, 'I don't re-member that!'"

These bulls were far stouter than at college, strong enough to wrench a big man's arm out, and Sampson adapted by doing what came naturally. To absorb their jerk he rode loose and cool, hung like a rag; the more his tiny body flopped, the less power Sampson had to fight. And to anchor his seat through the storm, he latched on with his legs for his well-deep hold, the pin for his pinwheel. No one else rode remotely like him. Soon he'd cracked the top fifteen in his first full year as a pro.

Outside the ring his adjustment took longer, if it took at all. In those days rookies were ignored till they proved themselves. But few were as lonely as Sampson. Shy by nature, he was, like Dightman before him, the only black cowboy going down the road full-bore. He traveled mostly by himself, hitching to backwater towns where fans glared as he outrode their favorite sons, to big cities that flew rebel flags. He had no credit cards, no money in his wallet but what the last few bulls had brought him.

Who could count the miles Sampson drowsed through? Who could count the meals he missed? Nine of ten young studs with the *right* paint job lost their nerve and ran home, to wish for what might have been. But Sampson endured; he was always tougher than he looked. And he found an ally in rodeo man Bob Tallman, a one-time bull rider who'd had a hearing problem behind the chutes: his knees kept rattling too loud. Sampson bugged the announcer to help him clean up his speech, to scrub out the East L.A. slang. Tallman drilled the young cowboy on tape till Sampson's voice homogenized.

Truth was, he could have talked like Johnny Cash and still never fit in. Many were the cowboys who hadn't known a black person beyond their childhood nannies. They took Sampson as "a novelty—they hadn't had nobody like me." He caught rides for a while with two Canadians, and one great day in Billings he hooked up with Donnie Gay and Monty "Hawkeye" Henson, the reigning kingpins of bull riding and saddle bronc.

"You got a place to stay?" asked Henson, a bluff character who'd worn spurs to the White House. "No? Hell, you come on and stay with us." Sampson got jerked down and kissed on the chin that night, and the two superstars left him to nurse his wound in their room while they went to the bar—they always went to the bar. Sampson wound up sharing Gay's bed.

"Donnie was going for a championship, and so was Monty," Sampson recalled. "That felt *real* good. Here I was a kid that just got popped in the head, and I'm with these champions." There weren't any black jokes with Gay or Henson. They knew Sampson was one of them, that he stalked the same high goal.

But regardless of his company, Sampson stayed safely on the margins, a stranger in a strange land. "I didn't chase the girls, because most of the girls were white," he said. "I didn't go and get drunk, and I didn't dance 'cause I couldn't dance country and western. I'd just hang in the corner and wait, and when my ride was ready, I was ready to go."

By August Sampson ranked eighth in the world, a twenty-two-year-old headed for the Finals. But in Sidney, Iowa, a bull stepped on his chest and crushed his sternum, shelving him for thirteen weeks. He used the time to court Marilyn Casmon, a Seattle woman even smaller and shier than he was. Sampson phoned every day. "I been rodeoin' all these years," he'd tell her, "and I don't have a girl, that's all I'm missing. I need somebody to love." After getting bucked off at the Cow Palace, his last-ditch attempt to make the NFR, Sampson caught the next flight to Seattle. Five years later they were married.

Missing the Finals stung Sampson deeply, all the more for feeling he'd been cheated of his chance. True, his injury had cost him. But he still would have made it, Sampson was sure, had some pinch-faced judges not connived against him. He caught their drift at the Fat Show in Fort Worth early that '79 season:

"The first go-round, I rode my bull for seventy-three points. My next bull, I make a great ride for eighty points and

I win second in that go-round. Now I'm winning the average—this little black kid they don't even know, he's winning this big rodeo.

"The final round comes along, I make a great bull ride, and by overall score I'm the champion. So they give me the plaque. But as I go to walk out of the arena, they come back from the judges' room, and they've moved a bull rider named Ken Henry up or they moved me down, and he beat me by one point for the average." When Sampson handed back the plaque he nearly cried.

It was Sampson's first raw deal in the PRCA, though hardly his last. Over the years he'd find the judges' pencils sharper than a bull's horns, and there was no dodging them. Bob Tallman figured Sampson should have won "thirty percent" more than he did. Donnie Gay himself conceded, "When Charley started, he was not getting the points he should have been." In many towns, Sampson found, the color of money was white.

Bull riders spat on alibis even when they were real, and Sampson refused to gripe. When rider friends called him "Buckwheat," he laughed right along: "If you take it too serious, how you going to be around somebody?" As late as the '91 Finals, he'd still hewed to the cowboy code. It was Myrtis who'd blazed the trail and borne the brunt of it, he'd insist. Sure, there were "mean people" in the stands and the towns, but at the rodeos themselves, he'd "never had any incidents."

It was only this evening, as he treated his leg at the Gold Coast, that Sampson finally let loose. "I'm learning to speak out against prejudice," he said. "I never understood it because I never dealt with it. Now that I'm older, now that I've looked at what I've been through—did judges ever cheat me? I never felt that, but now that I look at it, I think they might have.

"This is what they instill in white minds: a black person is second-class, a black person's a slave, a black person cleans house—a white person tells a black person what to do. Now you got that instilled in you, how you gonna feel that we're equal?"

Now Sampson took exception to put-downs of his flop and pop, his flash dance of arm and body. Over the years, the buzz was that Sampson boosted his scores by "dressing up" his bulls. For the record, he wasn't the first. The tradition dated to the "freight train" rides of Marvel Rogers, who'd blow smoke rings from a gold-holdered stogie at the peak of his bull's jump. Black cowboys had good reason to pour it on, noted Cleo Hearn, a calf roper of Rogers's era who now produced rodeos for "cowboys of color": "No matter how good we are, we know we got to do something to be better. We wake up every morning and have to prove ourselves, just to be equal."

Like writers and divas, bull riders take attacks on their style real personal. Donnie Gay earned a Ph.D. in body English; with a jump to go he'd let the bull suck him back to the end of his rope, losing just enough control—face contorted, veins a-poppin'—to sling off at the whistle as if shot from a gun. He got countless first-place checks on third-place bulls, but no one dared question Gay's scores, least not to his face.

"They say I flop and pop—well, I'm just one!" Sampson said. "There's ten million white cowboys, how do they ride? They don't flop and pop? They categorize Clint as riding great, and Tuff as riding great—they categorize all the white guys as riding great. But I'm a flop-and-popper. The black guy's wrong, the white guy's right."

Was the racial atmosphere any clearer, any fairer now than a decade ago?

Sampson pondered this some long seconds. He might have been thinking of Marvel Rogers, who'd find his boots pissed in and his bedding set afire; of Myrtis Dightman, who'd sometimes last for ten seconds and more, the horn held by a spiteful timer till the strong man finally surrendered. Or of Ervin Williams, the soft-spoken bull rider menaced just the year before in Vegas by a Louisiana steer wrestler. Williams's crime: addressing a white woman at the Stardust.

In 1992, the age of Michael Jordan and Barry Bonds, less than 2 percent of the PRCA's membership was black. That July Cleo Hearn had counted thirteen black cowboys among 1,150 contestants at Cheyenne's "absolutely open contest"— or three more than at his first appearance there, twenty-seven years before. And for some, it appeared, thirteen were yet too many. Here was a scrawl from inside the men's room at Cheyenne's best hotel: "*NIGGER* COWBOYS? THAT'S ALL, BROTHER!"

"Hell, no," Sampson said at last. Weightily, wearily. "And that's a *hell*, no—not just a no. It hasn't got no better."

CHAPTER 11

Little Big Man

AFTER LOSING 1980 TO AN-
other broken leg, Sampson came back strong the next season.
He easily made the Finals, even won a go-round; it was the
time of his life. Now Sampson understood why cowboys
pushed themselves without sleep to faceless burgs in Montana
and Saskatchewan. The Finals made it all worthwhile.

"This is your reward," he said. "You go to all those different rodeos and nobody knows who you are. Then you come
here, you get that NFR number on your back, you get that
NFR jacket, and you know you're the one they come to see.
You're a star for ten days, and it's a pretty good feeling."

Sampson finished the year ranked fourth, behind Denny
Flynn, the silken stylist from Arkansas; Bobby DelVecchio, the
Bronx bomber; and Donnie Gay. All three were big-name veterans, but only one concerned Sampson as he opened his '82
season. Flynn wasn't hungry enough to stop him, and
DelVecchio wasn't good enough. To beat Donnie Gay was to
win the world. It was that simple, and that hard.

Gay was the compleat cowboy, and a throw-out-the-mold original. While just a fair athlete, he prevailed with pig-iron grit and a flair for clutch performances. They said there were two ways to make sure that Donnie would ride his bull that night. One was to roll the TV cameras. The other was to tell him he couldn't do it.

Gay was seven years old when he first met Monty Henson at a Little League practice. This was how he said hello: "I'm

Donnie Gay, and I'm going to be the world champion bull rider." When your mother died when you were a toddler, and Neal Gay was your dad and Jim Shoulders your baby-sitter ("He was everything I wanted to be"), there wasn't much coddling in your life. Young Donnie was raised at the family's Mesquite Championship Rodeo arena, just east of Dallas, and turned bull crazy at a tender age. He might get on three dozen for practice in the space of two hours, and when he got bucked off or stepped on, his father wasn't big on sympathy. "You got your ass up and you didn't say anything," said Henson, who was there every day. "That was just the way things were."

Gay hit the trail the day he graduated from high school, and never wired home for money; he was an instant, single-minded success. With his rocker's hairstyle, wild shirts, and wilder stories, he was also the life of each party he crashed. Nobody danced later, joked louder, or brawled braver. Gay always anted up, and he wasn't fond of folding. He liked to fight and was meaner than most opponents, which meant that he usually won. "Gettin' pissed off," he observed, "is way better than gettin' pissed on."

Once Gay and his travel mates stopped at a saloon in Great Falls—"and Montana bars were the worst in the world," he recounted. "It was, 'Who Shit in Your Saddle Bags?' by Gene Autry. There wasn't a guy in there whose hands weren't this big, and there wasn't a girl that weighed under three hundred pounds."

Featured live that night was some older gent in formal wear, who sang almost too bad to be funny. As Gay and company loaded back in their car, one of the cowboys shouted something ugly at the locals. "This fat girl walked over and reached through the back window," Gay went on, "and she hit me right at the end of the nose, like to knocked me out. I went absolutely berserk. I crawled out of that car through the window and I drilled her. Now here comes the guy in the tuxedo, and he's pulled his coat open and he's got a thirty-eight stuck down his cummerbund, and that old fat girl she's a cryin', and my nose is hurtin' and my eyes are waterin'—and I had gone nuts."

The man glared at Gay and said, "Boy, I'm fixin' to blow you away."

And Gay said, "You better get to blowin', you fat son of a bitch." He snatched the gun and emptied its chamber into the parking lot while his buddies scattered like quail. Gay slapped the singer once for good measure, and moved on to the next town.

As Gay understood it, that was the point of fighting, or riding, or checkers: to win, every time, at any cost. Nobody lusted to win worse than Donnie Gay. His ego was big as his heart, and his heart had a few extra ventricles. Like Muhammad Ali, his boyhood hero, Gay loved to boast he was the greatest, then back it up. "Take a good look," he told Gary Leffew as he brandished his first gold buckle, in 1974. "That's just the hill on the way to the mountain."

Gay climbed that mountain every day, whatever it took. He might stay out half the night, but he'd sweat whiskey with the Jane Fonda workout at seven the next morning. He was a man obsessed. One year he went to 188 rodeos, catching sleep in his private plane or wolfing diet pills over the road. He'd appear in twenty cities in eleven days, dizzy and sore—and then he'd nod his head and look fresh as the morning paper.

More amazing still, Gay somehow saved his best efforts for the Finals, where healthier men wore down and out. Like Shoulders before him and Tuff to come, he rode the rankest bulls under the worst conditions. In 1979 Gay came to Oklahoma City with sixty-three fresh stitches in his side. In 1980 he tore some ribs but bounced back to win the following night. In 1981 he got mauled into a hospital bed by the bull of the year, and never skipped a beat. Gay opened 1982 defending a string of four straight titles and seven in eight years.

"He had a stranglehold on the championship," Sampson recalled. "Nobody believed they could beat him." Yet Sampson believed. His otherness now worked for him; he felt no need to bow before the king. He had one goal: to win the gold buckle. And there was one man blocking his path. "I ain't saying I had any animosity toward him, but it was like a vendetta—like a grudge," Sampson said. "I was not gonna let this man beat me like he had beat me before."

To strike the proper frame of mind, Sampson convinced himself that Gay won because he worked the system so well—wowing the fans, lobbying the judges. "He was the one they all felt was the best rider," Sampson noted, "and I said, 'Bullshit! If those bulls don't buck me off, how's Donnie Gay goin' to beat me? I'm better than Donnie Gay!'" But to get the world to agree, Sampson would not merely have to ride better. He would have to *style* better, blitz Gay at his own garish game. He'd wave his hands higher after jumping off a bull. Hurl his hat nearer the clouds. Smile till they could see his wisdom teeth.

And the funny thing was, it worked. In 1982 Sampson broke out on top of the standings and never looked back. He drew money bulls as if blessed, rode them as though possessed. On the rare days he fell off, Sampson's sleep would be troubled by Gay's mocking face—*Comin' at you, cowboy!*—and he would bounce back the next day, more urgent than ever.

Sampson was twenty-five years old, at his absolute physical peak. He ran every day; his body responded, fought off any hurt. By midyear he'd picked up a partner in Ted Nuce, then a bubbly youngster striving to make his first Finals. With Sampson at the helm, the pair crisscrossed the map, driving all night to shoot for a few hundred dollars—and a few hundred points toward the title.

"What are we going back *here* for?" Nuce would wonder as they gunned for Deadwood or Elk City or Wahoo, Nebraska.

"We're going to win," Sampson would reply. "I know where I'm going: I'll be number one, and I'll get you to the Finals. We're going to beat Donnie Gay—Donnie Gay can't beat me *and* you. This man can be beat! We're the hot men, we're the hot men now!"

It didn't hurt that Gay was disabled, on and off, with a groin that finally ripped in August like a rotten rubber band—"playing that cripple game," as the dry-eyed Sampson put it. Now that Gay was down, the arrogant champ with the shamrock chaps got as much compassion as the Damn Yankees in decline. The public was primed for a fresh story line. Sampson was the right character at the right time—a jockey-sized acrobat from Watts topping the fiercest bulls and steamrolling the competition, a hero irresistible for being so unlikely. After each wondrous ride he bowed to the crowd, and the fans roared back, and the judges were swept up in the high rising tide. And if Sampson got screwed in the scoring, the crowd's booing would scorch the ears, with a righteous bite that made a judge think twice the next time. But those incidents were few in 1982.

"In a sense, they *wanted* somebody to compete against Donnie Gay. They were needing that in rodeo," Sampson observed. "People were telling me, 'Rodeo ain't got nothing to sell, and all of a sudden you came along.' Everybody got excited about rodeo. Everybody wanted to see this little black guy on a bull. . . . It almost makes you think they set this up."

But they couldn't have set up his riding, which was astonishing that year. When George Michael's *Sports Machine* came to Texas for a bull riding, the TV host was stunned by Sampson's ride on Fort Apache. "That bull had what we call *gas*—the ability to back up, spin, and buck all at one time," Michael said. "But Charles rode—man, Charles rode that thing forever. It was the maximum determination, the maximum effort.

"There are certain rides I keep on a tape at home for inspiration, and that's one of them. And if things aren't so hot, or I need to get psyched about something, I'll watch it—to remind me to get up off my dead butt, and get in there and get the job done."

By the Finals Sampson led his closest pursuer by more than twenty thousand dollars, more than any bull rider had ever won at Oklahoma City. The end game was a formality. But there were still ten rank bulls to ride and survive, and to help get himself through—and repay an old debt—Sampson asked Myrtis Dightman to pull his rope in the chutes.

Dightman, by then retired from riding, still owned a right forearm as flat and wide as a steam iron. He could still pull a rope one-handed and put a bull on its belly. But his greater aid was his patience. After Sampson bucked off early on and lashed himself, Dightman counseled, "Be cool. Don't worry about the one behind you. Worry about them in front of you, that you haven't been on yet." Sampson settled and placed fourth in the average.

He wrapped up the crown by winning the ninth go-round on a cream-colored, one-horned, twenty-four-hundred-pound monster called Gallon of Velvet, so big it required two chutes. Sampson boarded his tenth and last bull in a trance: "I didn't care if I rode or not. All I wanted to do was get off safe."

"I'm proud," Dightman said, as he watched the press mob his protégé. "A black man has won." *If you try, you can do it, and if you* really *try, people will help you do it.* More than the new champ himself, Dightman knew what odds had been whipped.

The night Sampson got his gold buckle, he wore it to bed with him. It wasn't good for sleeping but it was *there,* strapped to his middle, a heavy-metal monument to how far he'd come. No one could take this one away from him. They'd have to kill him first.

As Sampson's fame rippled into the national talk-show circuit, something was rubbing him wrong. He kept getting introduced as the first *black* world champion. For one who'd lived so long in cowboy culture, where a man bears credit or blame for every step he takes, the label stole his very self.

Sampson could think of just one thing to do. He would win another title, "to show that they didn't give me this because I was black. More than anything, to show myself, because I was puzzled. What did I actually do? It was so easy, my first championship." He added wryly: "And since then it's been so brutal, man, I'm glad I got the one."

The 1983 season began in misery and plunged downhill from there. A broken leg in February, a concussion in May. Slowly Sampson climbed into the top fifteen. In September he won the Pendleton Round-Up, then placed in Albuquerque. The magic was rushing home to him. "I could just feel it starting to happen," he'd say. "That time of year I always get hot."

In October Sampson broke from his regular schedule for a command performance before President Ronald Reagan in Landover, Maryland. He carried with him an NFR jacket, sewn with Reagan's name above his own, to present to the old B-movie cowboy after he rode. It would be the high point of his life.

But Sampson never made it to the presidential box. He began to worry when he drew Kiss Me, a big white Charbray. Landover was supposed to be stocked with no-sweat, "banana pen" bulls. But the contractor, seeking his own splash, had crossed the riders up. Kiss Me, in particular, was a hooky, jerk-down terror. The bull was so dangerous that Sampson had turned it out the year before.

This time he had no graceful option but to cowboy up. With the rodeo running late, they rushed riders behind the chutes that night. Sampson slid up on his rope, took his deep hold, and called, "Let's go!" It was truly remarkable that he'd remember what happened next.

"That bull left so hard, so quick and strong, that I couldn't believe it. If I'd known he had that kind of power, I would have taken my time, no matter who was in the audience. He threw me a belly roll, and he stretched me out on the first jump. . . . I lifted, tried to gather up to get hold of him, but he jerked me down so fast and hard, I couldn't even get my free arm in front to push off. I mean I never *ever* got whipped down like that."

As he lay flat in the dirt, Sampson sensed the bullfighters kneeling over him, heard foggy snatches of their voices as they tried to stem his shock. *You're gonna be all right. . . . It's just a gash over your eye.*

But Donnie Gay, five chutes away, knew different as soon as he heard the hollow impact: "He's hurt *bad!*"

Sampson's face had smashed square into the ball of Kiss Me's skull, so hard that the man's forehead caved half an inch into his cranium. The doctors would refer to "a four-point injury" with "multiple shock trauma"—which is to say that Sampson's face imploded. Both orbital rims above his eyes were badly fractured. So was his lower jaw. His sinuses were shattered, and the first concern of Reagan's personal physician, on hand for the event, was to keep the cowboy breathing.

Four specialists labored that night to piece Sampson back together. He was lucky, the doctors would tell him straight-faced; he'd avoided meningitis, and he'd kept all his teeth. And somehow, in anatomical irony, his nose was unbroken.

The only person Sampson knew on the East Coast was George Michael, who took him into his Maryland home. There the cowboy rested, his jaw wired shut, a six-week Metrecal diet paring him to 108 pounds. Now he saw how fragile it all was. As Sampson told the *Sports News:* "One year you can have all the glory, and the next year you can have hell."

For all that, he was unsinkable. As his convalescence dragged on he took to "riding" in Michael's rec room, posting forward in his chair, his old energy streaming. Ten weeks after his accident, Sampson returned to the National Finals. He was no longer known as the first black world champion. Now he was *the black bull rider who survived near-death in the face of the president.* He'd lost too much time to defend his

title, but somehow beat seven of ten bulls and wound up sixth
in the world.

☆

There are those who'd say Sampson rode even better after
his accident. But it never felt quite the same inside. Sampson
had lost his moment. In 1984, Donnie Gay grabbed back the
headlines by coming out of retirement to win his eighth title.
Sampson finished second that year, but no one noticed. He
was black and talented and quotable, a maker of history. And
by 1984 he was also old news. "Time had already passed me
by," he said. "They didn't ease me down—they just cleared
me off and took me away. They couldn't sell rodeo with a
black person, because it's the only sport they have, they
think—the only sport in this country that blacks haven't dominated."

It didn't help that he kept getting hurt. He could hardly
remember all the wounds, the blur of torn knees and bruised
kidneys, of one dazed, rattled head after the next. He was
slogging uphill now, against age and expectation and judges
who never liked him much anyway. Of late it had seemed that
he just could not win: "Not that I wasn't trying—*they would
not let me win*. 'Charles Sampson is no longer the bull rider he
thinks he is,' in their eyes. 'Charles Sampson should *quit* riding bulls.'"

Then, too, there were other things on his mind. Shortly
after the 1987 Finals, Sampson was home in Arizona, moving
sand in the back of a pickup. Marilyn was inside; their three-
year-old son, L. C., was up on a bucking barrel about twenty
feet away. As Sampson backed his truck up the driveway, he
never saw the little boy dash behind him. He only felt an awful
bump: of a large tire passing over a small head.

The brain damage was severe and permanent, the doctors
told them in Phoenix, after L. C. came out of his coma.
Charles and Marilyn wouldn't believe it, *couldn't* believe it. At

a rodeo five months later, Sampson pointed at the bulls and urged his son, "Get him, get him, ride that bull!" And L. C. raised one hand like a tiny rider, and started spurring with his legs, and only then did his parents know for certain that the boy's brain was still there.

Who could weigh the father's guilt? "It was just the worst thing that could happen," said George Michael. "Marilyn called and said, 'You got to talk to Charles.' Well, what could I say? It was his *son*. There was nothing I could say except 'God does not punish children. It was an accident. It happened. You've got to get on with your life.' But sometimes you just can't."

Cowboys aren't much for wills or insurance, and Sampson had to get back and rodeo to pay for L. C.'s special needs. He cracked out as hard as his battered body allowed, maybe harder. Sampson was never home anymore. To some it seemed he was running from the pain in his life, but he never got far. There was a hum that nagged him from morning shower to his pillow at night. It stopped only inside the chute and for eight seconds after, when the cowboy's throbbing heart drowned it out.

Sampson's vices—the roads he drove too fast, the beer he drank too freely, the women who lingered—made as if to consume him. Even his best traits wound out of control. After winning the Cow Palace in 1989, days after the Bay Area earthquake, he signed over his four-figure check to the Red Cross, right there at the presentation—a costly impulse for a man who could scarcely pay his feed bills.

Fact was, he'd nearly skipped the Cow Palace that year. After Cheyenne he'd lost any love he had left for the business. Not *Lane*, Sampson moaned when the phone call came to Casa Grande. They'd talked just days before: "Lane had just come back from breaking his jaw, and he said, 'Charles, between me and you, we could write a book on injuries!' And I said, 'I know, Lane. If you ain't getting hurt, I'm getting hurt.' We was just kidding around, you know? We was always kidding.

"I was really, really, really, *really* hurt. I just went outside and fed my horses, and cried and cried and cried. It makes you look at what you do and wonder why you do it. I almost gave up rodeoin' in '89."

Every time Sampson thought of Frost he'd cuss into the next day. He got so he couldn't read the sports section, couldn't stand to hear of one more million-dollar free agent who'd yet to hit two-fifty. What was he doing? Why let those damn bulls abuse you?

Sampson had no answer, except to keep going, to "dig way down, because it's tough." To dig into yourself, because that *was* the answer, to find that hard part of you that would never give in.

Back in the hotel room, it was twenty-three hours and counting till the Finals' first go-round. Pastor Craig finished his sermon. Sampson peeled the electrodes from his leg. "I accept that this is the end," he said evenly. He was ready to become a businessman. He'd pour his energies into Bull Riders International and rove the globe as a cowboy ambassador. He'd push his luck no further. This would be his final Finals, the last ten bulls of his career.

Forty thousand dollars behind top-ranked Cody Custer, Sampson held out little hope to win the world. But there was still the NFR average—one of the few buckles to elude him— and piles of money for the taking. Sampson had always won at least one go-round at the Finals, a streak he took pride in. First-place money now exceeded eleven thousand dollars, which would shut up a lot of lenders.

And Sampson was prepared to be happy with less than that. Ten years after his breakthrough in Oklahoma City, he was a lion in winter. The old fire was damped. Now he aimed to "just survive it, and know deep in my heart that I honestly tried every bull I got on—that I wasn't afraid, I wasn't letting go."

He hadn't touched a bull in two months. He'd hardly worked out, and now he'd be tackling the rankest animals on the continent. During the season he'd picked and chosen his draws, turning out bulls with too much drop. At the Finals he'd have to show up every night. And many were those who doubted he'd make it through.

J. Pat Evans had warned Sampson that one awkward dismount—not to mention a bull's hoof—could snap the plates in his leg. "The metal will fatigue," the doctor noted. "It's just like if you take a coat hanger and bend it and bend it, and it finally breaks."

People looked at Sampson and saw a glass chin spoiling to shatter, with a forehead to match. A PRCA official likened him to a boxer who'd "been hit too many times, and it doesn't take a lot to knock him out. I don't want to put a hex on him, but there's a good chance he'll only ride once."

But the opinion Sampson cared about belonged to an eight-year-old boy. Five years after the accident, L. C. was thriving in school, teasing his little brother, zipping about in his walker. "He has a real life," Sampson said. "He's learning how to walk again—it just hasn't clicked in his mind that if he can take two or three steps, he can take another."

When your child makes miracles daily, it stretches your sense of the possible. Your days are inspired. If a boy could walk with a damaged brain, couldn't a bull rider win with a crushed leg? "He's overcome a lot—he's been through a lot more than I have," Sampson said of his son. "It's a battle for both of us just to show each other we're tough. He still wants to get on my back, and I can't let him know that daddy's got a sore leg. So I tell him, 'I can carry you, but I want you to walk, too—get your balance, get your balance, you can walk!'

"I'm here at the Finals financially embarrassed and injured. But I think I deserve to be here. I *know* I deserve to be here.

I'm riding on faith. Over the last three years, that's all I've been riding on."

He glanced at a list of bulls who'd be tested the next two nights. They were famous names in the trade: Dillinger, Kowabunga, Okeechobee Fats. The Finals, he mused, was "a good show, nothin' like it." He looked up with his old cocky grin. It was good to belong again, to ride with the best in the world. "Nothin' to it," Sampson said, breaking into a youthful laugh, "but just to do it!"

Sampson was pleased with his first two draws: Badlands and Skoal Tea Party. "I don't want to say they're easy—you hang around and they'll come after you, I guarantee—but they ain't gonna buck me off and *look* for me," he said. Best of all, both bulls normally turned and spun to the left, which would spare his hampered left leg. To hold his position he'd be squeezing with his right, outside the spin.

Earlier that day Sampson had greeted his fellow entrants at the arena and stood in line for the formalities—the bull riders' group picture, still photos for ESPN's file. He gave his autograph to a trio of barrel racers, joshing, "I'm here for a great time, not a long time, so enjoy me while you can." By late afternoon his limp had worsened, but his front never wavered.

"How ya feelin'?" a steer wrestler asked him.

"I'm feelin' a whole lot better," Sampson replied.

"You gonna be all right?"

"A little tape, a few aspirins, I'll be all right," Sampson said.

Positive thinking had its limits, though. The rust was plain when Sampson bucked off those first two bulls. He felt off-balance, out of rhythm. His free-arm moves, once instinctive, now demanded the briefest thought. In that split instant he'd lag a beat behind the bull's vortex, and the syncopation did him in.

It had to be frustrating. Yet each time Sampson trudged back to the dressing room, towing his belled rope behind him, smiling with relief that his leg hadn't crumpled. "I got a *lot* of encouragement," he'd say. "I'm just thankful I could get up and walk away."

He was riding great, Ted Nuce would assure him, until he'd stiffened up, or gotten too far over, or. . . . Sampson would weigh the words and head back to his hotel. He wasn't in Vegas to party, not this year.

On the fourth day Sampson left his room early for the Exceptional Rodeo. His partner was Raymond Freeman, an eight-year-old Las Vegan born without a left hand. Sampson cheered the child through a seesaw bull ride, and a wooden steer to be wrestled with a kick. When Raymond seemed upset after his rope missed a stationary calf, Sampson gently pushed him to hang in: "You can do it, Raymond! I *know* you can do it!" On his next throw the boy nailed his target.

"Some people look at these children and see only that they have problems," Sampson said afterward. "But I look at them and see that they are blessed, because I am also blessed. . . . You have to play the cards you've been dealt, and find out what in life is meant for you."

That night Sampson made the whistle but was goose-egged for whacking the rubbery hump of Arnie's Skoal with his right forearm. He managed to find humor in it: "You can't ride *every* bull with one hand!"

The fifth go-round featured the dread eliminators. Sampson's draw was a speckle-bellied Braford named Eli's Bandit. The bull burst out of the chute with three twisting leaps to the left, like some carousel gone haywire, and Sampson was in trouble from the gun. By the second jump the tiny rider was sliding a foot up and down the bull's loose hide, a bad sign. By the third jump he was getting whipped off to the right, outside the spin. To save himself, he knifed his free right arm up and sideways over his head.

It was the perfect move—except that Eli's Bandit chose that moment to reverse field, to the right. Now Sampson found himself whipped off to the left, worse than before. His weak left leg slid under the bull's belly. His shoulder caromed off the loosely roped exit gate. For two terrible seconds Sampson rode sideways, his torso parallel to the ground. It was time for any sane man to relent, as the next jump might send him upside down, his head among the cloven hooves.

Those two seconds showed the difference between bull riders and the rest of us. Sampson's left hand stayed fixed to its wrap. He would not let go to fight another day, for he had too few days left . . . and somehow he made it. The bull straightened, the break Sampson needed to hop back to base. Eli's Bandit had run out of moves, and the last few seconds were routine, a zigzag skittering to the horn. Sampson slid to the ground, his good leg taking the impact.

"What a recovery!" Tallman shouted from up above the chutes. Sampson received the great whooping roar of the fans—*his* fans, once more—by throwing his arms wide, as if to hug everyone in the joint. His grin spread to bare his seven false teeth and a dozen or more real ones.

Though he placed out of the money, Sampson was one of only five men to make the whistle that night. For George Michael it was a sweet reminder of great moments: "He'll never bail out—he just doesn't do that. He should have been thrown off and slammed into the gate. He should have been destroyed. There was no reason for him to hustle up and finish. But there's that talent and heart and desire." It was a ride, Michael figured, that just "might propel him to better things."

Two nights later Sampson drew Blue Bonnett Palace, the Cadillac-sized bull that had killed T. R. Sprague and bullied Clint Branger out of fifteen thousand dollars. It was a match made in rodeo hell. No bull going had more downdraft, and no rider was more prone to a "facial." Sammy Andrews counted the notches on his prize bucker's belt: "At Phoenix last year, he whipped Wacey Cathey down and busted him across the face. He wiped out Wade Leslie at Jackson. And he damn near got Clint Branger in Guthrie." Andrews didn't mention T. R. Sprague.

Sampson checked with Branger about the bull, absorbed the bad news, then promptly forgot it: "I wanted to have a positive outlook, and you have to block all those things out." When Sampson bumped into Cody Lambert, another rider down on his NFR luck, he pronounced, "Cody, we're gonna win the bull riding. You win second and I win first." It wasn't offhand; he really felt it.

Sampson was game-faced in the locker room that night. As the time approached he swapped his dental plate for a mouthpiece, then picked up his rope and moved into the corridor. Sammy Andrews collared him there with a storm watch. "Now pay attention," the contractor cautioned. "If you know you're gone, get the hell out of there." Sampson nodded politely and walked on. If he could ride the bull, there was no problem, and if he couldn't. . . . *Please, God, keep me strong.*

Inside the chute he pounded his wrap, and then, without fuss or delay, he nodded. Blue Bonnett Palace came out bucking in no special direction, all ill will and oblique angles. It gave three head fakes for every jump, flounced its massive crown about like a nervous stakes horse—if a horse had baseball bats curling above its ears. Sampson stayed deftly centered, but his job kept getting harder. Each kick was slightly higher, each landing that much heavier. By the end the bull's rear legs would be looping five feet off the ground, its front dropping so hard that you pitied the dirt.

Sampson countered by flinging his free arm straight back past his shoulder. His new rope was taut and stable. He felt finely tuned and flowing, but he couldn't help that he was five-foot-four. He couldn't help that his face skimmed ever closer to the tossing skull.

"Charlie, stay away from his head!" Tallman cried, as Marilyn Sampson prayed from her seat among the riders' wives. "Charlie, sit up, sit up, sit up, sit *up*, Charlie!"

Bull riders will tell you that some rides fly by and others crawl into the next week. Blue Bonnett Palace was a slow boat for Sampson. But when it was over he'd miss that bull, and the inhuman power he'd shared.

"*Eighty-six points!*" Tallman crowed after scanning the judges' number boards. "Oh, boy! *That's* the Charlie Sampson we've been waiting for!" On his victory lap Sampson took an easy canter on a pretty paint horse, waving his hat to the crowd like a beauty queen. There'd been times that year, more than a few, when he thought he'd never make that round again.

"What did I tell you?" Sampson bellowed to Cody Lambert, who'd earned an eighty but failed to place. The winner briskly stripped the double tape job and elastic bandage from his leg. He squeezed out of a hot-pink truss, a cowboy's best bet against groin pulls. And he smiled—modestly, as one who'd been there before—to accept the locker-room praise of his peers: "All right, Chuck!" "Good bull ride!"

As Blue Bonnett Palace bucked in slow motion on tape, the room hushed. Donnie Gay—no, he was a more dignified *Don* Gay now, champion emeritus and up-and-coming stock contractor—was struck by the slivered daylight between rider's chin and bull's head: "He's trying to *bring* you there!"

Sampson carefully pulled his jeans up over his legs. He was glowing shyly, like a soft-white bulb. To no one in particular, he said, "I seem to amaze myself."

Back at the Gold Coast, he and Marilyn took a back-door route to the Saloon, with Bart Walczak, a former tight end for the San Diego Chargers, running interference. The gang was all there. "Is this the greatest thing that ever happened?" bubbled Patrick O'Donnell, a Bull Riders International partner who spoke in exclamation points. He threw his arms around Sampson: "We did it, man! We rode that sucker!"

As Sampson awaited the ceremony and his go-round buckle (as always, bull riding came last), he found backstage haven in a small, cluttered dressing room. He parked heavily on a chair under a row of vanity lights. As adrenaline ebbed, the leg took to throbbing again. Sampson tapped his good foot to the beat of the band as it finished its set. And he took to talking, in a white-water rush of vindication.

"Nine years I've been to the Finals and won a go-round each year," he said. "I knew if I was patient, something would work out. I knew it, I just knew I could do it! I really felt strong tonight. That bull had a reputation, but I said, 'No, no, no—no more pain. Things are going too good for me.'"

It was Sampson's turn. He rose to stand behind the curtain, holding Marilyn's hand. Tallman, he of the handlebar mustache and Hawaiian tan, rambled into his prologue at the mike: "Here come this little black cat walkin' out of Watts, he weighed ninety-five pounds and his riggin' bag weighed a hundred and two. . . ."

Then Sampson came out, and the announcer turned it up a peg. "Charles Sampson," Tallman boomed, "we've punched his lights out a dozen times, broke his face, tore his ear off—I was there, I saw it. When I saw his draw tonight, I said, 'All right, we'll just kill him, it'll be over.'" Hearty laughter from the sardined crowd. "'We'll just kill him, get a half-size coffin, it's gonna be a cheap funeral, and that'll be it.'

"But you got by, you rode the bull, you get the buckle, it's a hell of a story—" And at that point even Tallman couldn't compete with the cheers that poured over the stage. It was an indelible moment—as close as Sampson had come to reliving the glory of '82, as close as he'd ever come again.

When they added things up they'd mark Sampson down for just one gold buckle. But his name would ring as loud as Shoulders's, or Mahan's, or Gay's. Because Charles Sampson won a title every time he nodded his head, whether ninety points or none—every time he threw his hands to the air for the crowd, *his* crowd, and seemed so much bigger than life.

As the music resumed, Sampson turned to his wife and asked, "Do you want to go back the way we came, or go out front?" Out front bobbed a beery sea of two-steppers and backslappers, of good old buddies who'd never really know him, of strangers who would point and shout his name.

"It's your night, baby," Marilyn said.

With Walczak clearing the way, Sampson strode forward. His chest puffed out. His limp was gone. "Let's go," he said, "and face the public."

CHAPTER 12

God and Country

*E*VERY YEAR WAS TOUGH FOR Clint Branger, even when things seemed in surface order, as in 1992. Black eyes aside, Branger had stayed injury free. He'd ridden superbly ever since he came off his two-week drunk in January, soft and jittery, to win a big jackpot in Phoenix. From July on he'd swamped the competition, jockeying with Cody Custer for top seed in the standings while knocking off rank ones like skeet.

But Branger's best season was also his worst of times. He was building a log house on his parents' spread in Roscoe, and took a pricey ride with a bad-news contractor. Then he broke off with his longtime fiancée. Bull riders tend to put their personal lives on automatic pilot, but sometimes the pilot malfunctions. As Branger ran like a loose goose from one crisis to the other, he had to keep cracking out, keep bearing down to make money, with nary a day to step back and breathe. Rodeo was less of a lark, more of a grudge match. It had been heading that way ever since Lane Frost died, but now it was worse. Now Branger hardly loved it even when he won.

Through it all the next Finals haunted him, closed in with each passing week. Some days Branger could hardly wait for it. Some days it scared him to death. If he didn't win the gold buckle this time around, he told the *Sports News* in September, "I won't look at it as the end of the earth. I'm ready to go to the Finals and have fun for the first time. I'm sick of going there and being all stressed out. . . . I'm not looking at it as a life-and-death situation."

When Donnie Gay caught wind of these remarks, he flared as if Branger had spit on his lizard-skinned boots and disrespected his mama. Here was bull-riding blasphemy—not that Gay bought it for one minute. "Not winning a world title's *okay?*" Gay said, at his rodeo in Palestine, Texas. "That's a dodge—that's just an excuse to pad the collision when it don't happen. He's sittin' there goin', 'Damn, I want it so bad I can taste it.'"

That Branger hadn't yet copped a title was a puzzlement to Gay. When he studied the Montanan in action, he saw a natural to match Denny Flynn, except that he liked Branger's style even better, "because we're the same size, and he does those little finesse things that I couldn't do—being completely limber, turning your toes out." But as Gay pointed out, "Pretty don't always get it."

Yet Gay found himself pulling for the man. In his view there was just one rider who had "the ability and toughness and winning values to beat Tuff and Sharp, and that's Branger. Cody Custer, he's a nice guy, but in my mind he ain't supposed to win." In Gay's two-toned world there were contenders and pretenders, the ones who weren't up to snuff. When a pretender won the championship Gay felt let down, as if the win devalued his gold buckles, the totems he'd spun his world around. Barring a long-shot charge by one of his partners, Branger was the only one who could make the season's story come out right.

Which by no means guaranteed he'd prevail—especially if he didn't "drop all this bullshit that all he's trying to do is have fun," Gay fumed. "If a man's goal is not to win a world title—'That would be nice, but second's all right'—he's gonna have to be luckier than a dog with two dicks to win one. I got no respect for somebody like that."

Gay meant his blast to get back to Branger, to sting the man into a more bull-riderly frame of mind. It stung, all right, and Branger shot back. "If I'm happy doing what I'm doing, I'm going to win the buckle—and if people don't like my attitude, that's—just—too—bad," he said, incensed. "Donnie won eight titles, so he can say whatever he wants now, and I respect the hell out of him. But if he's got a problem with my attitude, tell him to get his rope out. I don't care if he's thirty-five. Just strap it on a bull, let's go to it."

As he headed into Vegas, picked by Tuff as the man to beat, Branger told the press that he'd cleared his head of distractions. "To hell with the house," he said. "To hell with the relationship. I'm going to use the next ten days to do the best I can." Real life could wait.

Then again, it could be hard to tell real life from rodeo. Bull riding still drove Branger, and it was hard to imagine himself a family man—to have that "other life that I want to have"—while chasing his rope and his grail.

Branger was back in his Gold Coast suite after the first go-round and another glum Finals start. His bull had been clumsy, banged into the chute and wallowed about. ("Just kind of like me," Tuff observed. "Big, fat, and slow.") Branger scored a sixty-eight, and the judges sinned by denying a reride. Still, it was good to get by that first one and settle the nerves. And besides, the new Clint Branger took setbacks in stride. Except for the one that faced him at this minute past midnight, with a Patrick Swayze adventure kabooming on TV: Branger was out of chew.

"If it was just sitting there and I knew it was there, I wouldn't need it as bad," he explained. "But now that I know that I can't have it this hour, I can't have it next hour, I can't have it till *tomorrow*—that really makes me want it as bad as anything. It makes me mad, because I knew I had it in my pocket." He glared at his clean-cut roommate, Ron Kingston, a Montana circuit rider who hired out at the Brangers' cattle ranch and quoted the Bible in argument. "You stole it, didn't you?" Kingston protested his innocence.

Tobacco was the only vice Branger had left. He'd cut back on his Vegas nightlife; he'd wearied of the whole scene, of the cowboys' tough-guy force fields. "It ain't healthy," Branger said. "I guess that's why I've pulled away from bull riding, because everybody's so hard that way. Everybody's so cold about everything. I keep waiting for rodeo to change, but I guess it never will." So he'd resolved to change himself: "I worked very hard to get a reputation as a drinker and carouser and woman user and abuser, but I'm sick of that life. I *hate* it. . . . Patrick Swayze is just kicking ass. What did they do to the kids?"

"They killed half the Boy Scout camp," Kingston answered.

"That's why I'm building my house," Branger continued, "because I know I'm going to have to hang it up someday, and I'm scared if I don't have someplace to come back to, I may wind up just hurting myself." He designed the place with three bedrooms, to say he wouldn't be lonely forever.

In his old knockabout days, Branger didn't care if he used up his body or drained his bank account. Only the buckle mattered. He still yearned to win the world, "but it's not my number-one goal anymore. That buckle ain't gonna build a house, and it ain't gonna build a family. That buckle can do a lot of things, but it can't make me happy."

You wanted to believe that Branger could write Gay's happy ending. As Bryan McDonald had predicted, "When Clint quits trying to win the world so hard, he'll win it." But the turmoil of Branger's season seemed a shaky basis for a title run in Vegas, a place never kind to him. Earlier that Friday, at a model-home promotion to benefit the Justin Crisis Fund for disabled cowboys, Branger was dutifully signing when a man asked him brusquely, "You gonna win?"

"Hopefully," Branger said, a thin lid on his annoyance. "I'm here, ain't I?" But even as the words filed out he knew they were hollow.

Not that he was the only bull rider in town with something to prove. If Branger's confidence was in question, so was Cody Custer's toughness, Jim Sharp's consistency, and Tuff's ever-more-cynical attitude. Who would best wrestle his weakness to the mat? The next nine days would tell.

As the year wore on, the Carrillo twins seemed less identical. Those who knew them could tell Adam by the mole on his neck and a what-the-hell curl to his lips; Gilbert's face set softer, more serious. Adam could be reckless on a bull—he loved to spur the rank ones—and might count his money before the whistle. Gilbert was cautious and steady and took losing harder. By October, the differences began to tell; Gilbert had locked a Finals berth, while Adam staged a desperate rally to crack the top fifteen. It came down to the last night of the season, at Madison Square Garden's restored rodeo. Adam needed to place first for a ghost of a shot. You could tell how hard he was trying when he got jerked over the top and whirlybirded over the bull's horns before landing with a scraped arm and a dead dream. Only one twin would make the NFR that season.

Gilbert was subdued as he packed his gear in the Garden locker room, Adam silent and pink-faced. Wait till next year, someone said.

"Gonna mow 'em down next year," Gilbert agreed. He exhaled heavily. "Gonna be a whole different story next year." Adam left quickly, whistling an aimless tune as he headed into the urban night.

But the young are resilient. By the next day, as the twins sat down to lunch at a restaurant called the Cowgirl Hall of Fame, Adam fizzed with tourist fever. "Who would ever think me and Gilbert would be here in New York, bein' cowboys in this big ol' city?" he said. "Now we've seen it all."

The twins had figured out what hurt their season: girl trouble. To be specific, a girl Adam met two years before in Odessa, Texas, where the Carrillos went to college. "I always tried to tell Adam that she was too wild for him," Gilbert admonished. "She was a young girl, but she was wild for her age."

"It *was* kind of rocky," Adam conceded.

"She blew Adam away," Gilbert said, giggling into his barbecued-beef sandwich.

"Yes she did, she blew me away," Adam said. He'd ended it in September, and proceeded to win seventeen thousand dollars in four weeks—as much as he'd cashed the whole season to that point. "I guess you could say it was a lesson I learned," he said. "I need to concentrate on the bulls I draw and nothing else—just rodeo, and who cares what people think?"

Come December, Adam managed to share the Finals after all. John Growney found him a flank man's pass, which got him behind the chutes to pull his brother's rope. Midway through the rodeo he was spotted stepping into an elevator at the Gold Coast, wearing a canary-fed smile and a towering blonde on either side. "You caught me," he owned up the next day, then hastened to add: "One was for Gilbert."

Tuff cruised into the Finals in seventh place, his worst seeding ever, more than thirty thousand back of Cody Custer. He'd drawn frigid since Cheyenne, and his pulled groin pained him more than he let on; he wrapped the muscle with a bright red girdle under his Wranglers.

He was keeping busy, as usual. A few hours before the first go-round, Tuff's tongue stuck out in concentration as he worked on the handwritten lists papering the wet bar of his Roman emperor's suite, the place where big names stayed free when they played with hundred-dollar chips. There were twenty tickets to be unearthed and passed on for each night's performance ("I'm Mr. Ticketron"); shirts to be parceled out to fifty cowboys, to push Panhandle Slim's spring line; a room to find for a writer friend; a stack of posters to be autographed for his T-shirt sponsor. Then Tuff would change out of his Dallas Cowboys sweatpants for the model-home promotion, dash to the airport to pick up some new spurs (an old one had popped a button), and head straight to the Thomas and Mack to beat rodeo rush hour.

"It's all work and no play for me," Tuff said. Fighting a summer cold, he gulped some orange juice and cupped a hand over the mouthpiece of his phone, which might as well have been sutured to his ear. "I'm just a big-hearted guy."

Other riders reserved spare hours for naps or quiet time, but Tuff chugged on, following an old law: that it was harder to stop an object in motion. "I can rest when I'm dead," he liked to say.

These days Tuff was extra busy with Professional Bull Riders, a new corporation formed by thirty top cowboys to regulate the independent jackpots, lure sponsors, and ultimately produce its own events. Bull riders were becoming a hot boardroom item. They'd hired Michael Jordan's agent. They'd signed with Bud Light, which had seized the chance to trump arch-rival Coors, exclusive suds sponsor for the PRCA. Coming soon, a national magazine campaign and a series of televised contests. Down the road lay a full-scale bull-riding tour, patterned after Nascar or the pro golfers', with a year-end championship that would pay more than any bull rider had ever won at the National Finals.

Not all of the PRCA's honchos were elated to see a bunch of cowboys setting themselves apart—and outside the honchos' control. Tuff and Cody Lambert, the group's leaders, kept stressing that they weren't attacking the mother ship. In a sport as undermarketed as rodeo, there was room for everyone. And as the top bull riders became bigger, coast-to-coast stars, they would draw a new fan base to PRCA events as well.

"If rodeo is to make it to the year two thousand," declared one abrasive PBR official, since fired, "it's going to be because of us."

Yet there were undeniable points of friction between the bull riders and the PRCA, and at the '92 Finals they surfaced in Jacket Wars. For years every Finals contestant had received, free of charge, a colorful, wool-and-suede NFR jacket made by Rodeo America, a California apparel firm run by a cagey entrepreneur named Bob Bellino. It seemed like a swell deal; the contestants even had their names stitched on the front. And it was, till you figured what Bellino must be netting at 350 bucks a pop in jacket sales to the rodeo public, which would buy replica muslin horse blankets if their heroes were draped in them.

Therein lay the rub. Bellino paid the PRCA a royalty to use the National Finals logo, but declined to make any added payment to the cowboys. For the top bull riders, who'd been riled to see other companies use their names and likenesses without compensation, here was a line to draw. The fifteen riders in Las Vegas would not wear their maroon-and-yellow Rodeo America jackets. They would model instead a red wool and black leather number bearing the logo of Professional Bull Riders, for which they'd be paid a thousand dollars. The jackets were no threat to Giorgio Armani, and a Naugahyde fans' edition would be dumped at cost. But they were showy enough to send a buzz across a casino floor. Deep down, bull riders always knew they were different. Now they wore their uniqueness on their sleeves.

Tuff rode his first two bulls out of the money, just like all the other pigs and goats he'd drawn since summer. He hoped his luck would turn Sunday with John Growney's Cyanide, a big eight-year-old brindle, but the day's early omens weren't good. At blackjack that afternoon some pilgrim doubled down on a hard seventeen, which cost Tuff a winning card and two hundred dollars. Then his Dallas Cowboys won their game but fell short of the spread: another loss. Tuff wasn't superstitious as cowboys went—he brazenly wore yellow, left his hat on his bed—but he started to wonder how ol' Cyanide might perform that night.

As it turned out, Cyanide would buck quite nicely—before he lost his footing and slowed to a fox-trot. The judges, who'd seen more life in their London broils, gave sixty-seven points and a reride. Tuff took the option and concluded his black Sunday on a no-kicking scooter away from his hand, his least favorite kind of bull. He clicked his heels and missed the horn by half a second. Once again, he wouldn't ride all ten.

Though that reride would ultimately cost Tuff the NFR high-average buckle, he refused to second-guess himself: "I'd rather get my ass kicked trying to win than laying down and taking it." But he wasn't above zinging Don Kish when the two met up later at the casino.

"You could see the second jump he was going to be a pig," Kish said, abashed.

"Right," Tuff agreed, beer in hand.

"He had no intention of bucking," Kish said.

"Give him the knife."

"That's a ten-thousand-dollar knife."

"Looks to me like that's a nine-hundred-dollar knife now," Tuff said, citing the canners' going rate.

In the fourth go Tuff drew Dan Russell's Rocky, the '92 bull of the year. The Brangus had bucked off Ty Murray and Wacey Cathey at the Finals the year before, then been shipped to near every big dance since Denver. Rocky wasn't overly big or strong, but he always tried, never scored below the high eighties. Till he pulled a muscle in Salinas, that is, and came into Las Vegas packing a leg. McDonald kept him in the rank pen out of sentiment, and the bull earned seventy-six points with Tuff—eight points shy of the money—on heart alone.

Tuff plucked a money bull for sure the next round: Sammy Andrews's Hard Rock, a big eliminator he'd placed on three times in three tries. "An excellent draw in this pen," Tuff said before his ride. "A lot of kick, roll, action. The only thing I don't care for is he's skittish in the chute. He doesn't stand well, might go upside down."

It wasn't easy for a seventeen-hundred-pound bull to flip backward in a space no bigger than a grave, but Hard Rock gave it his best effort that night. He reared so high and fast—"the bronc mash," the cowboys called it—that the back of Tuff's head socked the iron chute with a sick thud.

"He absolutely couldn't of hit it any harder," said a *Sports Illustrated* photographer shooting a few feet away. "I have never seen anyone get hit like that. I was honestly surprised that he wasn't at the very least knocked cold."

But Tuff had a bull to ride, and a title to defend. When the bells stopped clanging he climbed back on the bull, took a new wrap, and logged a seventy-five and fourth place, his first check at the rodeo. "A *great* night," he'd proclaim. Ignoring the oozing scrape by his right temple, he unwound the tape over his girdle. "I got a loose tooth and a couple knots on my head, other than that I'm all right." He wiggled a canine; the force of the blow had knocked the tooth's cap off.

"You know, you turned white after you hit your head," George Michael informed him on camera.

"I placed—I'm tickled," Tuff said. "I'm happy. I love rodeo."

"You *do* love rodeo, don't you?" asked Michael, seeking reassurance.

"What else is there?" Tuff said. His laugh had no fun in it. He was sixty thousand out of the lead and the clock was ticking. The next night, after yet another dull score, he sat down at a celebrity blackjack tournament at the Rio with a vow: "I'm either gonna finish first or lose it all." He lost it all, the first player out.

But later that night, gambling for real, Tuff built a tidy hill of black chips. "If you win once, you can win twice," he said, pressing his bet. It was one o'clock, time for the Rio's famous Dolores Del Rio Memorial Conga Line. A dozen cocktail waitresses, in skyscraping headdresses and not much else, wound among the casino's tables and lush hanging plants, swinging their hips to some tropical tune.

"There is a God, ladies and gentlemen!" Tuff shouted, as more chips slid his way. The hill was a small mountain; by the time he stood up, close to dawn, he'd be several thousand to the good. And the money was the least of it for Tuff. It was the *winning* that counted, always had.

"This is my town," he bragged, as his hot streak ran on. "They were forgetting this is *my* town."

It was a bad week for bull riders. The third seed coming in, Aaron Semas, got kicked in the head and was mostly useless thereafter. The fourth seed, David Fournier, tore up a knee, tried it once ("The only way they'll keep me out of this is to shoot me"), felt like he *had* been shot, and sat out the rest of the way.

Branger's wounds were less obvious. After he bucked off in the third go-round, Donnie Gay saw danger in the rider's face. He stubbed out his cigarette and sat down next to Branger in the dressing room. "That wasn't the first time you hit the ground and it won't be the last, and you're way too good to let it bother you," Gay told him. "It's good to try, but you're already doing that. Just don't try too hard."

Branger was brutally underscored on a leaping, leaning rocket in the fourth round—"Three blind mice," Gay raged at the judges, "except there's four of them"—and bucked off again in the fifth when the rope slipped from his hand. Each night Branger would sink a little deeper into his hangdog silence and monotoned shirts, his small body folding in on itself, till he was barely visible as he watched the TV replays.

In the sixth round he drew Red Heat, one of Sammy Andrews's nice spinners. Though McDonald rated the bull's chances of throwing him at "less than zero," Branger overrode and fell off. Cody Custer won yet again, and now led him by thirty-nine thousand dollars.

Branger aimed to flee from the arena without a word, but got waylaid by George Michael's crew. "I wish Cody the best," Branger said for the camera. "I know I'm done." At that moment he longed to drive into the desert with a fifth of whiskey. He knew the drill by rote—how the booze would stop tasting bad around the third swig, how oblivion would cover him like a blanket. But Branger never made that drive. He went home to his Bible-toting roommate and a glass of cranberry juice, and then he called it a night.

Night upon glorious night at this Finals, after he'd taken his victory canter and untaped his sore muscles and completed his last sound bite for some thousand-watt radio station, Cody Custer rode an elevator up to the arena's ground level. The skinny Arizonan would hoof down the corridor and into a bright meeting room where he knew he'd find Stacey, his pregnant wife. By the time he got there the nightly Christian fellowship would be breaking into islands of conversation. Custer would slip in discreetly, modestly, as befit a man serving something higher than himself. He'd check in with his parents, collect Stacey, say a few hellos, get back to the hotel.

It never worked.

"You *stud*, you!" a young woman cried. "God bless you!"

"You looked great tonight, honey," grated a second, a middle-aged blackjack dealer in a sequined blouse. "When I saw you limping I was worried, but I knew you were all right, because we all prayed for you last night."

Other bull riders might be gunning for money or prestige. Only Custer rode expressly for God—and for a born-again community who saw in him a chance to spread the Good Word. After Custer won the second go-round, his mother declared that his purpose was too great to be derailed. "Cody can bring the Lord forth to people," Dixie Custer said. "He does it now, but he can do it ten times more by being a world champion. That's why Cody is where he is today, because he needs to be out there proclaiming Christ, *period*."

Most cowboys aren't famous as churchgoers, Sunday mornings being reserved for Our Lady of the Hangover. On the other hand, it didn't seem too bright to be an atheist when the afterlife coiled just eight seconds away, and you'd be hard-pressed to find a bull rider who hadn't mumbled some skyward plea before nodding his head. And if any still squatted on the fence, Custer's blitzkrieg at the '92 Finals was enough to make them look hard at their everlasting future.

In the thirty-four-year history of the NFR, no one had ever won four of the first six go-rounds—until Custer. He had picked up in Vegas where he'd left off the year before with Wolfman. He drew one sweet spinner after the next, like money from home, bulls that matched his style and wouldn't strain his nagging hurts. In the fifth go his luck seemed sure to sputter with Chucker, an out-of-line brindle subbed into the rank pen after another bull got disabled. Then the chute opened, and the big, bad eliminator turned back for the most rhythmic trip of its life—no day off, but no torment, either. Eighty-six points, and another go-round buckle for Custer.

Toward the rodeo's end, Donnie Gay shook down the bull riders for a light for his contraband cigarette. "It's hell to find a match around you healthy little bastards," he crabbed.

"How about Cody Custer's ass?" Tuff said. "I've never seen anything that hot."

Maybe Custer was due for some breaks. When he was seven years old, he lost two younger siblings in a carbon monoxide accident. When he was fifteen, his father fell from a horse and was paralyzed from the lips down for six months. As the firstborn son, Custer shed his adolescence and took a hand in the family buckle-crafting business. He drew into himself, and had yet to resurface.

No one questioned his talent. With his supple, leggy form, the way he kicked loose for new footholds, he could recall Lane Frost. A finesse man all the way, Custer was one of the best ever at riding rank bulls away from his hand. But he'd lacked a contender's consistency into the '88 Finals, where a Neal Gay bull kicked him, with feeling. The rider lay so still that Dixie was sure her son was dead, even after she'd run into the ring for a close-up. Custer stayed out for three minutes—a full round of boxing—till finally he moaned and stirred to make J. Pat Evans smile. Custer's neck wasn't broken. He would walk, and ride, again.

A concussion, a punctured lung—those were quickly mended. But that wreck rattled Custer to his bones, rubbed his face in a lesson he'd long known: that anyone, anytime, could be swept away. It was then, Custer said, that he realized he'd been "playing with God," that it was time to quit the party crowd and get serious: "I can sit and talk, I can yap-yap-yap all I want, but if I'm not living what I'm saying it don't mean anything."

Custer wasn't sure where the bulls fit in—*was this really the Plan for me?*—and he looked to his Bible for guidance. Seven months after his accident, the rider drew a big Charbray in Cody, Wyoming. The bull "was just going nuts," Custer recounted. "If you came near him he'd kick at you, try to go through the pen. I was pretty scared—I couldn't even get my rope on him." So Custer did what came naturally: he prayed. And lo, the bull calmed. Custer hooked his rope without fuss under the Charbray's girth, and when they met in the chute the animal stood like an ox. When the chute opened he turned back in his tracks and won Custer the rodeo. Here was faith rewarded, and from that point on Custer laid hands over each of his bulls a half hour before he rode, praying for a sound mind.

When the ride ended he knelt right there on the arena floor, giving glory to Jesus "because I don't want to get a big head."

With time there was more glory to pass. Each season Custer got a little stronger, rode a little better. In 1992 he turned twenty-seven, a good age for an athlete. That autumn he'd won the Pendleton Round-Up and the Coors Shoot-Out in Scottsdale, the Bull Riders Only finals and the Cow Palace in San Francisco. He had the lead and the momentum, and forgot how to hit the ground. It was his turn this year, he was sure of it. A title would lend a podium for Jesus, but Custer couldn't deny it was personal, too. That gold buckle would prove he wasn't some lame "hokey-pokey, that I do got what it takes."

The cowboy had grounds to be defensive. Among the hardest-core bull riders, there remained doubts about Custer, told mostly off the record, sotto voce. "He's a great bull rider, and a great guy, but I just don't think he wants it real bad," one said earlier that season. An undertone droned through the Finals: that Custer might be good enough but not quite tough enough. That his born-again testifying and high-fashion role modeling—"all that *ancillary* bullshit," as Donnie Gay put it—masked the fact that he lacked the right stuff. That something was missing.

Custer had indeed been "run through the wash," according to J. Pat Evans, but that was normal among bull riders in December. By the doc's estimate Tuff's groin pull was more serious, only Tuff wasn't one to gossip about a "personal problem," his scornful phrase for an alibi. Toward the end of the Finals, after Custer griped that an old shoulder injury had spoiled a free-arm move, Tuff arched an eyebrow and told a third party: "Sounds like a personal problem to me."

As the tough guys saw it, you could weigh a man not just by how he rode, but by how he fell off. Custer was betrayed, most of all, by his habit of getting packed out—by all the times he'd stayed down postwreck till a stretcher or less rubbery legs could carry him off.

In bull riding, packing out was the Wimp Factor. It was taboo for all but two classes of cowboys: the comatose and the dear departed. All others were expected to scramble up and out of harm's way, even if they collapsed into hemorrhage outside the ring. To just lie there was unseemly—a tacit plea for pity, a stain on the game's frontier fabric. If his horse ran off in the desert, would a real cowboy play dead for the rattlesnakes (who'd soon take him up on the deal)? Or would he shuffle off toward the far mountain, sipping cactus juice and whistling "The Streets of Laredo" till his tongue shriveled up like a sun-dried chili pepper? Which was roughly the whole point of bull riding: to overcome.

"I get my ass up and out of the arena unless I'm next to dead," said Ty Murray. "Every time I've seen Cody get bucked off he's hurt. I think they packed him out about every round last year. He ain't very tough." Ty furrowed his forehead, perplexed. He wasn't impressed that Custer had ridden with a broken collarbone in the last go-round in 1990, or that he'd solved Wolfman in '91 with his face a swollen mask after wrecking the night before.

"That's something that everybody has to deal with," Ty said dismissively. "That's part of our lives, right there—that's something you *have* to do, you know what I'm saying? That's a qualification."

They formed an exclusive club, men like Tuff and Ty and Donnie Gay, the guardians of their game. Their standards were extreme. In almost any other assembly, Cody Custer would rate as an exceedingly tough, brave man. But the best and truest bull riders are like astronauts, or samurai. They find themselves by pressing past others' limits, and stay alive by forgetting how to stop.

With just three days to go, and Custer's camp rehearsing its hosannas, one last challenge to the leader began to percolate. It came, fair enough, from the greatest bull-riding talent Tuff had ever seen: Jim Sharp.

In 1986, Sharp came out of the Texas "ammies" with a twenty-seven-inch waist, a cartoon sailor's forearms, and a manner so shy that "Yes, ma'am" was a lecture. But Sharp's riding spoke encyclopedias. He performed with Marine Corps posture, a black belt's control, and a fearless way of spurring that put bronc riders to shame. After setting a rookie earnings record at the age of twenty-one, he was tagged as the next Donnie Gay—a comparison unjust in both directions. Where Gay had outworked and outblustered other riders (and *lasted* at the top a full decade), Sharp killed them softly. When you owned strength and balance in ideal harmony, when you were out-and-out better than anyone else, trash talk went by the boards.

Sharp liked to reach a rodeo just in time to wolf a chicken leg or slice of Pizza Supreme, grab his wrap, nod his head, and get a check. The man was Robo Rider, so even-keeled it could be eerie. He never flared in anger, or even pique. The only sign of a nervous system was the rapid twitching of his eyelids, which gave birth to Sharp's mean nickname: "Blink."

Other cowboys might occasionally visit *the zone,* where they rode automatically, without doubt or error, but Sharp stayed there so often that he had to pay taxes. "Sometimes you think there ain't a bull that can throw you off," he'd say; once he rode fifty-seven in a row.

"Sharp's the most boring bull rider I've ever seen in my life," Gay said. "He looks exactly the same every time—consistent and real strong." If Sharp could be dull in action, he was a Thorazine cocktail in conversation. When asked about his strategy for a given bull, he'd deliver the same keep-it-simple-stupid prescription, in twangy monotone: "Toes out, and stay down."

After his first gold buckle Sharp poured it on. He took up karate and stowed dumbbells in his rigging bag, and soon he was bench-pressing 315 pounds, more than twice his weight. His welterweight frame took on mounds of muscle. "If you're strong, your body can take more," he reasoned. "I think weight lifting helps me. It makes me feel better, it makes me ride better." He gained ten pounds and traded up a size in Wranglers. By 1990, when he won his second title, Sharp had become a strength rider, simon-pure. There were times when it seemed that no bull alive could pry Jim Sharp loose, when it seemed like he'd beaten an unbeatable game.

But in 1991, when Sharp rode hurt all year, he started making those deadly little adjustments. At the NFR he topped seven bulls and finished seventh in the average—champagne for 'most anyone else, but Sharp's worst Finals ever. In '92 he started slow, got it going in early summer, and slumped again in late July, at one point falling off six of seven bulls.

When a colossus stumbles, theories abound. Some guessed that Sharp's tunnel vision had suffered as he'd left his social shell. Others noted that he no longer stuck his chest out and arched his back, but hunched over the bull instead, setting him back on his pockets. Gary Leffew maintained that Sharp had grown too "left-brained" from teaching at bull-riding schools—that he was thinking too much, like a pitcher guiding the ball.

The most popular theory was the simplest one: that Sharp was now too strong for his own good. The oldest cliché in rodeo said that you couldn't "out-stout" a bull, couldn't muscle one into submission—especially when it veered away from your hand, where all the biceps in the world couldn't add any leverage. "I think he's gonna have to learn how to ride again," Branger said. "He's worked out so much and he's filled out so much. . . . He needs to loosen up and just start *riding* more."

From the start Sharp was cradled by his talent. He'd always been better than the cowboys around him, and so he'd fairly assumed he'd wind up at the top. An athlete's ease is a part of him, like an architect's eye or a cook's nose, and it must have shaken Sharp to misplace it.

To his credit, he never panicked. Sharp came around a bit that fall, and at the Finals he switched on like old times. He entered Las Vegas ranked fifth, but rode six of his first seven bulls and placed four times. He'd need to sweep the last three rounds to have a shot at his third title, but he knew stranger things had happened at the NFR. "I still got that gold buckle in the back of my head," he said. "If I have anything to do with it, there's going to be a race."

For the eighth go Sharp drew Sammy Andrews's Mighty Whitey, who'd carried Custer to a first six nights before. The short-legged bull came out blowing left, shimmying madly as it spun. Sharp could have scored well by merely hanging on. But he needed every point he could squeeze, and, besides, he was feeling himself again. For eight wild seconds Sharp spurred like he had in his rookie year. Other top bull riders would scrape their spurs along a bull's ribs, less for style than stability. ("The only time I get to spur is in the chute," Tuff would tell you.) But Sharp was flinging his entire right leg clear off the bull's side, till three feet of daylight gaped tween boot and hide.

They hadn't seen spurring like that since the late '60s and the days of George Paul, maybe the greatest of them all till his small plane stopped a mountain when Paul was twenty-three. A mortal didn't move like that and stick on a rank bull, not with his face dialed somewhere between nonchalant and bored stiff. Sharp piled eighty-nine points and a tie for first in the go-round. With Custer bucking off, his race was alive.

As the riders trailed back to the dressing room, Tuff asked, "Don't you think Jim would have looked better while he was spurring if he'd puffed a cigarette now and then?"

"That's the way you're supposed to ride," said Donnie Gay, acting lots more excited than the victor.

In the ninth go-round Sharp drew the bull most riders feared, and the one he needed: Sammy Andrews's Bodacious. The color of clotted cream, Bodacious was a massive three-year-old—just a babe—with an action so freakishly heavy that the brawniest cowboys got airmailed over the top. When Bo-dacious bucked Ty off in the fifth round, you could see why a dozen riders had turned him out during the regular season. "He dropped so far," Ty said, "I just kept goin' down and down and down, and down some more, until. . . ."

Ty predicted that Sharp might fare better: "Jim really wants that bull, and he's so strong that I don't think he'll get all stretched out."

Sammy Andrews concurred: "If anybody here's gonna ride him it's gonna be Jim." If Sharp rode he'd be virtually sure to place first, and maybe build enough impetus to win the world. This Finals had finally found its drama. You could see it in Cody Custer's face, his tight lips, his strained courtesy. You could feel it in the room as the time approached.

And you could smell it in the arena as Sharp burst out with a perfect seat, his purple shirt a block of solid, stable color through each unbearable rear and drop. He looked so strong that Custer quit watching five seconds in, figuring the deal was done.

"Jim, that was the damnedest buck-off I ever seen in my life," said Ty, minutes later, as he stared at the replay. "I thought you had it rode. I would of bet a thousand dollars." The watch had stopped at seven-point-four seconds, the in-stant Sharp flipped into a one-and-a-half gainer, to land flat on his back and head. There'd been no warning, no hint of trou-ble—just the bull and then the ground.

"I don't remember nothin'—I don't remember comin' here tonight," Sharp said.

"You ought to have the doc look at your eyes," Ty said.

Sharp went obediently to the medical room, where J. Pat Evans quizzed him for a concussion: *How you feelin'*? "Not bad." *What happened*? "I lost." A drab exchange, but when Sharp recited his hotel room number, Evans was satisfied the damage was minor. The judges' ratings for Bodacious showed that Sharp would have scored in the mid-nineties, won the go-round, and preserved his run at the gold. Instead he left with

a scrape above his eye and the cold comfort that he'd given the best bull at the Finals all it could handle.

"It just all happened at once," he explained, after a night's sleep had calmed the bongo drummer behind his forehead. "I was in good shape, I thought, and then all of a sudden, *boom,* there it comes. I never had a bull bring me that fast.

"That was my chance and I blew it, right there, but I don't feel too bad about it. I was trying, I think. He was just trying harder. That's a great bull."

And sometimes the bull just gets you.

The rest was academic. While Cody Custer, giving way, would buck off his last three bulls, he still set a Finals earnings record for his event and coasted home ahead of Sharp, with Branger and Tuff next in line.

"It's the first time one of our guys hasn't won the world since '85," Tuff observed, driving off from the Thomas and Mack the final Sunday. He'd salvaged some pride and bankroll by taking the last go-round, plus the Lane Frost Memorial Award for the Finals' top bull ride. Another gift from Lane, who'd helped keep their remarkable streak alive: six straight gold buckles, all out of the same rented car. Tuff had once supposed that he and Lane and Sharp would share the championship indefinitely, till Branger was ready to take his turn. They were modern rodeo's dynasty; they were the best of friends.

Winning the world no longer made or broke Tuff like it used to. "You can't knock it downtown every time," he allowed. Still, it felt strange to see the title go out of the family. Felt like something dying too quick, and too young.

CHAPTER 13

The Last Pure American Cowboy

GREAT MATCHUPS DWELL at the heart of bull riding. Freckles Brown and Tornado, Lane Frost and Red Rock—both men and bulls were champs before they tangled, but their combat made them rodeo immortals. Ted Nuce spoke from that tradition when he advertised his yen to draw Bodacious or Grasshopper—Dan Russell's new unridden flagship—at the upcoming '93 Finals.

"They are super rodeo athletes," Nuce told the *Sports News.* "My blood pressure goes up and that adrenaline gets pumping. I know that if I stick him, I win. I love that feeling."

The brotherhood took Nuce's bravado with a pound of salt. Over the last few years he'd nursed a reputation for bailing at the first sign of trouble on the rank ones. In the fall of 1993, Nuce had backed off one step further. After drawing the rugged Grasshopper, who'd already jerked him down twice that season, the cowboy turned out. Never showed. Stood the bull up.

"I had a bunch of business I had to take care of," Nuce would explain. "If I'd of rode him I would of won two thousand dollars, and the business at hand had more priority."

Now a small scandal brewed. It was one thing for some Jello-kneed "jick," some dude with pockets on his chaps, to leave a rank bull cooling its hooves. It was another for a former world champion in perfect health—a man going to his record twelfth straight Finals—to duck a bull like Grasshopper. This time Nuce got called on his bluff.

"In my mind," Tuff said, "if he doesn't want to risk getting on one of the best bulls in the world, he should quit."

As Tuff's steam suggested, more than a bull ride was at stake. Nuce had dishonored the down-and-dirty tradition that made bull riding something special. The chain had run unbroken from Ken Roberts through Jim Shoulders, Freckles Brown through Ronnie Rossen, Donnie Gay to Tuff and Lane and the rest of their small tribe.

Now another old guard was wearing down. Cody Lambert edged toward his rodeo twilight. Tuff had turned thirty, the witching hour for bull riders, and was leaning toward hearth and home. Sharp and Branger were getting brittle, nearer the finish than the start of their careers. An era was ending, as all eras must.

But more than faces were changing. There were talented young bull riders in the wings, but not a one had yet grasped the baton to sprint forward. The next generation was running a different track, it seemed. If they lasted they'd become "professionals" like the golfers and baseball players. Shrewd and oh-so-competent and, at the end, bloodless.

Any of the new breed might win a title. But who could seize the next decade and put their stamp on the game? And who would sustain bull riding as more than an event that happened to go last on the card?

The PRCA's Bryan McDonald feared that the street-fighting bull rider was an endangered species. "If we don't develop one or two dominating kids with that kind of personality, it will be a totally different feel," he said. "You take the cowboy out of it and then there'll be just a bunch of guys who can ride good, and it'll be a slow death."

At its highest level, bull riding isn't something you do. It is something you *are,* your blessing and your curse. You hang on tight and try in every corner of your life. You may get scared, but you never run. You never safety up, because that's how you get hurt—and if you'd needed to be safe, you'd have stuck to team roping or Ping-Pong in the first place. As McDonald once wrote in his insiders' *Secret Agent Code Book:*

> I figure that bull riders have something to prove—maybe to others, and more probably to themselves. Either you were the leader of the pack—always into things—or maybe you were the little guy that was scared to death inside but never let it show. But now you're a professional bull rider . . . a gunfighter . . . a matador . . . bigger than life . . . or at least willin' to face life head-on.
>
> I call it "Pushin' Curtains." Pushin' life's curtains as far back as you can—just to see what's there. Makin' yourself do things a normal man wouldn't. It's a risky business—it's supposed to be—not everyone can do it. That's why it's important that you play the game right.

True bull riders ride because they love to ride, live to ride, because their days have jagged holes without it. Their passion may be crazy, may lead them to a poor old age, but it has kept their sport clean and real; it has preserved the wild West. It's no good for bull riders to weigh risk against reward, to baby their bodies and guard their slot in the Finals, because no bull is risk-free, and how much is it worth to get stomped on? How much can they pay you for your life? Somewhere down the line those price tags will prick at the core of you, till your self-esteem sags, and you aren't much good on a bull after that.

In 1993 Tuff became the first bull rider to earn a million dollars in his PRCA career. It was more money than he'd ever expected, and he'd been through enough to know what it had cost him. The new breed was different, if only because Tuff and Lambert had brought purpose to the cowboys' ranks. Now there were sponsors and endorsements; the first six-figure jackpot lay dead ahead. Soon any bull rider in the top thirty might make a decent living, with or without the NFR. Which was exactly what the veterans had fought for, except they hadn't counted on the cash changing people, or their game.

The wild West was killed by money, by railroads and the barons' barbed wire. Now bull riding, the frontier's love child, would face the same challenge. This time the threat would come from ratings points and market shares, and a seeping calculation that could spook the brave boys like no creature on four legs.

But just as the tough guys might have wondered what they'd wrought, they paused to watch someone throw his heart over the bar, three times a night. He was the sport's purest throwback and, no coincidence, an all-around champion. And after you thought you'd seen all from him, he kept turning fresh ground. In 1993 he'd built a long lead toward the gold buckle in bull riding, and showed no signs of looking back.

Ty Murray was only one man, but he was doing his best to keep the cowboy in it, at least for now.

Bull riding was Ty's birthright, the event he began with, like most any boy in rodeo country. From his first words he aimed to be a "boo rider." From his first toddling steps he was taming the back of the couch or gouging spur marks into the lid of his mother's sewing machine, hurling his left arm in the air in unmistakable mimickry.

"He's always been a bull rider first," said his mother, Joy Murray, a candid woman with a big laugh and a teased splendor of red hair. "The bulls would tickle Ty the most—he won't say it, but it's true. He walked and talked and lived and breathed them."

Joy Murray had ridden bulls herself in her youth, but Ty's idol was his father, Butch, an amateur roughstock cowboy who took his only son back of the chutes when the boy was two years old. Soon Ty wouldn't let them rest till they put him on a Holstein calf at their backyard arena in suburban Phoenix.

There the family found their routine. When Butch got home from work he'd set Ty on the calf, pull his rope, get his wrap. Joy was the announcer: "And now, ladies and gentlemen, here is Ty Murray, the next world's champion." Then she'd open the gate and the calf would hop out, with Butch running behind with two fingers in Ty's belt loop to keep his son from spilling. Joy would count aloud to eight—"*One* alligator, *two* alligators . . ."—and if she saw Ty slipping, about to dangle from his father's hand, she'd speed up to make sure he made eight. They had ten calves his size, and Ty would insist on running all of them in, then beg for second helpings. After six months, when Ty had turned three, he looked up at his father and said, "Dad, I don't need you anymore." From that point on he rode solo.

It wasn't much later when Joy began hauling him to junior rodeos in half a dozen states. When Ty won his debut and they handed the five-year-old his check for forty-four dollars, he told them to keep it. He clutched tight the real prize: his first buckle.

At nine came Ty's baptism into a world of hurt. He'd just graduated from steers to yearling bulls when he got flipped underneath one. The bull stepped on his face and broke the boy's jaw. Ty never seemed to feel pain like other kids. "Dad, it don't hurt that bad," he soothed Butch, who was crying. His one concern was the upcoming junior rodeo finals. The boy had to ride, wouldn't take no for an answer.

The family found a sympathetic surgeon, the kind that wore cowboy boots during office hours, and Ty went to that finals with a wired jaw and his Pop Warner football helmet. He won both go-rounds and the title, and took a lesson. Butch had long prodded him to turn his feet out and take a hold with his spurs, but Ty wouldn't do it—till after his wreck. "It's like the old saying," Ty considered, years later. "Either you win something or you learn something."

In those formative Arizona years rodeo hung in the air, as basic as sand and sky. Cowboys got respect not just for their talent, but for the honor of their word. Their handshake meant something. How could a boy not want to be like them? Ty lionized Larry Mahan and Donnie Gay, and held a special wonder for Denny Flynn, the knockout stylist of his day. "In my eyes they were gods," Ty would recall. "They *looked* the best. Like Michael Jordan—when you watch him you know why he's the best."

But Ty's biggest hero, the man he hoped to become, remained the first cowboy he'd ever known, a quiet man with a hell-raiser's grin and a taste for the wild side. Butch Murray never had to push his son. He simply shared his life. The two tackled colts in the breaking pen for eight hours at a stretch and it was play for them, though Butch got paid for it. When Ty bucked off a calf—then a steer, then a bull—Butch taught with a question: *What did we do wrong?* A patient father raised a son who'd neither fear failure nor accept it.

Life came to Ty sooner than others. He knew his course in the third grade, when a teacher's survey asked, "If you could accomplish anything, what would it be?" Simple stuff: he'd top Larry Mahan's record of six all-around titles. A second question: "If you could wish and change anything about yourself, what would it be?" From his classmates came the stock replies: "I wish I were skinny." "I wish my eyes were brown." "I wish I had curly hair."

Ty was the only student who'd ever answered with this single word: *Nothing*. He had no time for wishing; he was busy becoming. At ten he honed his balance on a unicycle. At twelve he bought a bucking machine and practiced till his thighs bled.

By freshman year in high school, Ty was riding the big bulls at only eighty-seven pounds. One afternoon he came home to ask, "Mom, is there something wrong with me?"

"What do you mean, Ty?"

"There's only two kids smaller than me in the whole school," the youth said, "and they both have bad diseases."

Ty would change his pant size three times that year. Soon he'd grow into the ideal roughstock body: five-eight and 150 pounds, strong but streamlined, big-boned but compact. At twenty he became the youngest all-around champion in PRCA history. Some were astonished at his progress, but for Ty it was high time. In his eyes he'd worked toward that gold buckle ever since he was two years old.

After the fourth go-round of the '92 Finals, the cowboys paid Ty their highest praise: they replayed his ride. Not once, but four times. Bull rides always looked slower on tape, but this one jumped out of the screen. The bull, a hot young brindle named Gun Slinger, got added to the NFR field after Bryan McDonald watched him buck for two seconds; the director was sold when he glanced up to see the bottoms of Gun Slinger's hooves. Ty scored an eighty-four that night, good for fourth in the rank pen. His form was less than classic. But the cowboy's bold spurring and his sweeping, arch-backed moves—the way he battled at the end of his rope to keep from whipping over the bull's head—made it the high-risk ride of the round.

"His ass went completely on out," said Wacey Cathey, stuck to the screen.

"He's leanin' back farther. . . ." Tuff said.

"He's comin' in that back door, isn't he?" Branger said.

"You ain't kiddin' me," Tuff said.

"And he lands on his feet—oh, god," said Donnie Gay, chuckling at Ty and his trace of a swagger.

Gay was still excited after the set went cold. "Ty tried about as hard as a human being can try," he said. "I don't care how old you are, how much you've won, when a guy tries like that, it pumps everybody up. That's why we ride bulls.

"Ty's in shape and all that, but havin' a lot of muscle don't mean anything. It's what's under that left shirt pocket that makes a guy try like that."

Riding a Gun Slinger "ain't no beauty pageant," Ty said in the med room, a trainer kneading his neck. "Them's the juice of the juice. With those rank-assed bulls you don't ever get a comfortable position." So to hell with how he looked; once the gate swung Ty never pondered his free arm, his weight shift. He was not, he'd allow, a "mental" or "heady" person. When a little boy he'd asked his father what a spinning bull felt like, and Butch Murray replied, "Just like one that goes straight, but it's in a circle."

The good riders avoided thinking too much. "You want to just keep winning, because it's all based on repetition," Gay noted. "You don't want to talk yourself out of making the whistle, and you can. It's real easy to do." When Ty was in high school, where he'd competed in six events, there'd been no time to plot strategies. Now he spurned plans out of principle.

"If I find out what a bull does, it usually ends up hurting me," Ty said. "Say a bull is supposed to spin to the left and he's kind of welly. Subconsciously you might not get around there like you should. And then that day if he ain't welly, you're screwed. . . . I just try to get on and stay on—that's what works for me."

It was no accident that Ty became but the second man to ride Mr. T, or the only right-hander to beat Wolfman. As the wildest bulls were also least predictable, a rider couldn't hope to cheat or outwit them; he'd have to *ride* them, reacting one jump at a time. In those charged moments, all a man might control was his own hardheaded gumption.

"I've seen it proved over and over," Ty said. "You just keep tryin' when the gate opens, and you can't quit the whole way through. You try the hardest, and you'll win."

If there were any questions about Ty's approach, they were laid to rest in 1993. He was a five-year pro now, a young vet in his prime, and in July he became the seventh cowboy to earn a million dollars at PRCA events—in half the time of any before him. While Ty's bronc riding was outstanding, as usual, he took his bull riding to the next rare level. He no longer counted on talent to cover technical errors; those errors were few now. Boarding bulls at only fifty-eight rodeos, Ty placed a phenomenal fifty-one times. His bulls could stumble, or carom off the chute, or twist their bellies to the sky, and none of it made any difference.

Bull riding was "so hard to do," Ty once noted, "but yet when you're tapped off and things are really clicking, it's so easy—everything's just smooth." In '93 things clicked all year long. When Ty bucked off it was news. He dominated as Tuff and Lane had at their best. There were days and nights when Ty seemed the hot man for all time, a mingling of all the great ones who'd come before. You could glimpse in him Harry Tompkins's balance and Jim Shoulders's lunar pain threshold; Larry Mahan's aggression and Donnie Gay's fiery try; Tuff's endurance and Jim Sharp's chiseled strength; and the stylish joy of Lane Frost in the thick of a storm.

"I know how to ride bulls," Ty explained, matter-of-factly. "I've been ridin' bulls for twenty-two years, countin' calves, and when things go right I feel like I can ride any bull in the world." At that point he was running off with his fifth straight all-around title, just one shy of Mahan's record. But the talk was about that other gold buckle, the one Ty had never won: the bull-riding buckle. By the end of October he led Tuff, sitting second, by nearly thirty thousand dollars.

"It's real important to me," he said, after riding at the Cow Palace, the last big show of the regular season. "It's a self-satisfaction deal. I'm not doing it for the press or the fans. I want to prove to myself that I can do it. Just because I love to ride, and to win the world means you're the best."

In the next breath Ty seemed vexed by his own talk. He'd never been one to set goals—in public, anyway—beyond the next winning ride. He figured he had a fifty-fifty chance of winning the title: "Either I'm gonna do it or I ain't."

But those closest to him knew he cared. They knew that Ty hadn't changed since his first Holstein calf, that one event thrilled him like no other. That his first love was still his truest. "In his heart, the bull riding means more than anything," said Julie Adair, Ty's girlfriend, a movie stunt rider and former all-around collegiate rodeo champ. "He's never said that to me, but I know how he reacts to a really good ride. He looks up to the guys he rides against—he thinks they're so great—and then when he wins it makes it all that much more special. . . . He would never say that he is more nervous this year, but I know he is."

Would the heat get to him? As the regular season wound down, some were guessing that Ty might falter at the Finals. He was new to front-running pressure, after all, and those thirty head in ten days would take their toll. But Gay, who knew a little about what it took to win, scoffed at such talk. Unless Ty got banged up early, Gay said, he would win going away: "He's beginning to really *like* it. I can tell by the way he's riding. His confidence level has jumped up times two."

One other ex-champion agreed, wholeheartedly. After an up-and-down season Tuff had finished strong, even rode Bodacious for ninety-four points. But he was ever the realist. "You don't want to spot the best cowboy in the world twenty-nine thousand going into the Finals," he said over a beer in San Francisco. And the pressure? Tuff tilted back in his chair and smiled thinly. "I don't think that he ever feels the pressure, does he?"

As the last pure American cowboy zeroed in on the ultimate western event, his rivals fell away, beaten or exhausted or hurt. Some blamed the rash of injuries on all the big-money bull ridings. In no other era had riders tried so many rank bulls, and while the practice surely made them better, it also wore them down. The odds against them stacked taller. Jim Sharp busted a rack of ribs, then pulled a groin. Clint Branger got his leg stepped on; he, too, was out of the Finals. Cody

Custer tore the biceps of his riding arm clean off the tendon, the muscle riding up like a curtain shade.

With the field thinned, the door opened for lesser lights—which could only help Ty, who seemed sure to place high in the average. Yet he too would miss the familiar faces, the raucous gang that had shared the same dressing room so many Decembers in a row.

For those who missed the cut and came to Vegas to watch, it was time to check their life's compass, reconsider old goals. Custer, for one, had found his gold buckle less alluring to own than to shoot for. "I think that was part of my problem—I was playing the role of the Champ," he confessed. "I got big-headed, self-centered. I stopped reading my Bible. I wasn't handling it with any dignity at all."

He'd worked all his grown life for that prize, and now he'd found that winning could muddle things all the more. "I didn't realize there was that much involved with being the world champion," Custer said. "I thought it was the buckle and the title, but it was a little more than that."

Branger, meanwhile, had found a separate peace. At first he'd suffered through his layoff, watching his name sink slowly in the standings, averting his eyes from the gear bag he'd stowed in a corner of his log house in Roscoe. Tuff called him religiously, once a week, but Branger couldn't bring himself to go to a rodeo, not when he'd have no place there.

Then he learned to fly-fish in the stream that burbled by his house, and his thinking took to shifting, and shifting, till it turned upside down—or right side up. "I was good enough as a bull rider to make a living at it," Branger mused as he waited to get on at the Cow Palace, shortly after eight screws came out of his leg. "I had a certain God-given talent and I thought it was my destiny. And then I laid off five months in Montana, and I was workin' cattle, breakin' horses, and ranchin', and I found out I could be just as happy doing that. And that's what I'm going to do after I rodeo a couple years—go home and run the ranch. Buy a truck and have a basic life, with three meals a day.

"I still have things I want to do in rodeo, but if my career ends tomorrow I'll be happy with what I achieved. If I won the gold buckle, it wouldn't mean as much to me as it did three years ago. Back then I was looking for an identity. Now I'm finding out who I am, that I wasted all those years wrapped up in that one goal. I never had enough time to realize that, because rodeo was my life. . . . Now I'm happy with what I've got."

Branger had begun his discoveries a year earlier, when his life was in shambles and he'd furloughed from the circuit. Now he disclosed where he'd gone instead: to a twenty-eight-day alcohol-rehabilitation program in Cody, Wyoming. Never again, Branger felt sure, would he need to pickle his pain to bring in the new year. Win or lose in Vegas, that crystal stream would thaw come spring, and the trout would strike, and the calves would need branding. He had a life ahead of him now, and he'd live it more than eight seconds at a time.

In San Francisco that night Branger's bull turned back just right. The Swiss-watch rider turned back with him, moving just right, so subtle and smooth that he made it look easy. "Seventy-nine points for the ranger from Roscoe!" the announcer sang out. The night's high score, it rang of what might have been, and what might yet be.

★

After placing fourth in the first go-round, Ty devoted the next day to business meetings and autograph sessions. By the time he reached a suburban mall that shopped his signature T-shirts, his patience was wearing thin. "One or two days of this is about all I can take," he said. Just outside the shop he spotted a fellow sufferer. "Hey, Pig!"

"Hey, Pud!" answered Tuff. There was a story behind Ty's nickname, but it didn't make much sense. The two cowboys slumped behind card tables as a line of pink faces snaked in on them. Ty looked each fan straight in the eye. He was always mannerly, and more than that with children: "Hi, pardner, how ya doin'?" But Ty lacked the electric-blanket warmth, the canned smile, the tools for instant rapport.

When Ty was thirteen years old, he spent his summer on Larry Mahan's ranch. Mahan was rodeo's pioneer in public relations. He could charm any writer within fifty yards, disarm graybeards in tennis shoes or punksters with purple hair. As Ty watched the ex-champ do a telecast, or give a speech, or work a crowd, the youngster thought: This was how you dealt with people. But ten years later fame still bewildered him.

By break time Ty was in a fairly foul mood. He chatted with Tuff, whose bubble gum reminded Ty of some tobacco a business associate had made off with: "Sam took my last chew—where is he? I'm gonna kill him. I'm gonna stab him."

"Here, I got something in my pocket," said Tuff, fishing in his jeans.

"You got some chew?"

"Nah," said Tuff, blowing a bubble, "a knife."

Celebrity did have its perks. Once Julie Adair was stopped at a Gold Coast elevator bank with Ty's tiny pet dog in her arms. The guard phoned his boss, then begged pardon, red-faced: "The manager says it's okay—if Ty wants to keep his *horse* in the room, it's okay."

But more often Ty felt cornered by the spotlight, smothered by the gush of compliments. Bob Tallman outdid himself this time at the NFR welcome reception: "The winningest, most blessed individual and the greatest leader and hero we could have in any place in the world today, in any sport, I present to you Mr. Ty Murray. . . ." Ty took Tallman in stride—"I think he's been sniffing too much glue"—but he'd be wishing to disappear.

In Ty this ran deeper than modesty, or youthful carelessness. ("Till you get to be thirty," Donnie Gay has observed, "you can pretty well tell the media to kiss your butt.") It was ingrained to the bone; he was the Anti-Star. He gave his all in the ring—but was that enough? Rodeo had always had an envoy, one singular man to carry the sport, a lightning rod for *Sports Illustrated* and the third-grader in Amarillo alike. Casey Tibbs was an envoy, and Mahan, and Gay. Lane Frost was born an envoy, never short on patience or enthusiasm. Tuff had to grow into the job after Lane's death. He learned to shoulder the big cheese's burden, then to enjoy it.

Now it was Ty's turn, and the stakes were high. With rodeo marketing on the rise, the sport needed that bigger-than-life persona as a hook. The program for the '93 National Finals pictured Ty stretched back on a bronc jumping over the moon, with the Milky Way for a backdrop and a title in Superman-comic typeface: "TY MURRAY—ALL AROUND CHAMPION OF THE UNIVERSE!"

There was just one catch to this envoy business: Ty wanted no part of it. It was hard to sell a sport when you cared nothing for selling yourself. "No, Ty's not seeking that role," Cody Lambert agreed. "Ty just wants to be himself—straight. He does try to do more, but he tries not to lose himself in it.

"Some guys would like to be rich, and some just want to be famous. Ty wants to be a cowboy."

CHAPTER 14

To the Brink

*T*UFF STARTED HIS FOURTH-quarter drive early at the '93 Finals. He won the second go-round, placed second the next night, tied for third the next. After the prior year's letdown, it all came back to him—how much he lived for these ten days in Las Vegas, how he still could step up his game when it counted. In three days he'd cut Ty's lead to six thousand dollars, and the *way* he was riding impressed most of all: with high authority and not a jot of trouble. He couldn't remember feeling quite this confident.

Ty, meanwhile, was fighting his most dangerous foe: himself. He felt healthy enough, but something was off. In the second round Ty got floored in five seconds. In the fourth round, a nice pen of even spinners, Growney's Rollin' Thunder faked right, then swung left and away from Ty's hand. Once again Ty got raised up and back, and this time he dumped even quicker. The crowd murmured its surprise as its tight-faced hero collected his rope.

"That bull just gets me up," Ty said later, as a trainer massaged another neck spasm. "Bucked me off last year, and that bull shouldn't buck nobody off. I tried to stay down, I don't know what. . . ." After a slump-free season, Ty seemed baffled. It was one of those times, he'd confess, when he'd have welcomed his dad's hand in his belt loop.

In the dressing room Donnie Gay studied the ride in slow motion. He watched Ty finish each jump in perfect shape . . . and then wind his free arm back another six inches, bareback style, as if unable to contain the exuberance of his move. On the tape you could see that hand pulling Ty's body back with it, farther each time, till he'd reached the land of no return. It was a minor mechanical error, one that might not cost Ty on a mediocre draw. But Finals bulls were less forgiving.

"He's trying too hard right now to make things happen, and letting his pride outrun his ride," Gay said. "He tries to cowboy a little too much. I still think he'll find one that fits him, and he'll spur the juice out of that son of a bitch, and then look out." Gay passed his observation to Lambert, the best messenger for the job.

By the time Ty rejoined the troops, he'd come to his own conclusions. "I'm a puss!" he declared. "You know what I did wrong, Donnie? I didn't stay on that mother. I've been thinking too much. That thinking don't work for me."

He seemed annoyed but unshaken, even as his lead dried up, even as Tuff bore down on him like a speeding truck. Once, when Ty was seven years old and got bucked off a steer, Joy Murray took her furious son in hand and said, "They might get you once, but they can't get you twice." When it happened again at the next rodeo, she told him, "They might get you twice, but they will *never* get you three times. It's not in you." That third time Ty rode his steer. Joy still made the same promise whenever her young man struggled. It was a joke between them now, but with a point.

The next night Ty headed out to the arena with Lambert, well ahead of the other bull riders. This was the partners' private time amid the Vegas hubbub. For a few minutes it could almost seem like July in Oklahoma or September in Oregon—like just another rodeo.

"Ty's got to come out early because he doesn't have time to get ready during the rodeo," Lambert explained from behind the wheel. "I come out early because Ty doesn't charge me any money for gas."

"I like to ride out with Cody because I get to listen to cornball junk all the way out here," Ty retorted. "There's a lot of guys who'll laugh at Cody's jokes, but I'm the only one who'll *keep* laughin' at 'em."

Ty stopped laughing about four hours later, when the little brindle he'd drawn in the rank pen, the one he'd had ninety-two on in Nampa and wanted more than any other, jumped and fell on its side just as the gate opened. Nine of ten bull riders would have taken off right there. But Ty cowboyed up and waited the bull out, squandering precious seconds before they left the chute. The score was low, ordinarily worthless. That night, however, only three other men would ride, which meant that Ty's fiasco was automatically worth fourth place and three thousand dollars. If he passed up the optional reride, he'd be sure to hold his rung in the average. But if Ty took his option and failed on his third bull in four nights, the gold buckle damage might be fatal, even to the coolest hand in Vegas.

Ty didn't hesitate: he'd take the reride. "I didn't come here to hang in the average," he'd say later. "Everyone acts like that was a big decision. Hell, there wasn't no decidin'. I came here to try to win first. I'd rather win nothin' than settle for fourth." Though his reride bull would tip Ty into his riding hand, Gay's message had gotten through. Ty's free arm stopped at the perpendicular, right where it belonged. The cowboy held on for the horn and scored eighty points, good for second.

Tuff, still closing, rode toward the end of the round. He seemed in great shape on Dog Face when, with odd abruptness, he sprawled over the bull's hump and dropped hard onto the dirt. Tuff took an extra few seconds to rise to his feet. In the dressing room he wrung his hands, which tingled as if asleep, then plunged them into warm water. When the tingling persisted, he checked in at the med room.

"It feels like little ant bites," Tuff told Don Andrews, as the trainer manipulated his neck. "I thought I hit my elbow."

Andrews kept working and said, "It could be the ulnar nerve if one hand felt that way, but if it's both, it's usually coming from up here."

"It was a good bull," Tuff lamented. "The bad thing about it was I had a good seat, a hell of a seat." He made a sour face. "My hands are just stinging. . . . Fudge, fudge, fudge." The stinging didn't bother him; it was falling off that got his craw. No ten bulls for him. "You win one, lose a few," he said.

"Hold my hands and pull hard," Andrews ordered. He set up an X ray for the morning; it would come back negative.

"Good ride, Pud," said Tuff, peeling off a few C-notes in the dressing room to pay back a blackjack loan.

"Tuff, are you angry?" Lambert asked, with a hint of mischief.

"No," Tuff said, unconvincingly.

It reminded Ty of the night Tuff bucked off at Calgary. *I'm all right*, Tuff kept insisting. *I'm all right*. "And then he threw his boot through the television."

Marty Staneart was cracking. You could see him falling apart, day by day. The guy had always been a little suspect—though not for his bull riding, which was solid as his barrel chest and had taken him to six NFRs. And not for his toughness; he'd ridden for months in '92 with torn ligaments in his wrist. But Staneart was strictly an amateur in the liquor department. Loud and pushy when sober, he could be positively obnoxious when drunk. That fall he'd gotten his lantern jaw in Tuff's face once too often, and Tuff had popped him with a right jab.

One month from his thirty-fifth birthday, with thinning hair and crosshatched scars, Staneart looked like an old sparring partner. But he'd ridden good as ever this year, won ten thousand at Cheyenne, and recently brushed off the notion of hanging it up. "Age is just a number," he'd said. "I'm beating these kids, I'm winning just as much as they are or more. Why should I quit?" Staneart came into the '93 Finals full of vinegar, and won the first round, but then he started falling off and taking it to heart. The first bad sign came after the third go, when he slammed his rope off the dressing-room wall and blamed his fellows for bad advice on how to ride his whippy bull. Two nights later Staneart complained, "I had a good start, but I've had hell since."

"You got twelve thousand and you ain't limping—you ain't had hell," Gay disputed. But Staneart wasn't looking at the bright side. In the seventh round he bucked off his sixth straight bull and got tromped on, roughed up more than hurt. As he sat to watch the replay he shook his head and muttered, "You got to be crazy to be doing this at thirty-five."

The next day Marty Staneart quit, turning out his last three Finals bulls. After fifteen years as a professional he was through. The press report noted that he'd broken a toe, but everyone knew that Staneart could have ridden that night.

The news didn't play well behind the chutes. Staneart had sold his saddle, disgraced himself. He'd done what bull riders despised most in others, and feared most in themselves: he'd given in. It was one thing to retire. That happened to every cowboy, unless he was killed first. Riding bulls was like going to war, and battle fatigue set in sooner or later. One day the mind stopped responding to its daily dose of adrenaline. It got flooded with the stuff, refused to start up, like an old Ford in February.

No, it wasn't any crime to bid farewell to arms. But there was a way to leave with dignity, and it sure as hell wasn't in the middle of the Finals with no better out than a hangnail. "Marty went out with his white flag up, didn't he?" Tuff said, dripping acid.

"He couldn't even retire right," Lambert said. "When that twelve thousand's gone, and reality sets in and the pain goes away, he'll be back."

When Staneart walked into the dressing room that night, his NFR contestant number still pinned to his broad back, the bull riders fell quiet. Finally Nuce piped up: "You still got time. You sure you don't want to get on?"

"They already turned the bull out," Staneart said. He sat down on a bench, his big, scabbed hands clasped in his lap. He pretended to watch the calf ropers, but his eyes kept dropping to the soiled linoleum. *What would he do for the rest of the night? What would he do with the rest of his life?* When the bull riders left to get ready, Staneart moved to the keg of Coors: "Have something to drink here, loosen up my vocal cords and root for the boys." Then to the sandwich buffet: "A year from now I'll probably be a big, old, fat team roper." He forced a laugh.

"There's a line that everyone's got to go through," Staneart said slowly, leaning on the cinder-block wall, trying to sort it all out. "I feel a slowness in my reflexes. My body don't move as good as it used to, and it's not going to get any better. I feel a notch below. It hurts my pride, it hurts my heart." He pressed two thick fingers to his chest.

Next to nodding for the gate, retirement was a bull rider's toughest call. You were in or out; there was no halfway. You didn't want to go too soon. As Jonnie Jonckowski put it, "It's hard to walk into the shade as long as the sun still shines on your face." Gay took that walk in 1983, after he'd torn his groin and lost his title to Sampson. Quit while you're ahead, people told him. Get on with your life. Gay quit, but he was only thirty years old—too young to die an athlete's first death.

"I'd keep waking up in the middle of the night," he recalled, "and I knew there was something amiss, but I couldn't figure out what it was. Finally I figured it out—I wasn't hurtin'. I'd wake up because my groins weren't hurtin', and I'd think, What is wrong with me?" The next year Gay came out of hiding to win his eighth gold buckle, snapping Jim Shoulders's bull-riding record.

Still, you didn't want to go too late. There was a right time for each man. Tuff figured that Lane Frost had been nearing that time when he was killed. Bull riding was taking too much out of Lane, body and soul, for him to win another title or take pleasure in pursuing one. And now Tuff knew that his own time was drawing short.

"I may not be over the hill, but I can definitely see the top of it," he said. "Rest assured, if you see me at thirty-five years old and still riding bulls, you shoot me in the head."

That Friday, with three bulls to go, four riders remained in the gold buckle hunt: Ty, Tuff, Darryl Mills, and Ted Nuce. Tuff had ridden the previous two nights without placing, with a foam horseshoe to cushion his sore neck. His hands were aching more than tingling now, which the docs took as a good sign. Tuff just ignored it. On the Finals' last weekend, champions found a way to get it done.

At the cowboys' arena entrance, Tuff said good-bye to Tracy and Robert Lane, now a sturdy two-year-old.

"Give me some skin!" Tuff said.

"Bear down, Tuff," urged his son.

It was a typical rock 'em, sock 'em night at the Thomas and Mack. Aaron Semas got kissed by Big Kahouna and came up for air, punch-drunk, with an extra crease in his hat. Jerome Davis had his bull fall sideways on his leg; Brent Thurman sprained his ankle on his dismount.

Tuff rode twelfth, and for six seconds was fixing to win the round. "He was the big one that got away," Tuff would say, days after it was over. "I was reeling him in and he jerked back. Not only did he get my pole, but he pulled me over and ate me." Dodge Magnum Power blew out strong to the left, into Tuff's hand, but Tuff stuck right in the middle. Then the bull turned back to spin right—good for a few more points, but nothing out of the ordinary. Tuff twisted to move with him, in perfect shape, and then he lost it. He tipped into his hand and fell as if shot. He found the ground chest-first and rolled to his back.

It was a routine lick, not one to knock Tuff out or even daze him. He raised his neck to get up and then something strange happened. His body went on strike. Tuff's hands made small fluttery motions on their own, and his legs were dead. The left one stuck straight out and the right one splayed at the diagonal, but neither belonged to him. Tuff's head sank back to the earth. His diaphragm heaved, more from fright than exertion. He tried praying, but it was hard to pray through a waking nightmare: of a man chair-bound, of a life of pale dependence.

By that time J. Pat Evans and his medical team had hustled to his side, but the first face Tuff saw was Cody Lambert's, peering anxiously as he knelt over him. Lambert had seen lots of bull riders stunned and still after a fall, but as the seconds ticked by he sensed this was different.

When Tuff heard his own voice, he was surprised at how calm it played against the arena's silence: "I must of broke my neck or something, 'cause I'm paralyzed. I can't feel my legs or feet—I can't feel nothin'." It took three minutes for Evans to fit a stiff plastic cervical collar around Tuff's neck and get the cowboy slid onto a stretcher. Tuff strained vainly for some shred of sensation in a limb. As he was borne away to muted applause, he realized he had never truly been scared, not before this.

Tuff didn't begin to get his life back till five minutes after the crash. Outside the Justin Healer room he asked Lambert to squeeze his foot. Tuff closed his eyes . . . and felt the soft pressure. "Just wiggle them for me one time," Lambert pleaded. Tuff sent the message, and this time he got an answer. The sight of his own swaying boots was the sweetest moment of his life. Maybe it was just a pinched nerve, Lambert thought, and he left Tuff to the doctors.

As they took Tuff's vital signs and prepped him for the hospital, Ted Nuce climbed aboard Slam Dunk, the last bull of the night. Nuce had already won two go-rounds with his old flop-and-pop magic, but this time he flopped back too far. When Slam Dunk reared, Nuce's body shot forward, like the spring of a trap—and when the bull threw his head back, it struck Nuce flush in the face. The bull rider flew into a twisting, rag-doll somersault before thunking heavily on his back. J. Pat Evans could tell from the flight path that the man was unconscious, and when the doctor trotted back into the ring—to see two eyes staring off, a blank face, a puppet's slack neck—he feared Nuce's spine had snapped. Evans gave the case priority, and Nuce was rushed down the long corridor toward the first ambulance. A suction tube drooped from his mouth; his eyes had rolled up. His mother shoved past a clot of onlookers as she trailed the gurney: "Excuse us, we're Teddy's family, we're Teddy's family!"

"Tough night," said Charles Sampson, who ought to know one. "That's as bad as I've ever seen."

Marty Staneart stood quavering in the corridor in Nuce's wake: "We don't think it will ever happen to any one of us, but once in a while it does. It happens. . . ." As the burly man cried you began to grasp why he'd retired, beyond his limp reasons of soreness or discouragement. Staneart had quit out of terror. He'd lost that blood taste in his mouth, that greed for a challenge that had earned him a living and helped keep him alive. And he'd seen enough carnage to know that the rank bulls of Vegas would make him pay.

It would be another half hour before Tuff emerged from the med room. Two dozen friends and relatives waited at the end of the hall, near the elevator. Among them were Clyde and Elsie Frost, Lane's parents—the woman straight-backed and red-faced, the man leathery and impassive, holding to one another as they had on so many hard nights.

Tuff had been the one to call Elsie with the news from Cheyenne—was it four years ago already, so soon? With Lambert he'd escorted Lane's bagged body in a tiny plane to Atoka, a wordless flight that took two eternities. Tuff had washed the mud off Lane's chaps and boots, and picked out a shirt—black and white, Lane's favorite plaid—for the funeral. Then he'd bought an interest in Clyde's cattle and helped with the ranch work that Lane once shouldered. And when Robert Lane Hedeman was born, Tuff called Elsie again: "You're a grandma now." He could never replace the son who'd been lost, none of them kidded themselves on that score, but the three were family just the same.

Finally Tuff was wheeled out, his body rigid to the white socks that stuck beyond the sheet's border. His eyes were open, his face drained and clammy. As he passed to the elevator Elsie reached out to clasp his hand.

By ten o'clock the vigil had shifted to a cramped waiting room at Memorial Hospital. From a couch Nuce's wife kept repeating, "Ted's a tough guy, so healthy, such a strong guy. . . ." With Sampson at her side, she'd just left her husband's room, shaken to find him delirious. Nuce had one eye swollen shut and a string of fresh stitches in his face, but he insisted he'd ride his next bull. "Got to cowboy up!" he kept shouting.

"Remember when I got hurt worse than this, in the presidential rodeo?" Sampson prodded him.

"Who are you?" Nuce demanded of his old friend.

"I'm your brother. I love you."

"Get this black man out of my face!" Nuce shouted.

Nuce's wife smiled as she told the story, but she never stopped crying. The doctors feared there might be bleeding inside Nuce's brain, which would force them to operate. "Tuff's better off than Ted," she told Tracy. In fact, Nuce had suffered a severe concussion but nothing more. He was through for the Finals, but he'd stagger out of the hospital the next day.

The waiting room hushed as the story played out over local news on a small television: "Bull riding is at the very core of rodeo. Bull riders are among the toughest athletes in sports, but fate caught up with a couple superstar cowboys. . . ."

"It goes with the territory," sighed Claryce Hedeman, Tuff's mother.

"Doesn't make you like it any better, though," Bryan McDonald said.

"You can never be prepared for it," Clyde Frost said. "Been to a lot of hospitals, Bryan?"

"Hospitals all over," McDonald said.

The trauma center was busy that night. It was near eleven when Mark Kabins, a young spinal surgeon, came out to meet with the rodeo folk. There were no fractures, no displaced vertebrae—that was the good news. What Tuff had instead, to be confirmed by an MRI the next day, was *spinal stenosis,* a narrowing of the bony column that housed the spinal cord. Stenosis was harmless of itself, and often went unnoticed through a lifetime. But once a disk bulged and protruded into the column, as it had in Tuff at this Finals, the spinal cord could be pinched, producing numbness—the tingling in his hands—or temporary paralysis.

"He's up and walking around," Kabins said, "but it would be a real big mistake for him to ride tomorrow. You have a lot to be proud of—he's a fine young man."

Relieved, Tracy and McDonald went to visit their cowboy's room. Tuff lay on his back, hands folded over a green hospital gown. Above his head a beeping monitor tracked his heart rate, blood pressure, breathing. Tuff asked what he'd drawn for the ninth go. It was Copenhagen Chase, the bull that won the first round for Staneart, a draw that could have helped a man to his fourth gold buckle. Then Tuff indulged some hoarse-throated regret for the ride just past, the one that got away: "I'd of placed for sure—oh, well."

"You won a hell of a lot more than twelve thousand dollars," McDonald told him.

On Saturday the news hardened. Tuff's numbness had crept up one arm, and Kabins didn't dare wait; he'd operate on Sunday to remove the bulging disk and relieve the spinal pressure. It was a routine procedure, common with football players, and Tuff could expect a full recovery. But no more bulls, Kabins said—for good. As he listened to the surgeon Tuff's legs started shaking and he could barely catch his breath. He felt, he'd say later, as if Kabins had cut his heart out. Then he swallowed hard and called Elsie Frost. "I'm history," he told her.

When the grapevine reached Ty that afternoon, he was dumbfounded. "I can't believe it," he said. "I didn't think it was that serious. God-*damn*." As thick-skinned as Ty seemed, he didn't take loss easy. After Lane died he came home to his folks and stayed inside for three days, either staring or crying.

It would be hard on Tuff to step away, Lambert thought, as he entered the arena Saturday night: "He loves the spotlight, and he really likes to ride. We promised each other when the time came that it was over, if we saw that the other one couldn't do it anymore, we'd tell him—we'd hurt each other's feelings. Now I don't know how everything is going to turn out, but the way it appears, he's going to have to hurt my feelings."

The bull riders' dressing room had been muted all Finals, what with seven first-timers meekly making their way, but tonight it was choked and dead. Tuff and Nuce were as bullet proof a pair of cowboys as the last decade had seen, and now they were out. It wasn't news that bull riding was hazardous to your health, but the past twenty-four hours had hammered the fact home. Now the survivors were looking at two of the most violent pens of bulls ever assembled. There didn't seem to be much to talk about.

Then Lambert came in and grabbed Tuff's folding chair, the rooster's perch. He didn't hold center stage by the television, as Tuff had, but he did sit down in it off to the side, and soon he was cracking his cornball jokes. The room loosened just a notch. As always, the show would go on.

And then there were two. Heading into the finale on Sunday afternoon, a single man stood between Ty and the gold buckle in bull riding: Darryl Mills, the two-time Canadian champion from Pink Mountain, British Columbia. Short and stocky, a world-class wrestler, Mills couldn't have been more different than the man he was chasing. He was a plugger, a plodder, the tortoise to Ty's hare.

"The average has always been my deal," Mills would say. "I don't ride like a Jim Sharp or a Ty Murray. Those guys are spectacular bull riders, but they expose themselves a little more than I do. Consistency is my deal. I like to be there when the average money is paid out."

At this Finals he'd been true to form, bucking off but two bulls. Mills had sliced Ty's lead from thirty-two thousand to ten, and he stood to chop away four thousand more if he held his lead in the average. If Ty rode his last bull, or if Mills bucked off, the Texan would be almost sure to clinch. But if Ty bucked off and Mills rode and placed, the Canadian could finish the biggest comeback in NFR history.

That scenario loomed closer after the random draw for matchups in the tenth go. Mills had outdrawn Ty all week, and he did it again by catching Grasshopper, the '93 bull of the year. Though still unridden, Grasshopper had weakened toward season's end. He was strong but slow, a good fit for Mills.

Ty, meanwhile, had drawn Bodacious, the freakish yellow Goliath who'd dropped him at the '92 Finals before knocking Sharp silly and out of a title. Butch Murray feared the worst: "That's the last one I'd of picked, the very last one. Now I'm nervous."

At 1:20 that afternoon, Donnie Gay popped into the dressing room to announce, "Tuff's in recovery and the deal went even better than they thought." Twenty minutes later, just before the bull riding began, Bob Tallman passed the news to the crowd: "The Lord has brought our three-time champion out of surgery with excellence."

Mills and Ty were the last to ride. Grasshopper came out bucking but seemed to lose his way, snowplowing rather than spinning to the horn. Mills just barely held on to the end; his seventy-six would get him third place and six thousand dollars. Then Bodacious busted out with his terrible drop, like the vanguard of a different species—new, improved, lethal. Ty had a terrific seat, but at the second jump he knew he was doomed; his rope had slipped to the last knuckle of his fingers. He rode four more seconds on sheer touch and stubbornness, but no one bobbled on Bodacious and made money on the deal. After picking himself up Ty tipped his hat for the crowd, then dragged the failed rope from the arena. Finally his head hung low. He'd lost; he'd choked. It was over.

But Mills wasn't sure he'd won it, and neither was Tallman. Without a stat man at the ready, it was too close for a quick call. As the house lights went dark for a presentation, Butch Murray took off from his seat to the still-lit concourse, to scratch out his own figures on a program. He added them twice, to make sure, and then he broke into his broadest, crinkle-eyed, kick-ass grin. Ty had finished the season with $124,659—exactly ninety-five dollars more than Darryl Mills.

Banshee screams rang from the bareback dressing room, where Ty had gotten the word. "I think I better get another pull of whiskey," he said, his mug glowing now.

Ty had won his bull-riding buckle in the grand tradition of Donnie Gay. He'd ridden best by far all year, then well enough at the Finals to finish second in the average. He'd won by daring bold decisions for twelve testing months, not the least of them that reride option in the fifth round's rank pen. He'd never settled for less than first, and now he wouldn't have to.

Over in a jammed pressroom, Ty sat down to hack and sniffle his way through a parade of interviews, his flu-ridden head propped on his hand. Most questions centered on the title some said Ty would never win. Now his truth could be told: "The bull-riding gold buckle means more to me than anybody knows, except maybe my mom and my dad. It's such a relief to win the world, because there's nothing anybody can do now to take it away. And I'm just the happiest sumbitch in the world."

It was after three when Ty escaped to his family in the hallway. He bent down for hugs from his mother and sister, but his longest, deepest embrace was reserved for the man dabbing at his eyes with a white handkerchief, the man who'd kept him from falling off those crazy-legged calves, who'd always run just one more into the chute.

Riding back to the Gold Coast, Ty held his dog in his lap and cooed to the pink-sweatered shih tzu through a huge wad of tobacco: "Are you a good little dog? You're a good little dog." He'd pick up his two gold buckles at the Caesar's Palace banquet that evening, where Tallman would proclaim him "on loan from God," then stop by the hospital to see Tuff. It was the kind of day that could make a twenty-four-year-old wax nostalgic.

"It seems the other day when I was watching Tuff on TV, his first year at the NFR," Ty said. "I can remember he wore a black vest, and it looked like he could barely walk. His back looked like it was five feet long and his legs looked like they were two and a half feet long—like he was tipping over. When I first saw it, I said, 'Geez, *look* at this guy.'

"You get used to certain guys, like that's how it's always been and how it'll always be, but there's a new wave now. Cody, it makes me sick to think about, but he's getting up there. You know, this is my sixth year of rodeoin' professionally. That's hard to believe, isn't it? It's just horrible to think about how fast your time goes by."

No one lasted too long in this game. The pace was too quick, the strain too great. Even if you were leased from the Man Upstairs. Even if you were the greatest rodeo cowboy ever. But it wasn't where you ended that mattered, as Tuff and Charles Sampson and Clint Branger now knew, as Ty was coming to figure out. It was the trip that counted, the road you chose. And how you traveled along the way.

Afterword

ON JUNE 6, 1994, THE RED Bluff neighbor who fed Red Rock saw something was wrong. The animal kept refusing his grain; it turned out he'd had a stroke. John Growney was summoned home. Two days later, as a vet tended him, the smartest bucking bull of all time lay down and died, at the ripe age of eighteen. He was buried under a big shade oak in his private field.

An emotional man, Growney needed weeks before he could talk about Red Rock without a full throat. It wasn't so much the bull, who'd had a full run in the arena and a pampered retirement. It was Lane Frost whom Growney missed. Whenever the contractor had glanced out his picture window and seen Red Rock, he'd remember the cowboy born to ride him. Lane and Red Rock were inducted into the ProRodeo Hall of Fame together; they'd been featured in a movie and a country song. But now Red Rock too was gone, and Lane would soon recede from flesh to legend, even for those who'd loved him most.

"It was the final chapter, Red Rock dying," Growney said, looking out at an empty field. "That sort of just ended that whole thing."

☆

A few years back, a national sportswriters' group polled itself to choose the most dangerous sport in the world. Boxing and auto racing got a number of votes, but rodeo bull riding swamped the field.

No one called for a recount in 1994, when top-ranked bull riders dropped like first lieutenants in a firefight. Cody Lambert broke his leg. Mike Gaffney and Cody Custer had shoulder surgery. David Fournier went under the knife for his ripped left knee. And Gilbert Carrillo lost his spleen and part of his pancreas after a bull stepped on his stomach—and after Carrillo took a four-hour flight before seeking treatment.

Jim Sharp, the brightest talent since George Paul, twice a world champion and still but twenty-eight years old, fought a wound beyond J. Pat Evans's care: ruptured confidence. When asked about his old traveling buddy, Tuff replied in gloom and wonder, "He just can't stay on."

None of these big names made the National Finals cut. Nor did Charles Sampson, who finally laid his rosin aside for good in March, after sixteen years and more than a hundred broken bones. "I felt I could still be competitive, and I was," Sampson said. "But that drive for a world title wasn't there."

Sampson's warm spirit would still make its mark. Two years before, he'd imported his protégé, a Brazilian champ named Adriano Moraes. The rage of Sao Paulo adapted quickly. In 1994 Moraes rode away with the title for the Bud Light Cup Series, the Professional Bull Riders's new eight-event circuit. (Ted Nuce, still a threat for the big checks, won the first PBR Finals—and forty-five thousand dollars—at the MGM Grand in Las Vegas.) In his debut National Finals that December, Moraes made the whistle on ten straight, a small miracle. At twenty-four he was the fresh stud the sport needed: technically flawless, slightly exotic, ever sunny, and dashing enough to rev the crowds.

Once again Ty Murray ruled the PRCA standings from early on. He entered the '94 Finals as top seed, then bucked off five of his first six bulls to spoil his chances. (Though he did, by the by, win his sixth straight all-around world championship, tying Larry Mahan's record.) Ty had torn a ligament in his riding wrist that fall, iced it down after each bull and yanking bareback, but he made no excuses. Never did and never would.

"Everybody wants to know what was troubling me, if I'd lost my drive," he said. "I don't know why I was off—there ain't no answers. It's like a batter when he can't even hit the ball. You just got to ride it out." And, turning wry: "I got a couple years left in me, I think."

The gold buckle in bull riding went to Darryl Mills—"that little biscuit-snatcher," as Ty called him. Mills prevailed when all three top finishers bucked off their last bull, and when Clint Branger's draw flagged to a seventy-nine, stranding the Montanan in fourth place.

Still and all, Branger was actually seen smiling of late. He had a new fiancée, a ranch-bred, kind-faced woman named Amy, who was fixing to move into the log cabin and make it the home he'd pined for. There was wedding talk for the following fall.

Branger's dad had gotten some fancy offers from the ranchette crowd for his spread near the Crazy Mountains, a million dollars and more, but he'd turned them all down, and the son was glad. "I don't have to be rich," Branger said. "I want to live where I live." Once he'd put rodeo behind him, Clint would be the family's fourth generation to run cattle on that grassy land near Roscoe. Now he knew a fifth generation would be coming, to share the sky and striking trout.

The '94 Finals ended the worst way it could. In the last go-round, twenty-five-year-old Brent Thurman—a Texan prized for his warm wit and toothless grin—got thrown under an eighteen-hundred-pound brindle named Red Wolf. Thurman was one of the toughest cowboys going, the best kind of throwback, but the bull had stamped square on his head; he held on for six days of coma, then gave out. It marked the first fatality in the Finals' thirty-six-year history, and the third professional bull rider to be killed in the ring that year.

Red Wolf was not "a particularly vicious or malicious animal," said a PRCA spokesman. "It was just a freak accident." He said this after two thousand people thronged the funeral at an exhibition center in Austin; the coffin made its slow circle in a horse-drawn covered wagon, trailed by a single big-humped bull. The spokesman was right, of course, but the words held no balm. They never could, when a man risked all and the debt came due—when he honored the bargain, it was way too soon for the ones left behind.

Tuff Hedeman wasn't exactly off rocking on his porch in 1994. By May he was team roping on the weekends for a sip of competition. He helped run the PBR, served up bull riding commentary on the Nashville Network, posed for several regional ad campaigns, and opened stores for a swelling roster of sponsors.

"You can count on two hands the people who can help you sell your product, and Tuff's one of them," said Ron Pack, a vice president with Panhandle Slim. "Rodeo's a relationship sport. As long as he keeps his face before the public, his aura will still be there."

Tuff's friends watched him cope with a mix of sadness and relief. Some took his injury as a sign, a word to the wise. Said Kellie Macy, who'd remarried into a West Texas ranching family four years after Lane Frost's death, "I think it's Lane telling him he's won enough money, and it's time to stop."

One day, months into his bull riding retirement, Tuff remarked to Larry Mahan that he'd had no pain from his spinal surgery, that he felt normal again.

"You wouldn't know what normal felt like," Mahan dryly replied.

Tuff couldn't argue with that, but his body was stubborn. It acted so damn healthy, and it kept blurting this message to his head: *You're not done yet.*

As a three-time world champion, Tuff's reputation stood secure. He had nothing to prove. His world was whole—except for the fact he missed riding. As the Finals approached, Tuff missed it worse. By November he'd cut a deal with John Growney: a ten thousand dollar match of Tuff versus Wolfman, the little bull he'd never tried, still spinning like mad after four years in the biz. They'd do it the following March, on the first night of the fifty-five thousand dollar Tuff Hedeman Championship Challenge in Fort Worth, the annual bull riding Tuff produced with Ron Pack. One shot. Winner take all.

By that time Tuff and Tracy had already huddled with J. Pat Evans. The doc gave it to them straight: A "prudent" person wouldn't re-enlist. Tuff's operation was designed to fuse two vertebrae, Evans explained, and had made the point of injury stronger than before. At the same time, it left the segment above that point *more* vulnerable, subject to more stress. If another disc were to bulge out, Tuff could face a repeat of his scare in '93. And if a vertebra were to fracture or dislocate, it might damage the spinal cord for good.

At worst, Tuff would lose everything from his shoulders down. His next rough landing might be his last.

Tuff granted that he ran "a greater risk of being paralyzed or even dead, but that could happen to anyone. There's always that risk in bull riding."

"He could get hurt driving to the grocery store," Evans agreed. "These guys accept the risks; it's a part of their life." A prudent person wouldn't ride bulls to begin with. Evans left the call to his patient; he understood cowboys.

Some well-meaning folks wondered aloud if Tuff might be setting a reckless example for the youth who adored him, or putting ego before family. But the hard core knew the equation was simpler than that. If Tuff truly hungered to ride, Donnie Gay declared, he had no real choice. "If you quit before you're ready," Gay warned him, "that'll be a void you'll never fill."

The inner circle's sole concern was that Tuff return as he'd left. They didn't want him back as just another cowboy—as Branger put it, "That would hurt your feelings." For Tuff's part, he figured he had to practice some before testing a Wolfman, and he might as well do it for pay. So he surfaced at Denver, the first big show of '95, and rode his first bull in a safety vest developed by Cody Lambert. Tuff felt a tad stiff, but the try was there, and he sensed he'd be all right.

To pound that sense home—or maybe just for the hell of it—Tuff entered the Cowboy Downhill Stampede in nearby Steamboat Springs, a ski race he'd never missed before the accident. He pushed off with seventy-two other wild men in chaps and Resistols. He shot past the finish line with seventy-two behind him. He would not play safe.

Going with Ty and Lambert, a wiseass brigade for all time, Tuff placed at Fort Worth and Tucson and won the whole shooting match at Kissimmee, Florida. His comrades relaxed. "You can't take away the toughness and experience of doing so well for so many years," Branger said. "He knows how to win, and that's not going to change."

Best of all was the first weekend in February, when Tuff won his third Bullnanza in Guthrie, Oklahoma, the red-letter event that kicked off the PBR's new season. He earned an eighty-six on Grasshopper to clinch the title, one point in front of Branger. In a rush he recalled what he'd missed—to compete with the very best cowboys, to last on a bull few men could handle. "When I got off at Guthrie," Tuff said, "that was probably more satisfying than anything I'd ever done."

Now the Wolfman match was gravy. Coming into Fort Worth Tuff ranked seventh in the world. He'd ridden sixteen of nineteen bulls, and the three who'd bucked him off were the miserable, scooting, no-kick panthers who'd always plagued him, who'd tip his big torso back. On Friday night, as Tuff slapped his riding arm in the locker room, he looked lit from within. "I've never felt better in all my life," he said. He'd had a thousand and one details to handle that month—with the PBR and the contractors he'd hired, with interviews and ticket sales, with Justin Boots and Cripple Creek Jackets—but now it was time to ride. To revisit the place it began for him, with a bull and a crowd and a bunch of lean-and-hungries bent on the same buckle.

"After I was hurt, I thought that I wasn't going to be able to ride anymore," Tuff reflected. "So I just left it behind. I didn't mope around. I moved on and went to doing different things. But this is still what I love to do—to get my spurs, get my chaps, get to the back of the chutes."

The other day he and Ty had got to talking about "the glory days"—all of five years back—when life was simpler. "We had one responsibility, and that was show up to the rodeo and nod," Tuff said. "Show up, ride, win something, go get a beer, sleep late the next morning if we could, get up, fly to another and do the same thing. . . . That was easy. That was the good life."

One by one, the first twenty-five bull riders strode through the out gate into a darkened Will Rogers Coliseum. Amid echoing applause, a Hollywood smoke machine took to spewing, and then a superstar quartet stepped out of the mist: Cody Lambert . . . Jim Sharp . . . Adriano Moraes . . . Ty Murray.

The sell-out crowd was fully fevered by the time one last cowboy emerged. At first he was spied in silhouette, bigger in profile than the rest, with that familiar, stiff-legged gait. Then the spotlights kicked in, and Fort Worth, the original cowtown, rose to greet its favorite son. The fans reclaimed him as Chicago would reclaim Michael Jordan two weeks later—as someone more precious for having once left them. Tuff thanked them with a savoring wave of his hat.

He'd go twice that night as part of the main contest, before tackling Wolfman at the end. First he drew rank with a juicy red longhorn named Palace Station. The bull spun left from the gun, and Tuff moved with his old sureness, in that blunt-edged style that made grace a side issue. There is a cowboy domain, known only to a few, where choice bulls like these are like cake: they go down easy. Tuff earned eighty-seven points, good for second in the round.

His next draw was a different story. As fans took up a rhythmic clapping, the spotted Mo Betta peeled off to the right, away from Tuff's hand; Tuff sagged outside the axis of the spin. But the bull was too small, the rider too hard. Tuff dug in with his right foot and inched back toward the middle. He kept at it till it was time to slide off and shoot his hands to the roof, to let the pleasure-drunken crowd embrace him. He'd won the round with an eighty-nine; he'd lead the average into Saturday. He was their once and future king.

Grinning to beat a Cotton Bowl band, Tuff set a personal best for the hat throw, flipping the black felt clear over a bucking chute and into a clutch of cameras. More pandemonium. In the VIP seats Tracy beamed next to Clyde and Elsie Frost; Kellie Macy, baby son in her lap, must have felt the tug of another time.

When bulls write the script, fairy tales take detours. Less than thirty minutes later, Wolfman half-stumbled from the chute, rocking Tuff left. The young Wolfman might have taken his twisting signature leap, might have given Tuff time to reload while in the air. But the older "T. Q. Hot" Wolfman (to honor John Growney's new top-shelf tequila sponsor) was less predictable now, and he cut to the chase—like a mini-Lamborghini—away from Tuff's hand. Tuff took his one shot to recover, but there was no way to calibrate a bull this quick, and he overrode to the right.

Now Tuff was tumbling to the inside, where a nasty hang-up awaited. He reached high with his free arm, desperate to pick himself up, and then he knew Wolfman was gone, like a satellite sprung from orbit, and it was time to save himself. Tuff grabbed the bull's hump and jostled off to the outside and safety; at some point a horn grazed his forehead, scraping a red band over his eye.

It was over in three seconds. Don Kish would take the sponsors' ten thousand dollars back to Red Bluff, to breed more little Wolfmans and bedevil more cowboys.

On Saturday Tuff bucked off twice; Gilbert Carrillo, another comeback kid, won the event. Even so, the weekend was one big sermon in overcoming discouragement. Tuff had proved wrong the skeptics who'd advised him he'd never ride like before. As Tuff pointed out, "I'm bad if they tell me I can't do it; then I'm going to see to it that I can." Going into Denver, he himself had wondered—in the dark, before sleep claimed him—but now he'd put his doubts to rest.

"I expect more out of myself than anybody," Tuff said, back in the Fort Worth rodeo office Sunday morning, counting receipts. His baseball cap sat backwards; it was time to take a breath. "If I couldn't come back and be competitive—world title contender, top-five kind of guy—then I'd be gone.

"But I still love to do it. As long as I can put out the effort, I can compete with anybody. That's all riding bulls is—effort. That's all anything is."

For Tuff there were no guarantees, save that one. Win or lose, he'd be out there trying.

On July 30, 1995, six years to the day after Lane Frost was killed there, Tuff Hedeman won the bull riding at Cheyenne Frontier Days, the biggest outdoor rodeo in the world.